PRAISE FOR *THE TIME OF THE TANS*

History, it is said, is written by the victors, which is why their self-serving accounts, letters and official papers became the rule for the predominant narrative of any conflict. Tomás Mac Conmara, on the other hand, digs deeper than that, down to the grass roots, painstakingly spending years speaking to and recording the actual people who lived and made history, their contemporaries, and their children – the carriers of folk memory. And so, what leaps off his pages is the great humanity involved. Without writers like Mac Conmara, history would be poorer, certainly distorted, individualistic and, let's face it, merely academic. By insisting on giving voice to the local, he offers us a deeper understanding of what really happened, the energy and power behind momentous change, and, not least, the debt we today owe to so many selfless men and women of the past.

Danny Morrison, writer and former republican activist

This book by Tomás Mac Conmara is an exemplary and riveting exercise in the use of oral history to illuminate a dark time in Irish history, which we all must revisit as part of our useful and instructive decade of centenaries. The nature of memory is explored, so that the reader can gauge the areas of certainty and uncertainty which proceed from people's recollections. The stories are extraordinary, and remind us that trauma lingers on over generations. The methodology is impeccable. Mac Conmara has spent many years excavating the oral history of County Clare and across Ireland, and has now produced a comprehensive gathering of stories and reminiscences of a pivotal time in our history.

Catriona Crowe, former head of special projects at the National Archives of Ireland

THE TIME OF THE TANS

AN ORAL HISTORY OF THE WAR OF INDEPENDENCE IN COUNTY CLARE

Tómas Mac Conmara

MERCIER PRESS

MERCIER PRESS
Cork
www.mercierpress.ie

© Tomás Mac Conmara, 2019
POD ISBN 978 1 78117 813 3

A CIP record for this title is available from the British Library

This book is sold subject to the condition that it shall not, by way of trade or otherwise, be lent, resold, hired out or otherwise circulated without the publisher's prior consent in any form of binding or cover other than that in which it is published and without a similar condition including this condition being imposed on the subsequent purchaser.

No part of this publication may be reproduced or transmitted in any form or by any means, electronic or mechanical, including photocopying, recording or any information or retrieval system, without the prior permission of the publisher in writing.

To my friend, Mae Tuohy,
Kilbarron, Feakle (1916–2017).

'One day men will be gathering even the slightest memory of those years …'

J.J. Walsh, *Recollections of a Rebel*

CONTENTS

List of Abbreviations — 11

Acknowledgements — 13

A Note on Memory — 15

A Note on Transcription — 17

Introduction — 19

1. 'The Criminals of England' — 28
   Stories of Memory

2. 'Run for it' — 74
   Stories of Experience

3. 'All their own sons' — 144
   Stories of Community

4. 'Born wild' — 189
   Stories of the Extraordinary

5. 'A corner of the grave' — 212
   Stories of Silence

6. Carrying Wounds — 222
   Stories of Pain

7	'Dormant sympathies' Stories of Death	236

Conclusion 266

Appendix 270
Exploring Memory

Endnotes 274

Bibliography 309

Index 316

About the Author 328

LIST OF ABBREVIATIONS

ASU	Active Service Unit
BMH	Bureau of Military History
CACA	Cuimhneamh an Chláir Archive
CO	Colonial Office papers
DCM	Distinguished Conduct Medal
GAA	Gaelic Athletic Association
NAUK	National Archive, Kew, UK
NFCS	National Folklore Collection Schools' Folklore Scheme
RIC	Royal Irish Constabulary
SSHP	Shannon Social History Project
WO	War Office papers
WS	Witness Statement

ACKNOWLEDGEMENTS

Firstly, my most sincere gratitude to the many people across Co. Clare and beyond who opened their doors and allowed me within the fold of their family memory; you are the true historians. Since I first began recording as a teenager in the mid-1990s, I have been increasingly struck with the generosity of memory that I have encountered. To the many who have moved to another place, my memory of them and their memory of distant days will endure. Many thanks to Mary Feehan, Wendy Logue, Noel O'Regan, Deirdre Roberts and all the team at Mercier Press for supporting my work. Special thanks to Professor Bernadette Whelan of the Department of History at University of Limerick for her guidance and support during my doctoral research. Thanks to the Military Archives of Ireland and, in particular, Noelle Grothier, Captain Daniel Ayiotis, Commandant Stephen Mac Eoin, Commandant Pádraig Kennedy and Commandant Claire Mortimer. To Dr Cliona O'Carroll and the Department of Folklore and Ethnology, UCC; Dr Crióstóir Mac Cárthaigh, National Folklore Collection, UCD; Dr Kelly Fitzgerald, School of Irish, Celtic Studies and Folklore, UCD; Clare County Librarian Helen Walsh; and Peter Beirne, Clare Local Studies, thanks for your continued support. To Dr Guy Beiner for his encouragement to continue my work on memory; to Tom Toomey and Dr Pádraig Óg Ó Ruairc, who have done tremendous work for Limerick and Clare history; and to historian Daniel McCarthy for his support and advice over many years; to Dr Arlene Crampsie, Adrian Roche, Dr Eve Morrison and Regina Fitzpatrick from the Oral History Network of Ireland for their continued advocacy; and to Austin Hobbes, former editor of the *Clare Champion*, as well as

Jackie Elger and John Kelly for the use of photos. Special thanks to friends Cllr Pat Hayes, Frances Madigan, Gerry O'Grady, Peter and Brian Flannery, Jack McCormack, Jimmy Walsh, Moira Talty, Patricia Sheehan, Seán McNamara, John Moroney, Carol Gleeson, Paul Minihan, Tomás Madigan, Jim and Ruth Minogue, Dr Ciarán Ó Murchadha, John Walsh, J.T. Larkin, Pat Hanrahan, Risteard Ua Cróinín, Congella McGuire, Clive Kelleher, Kieran Brennan, Shane O'Doherty, Brendan McMahon, Rob Dunne, Brian Marrinan, Kevin Cullinan, Emer O'Flaherty, Bridget and Oliver Garry, Mary McInerney, Kyran Kennedy, Seán and Maura Keating, Tommy Holland, Tony Diviney, Flan Garvey, Helen and Christy Venner, Derek and Elaine Venner King, Ciarán and Joanne Maynes, P.J. and Cathy Kelleher, Patrick Blake, Br Seán McNamara, Dennis McBride, Frances O'Neill, Joe Garrihy, Paula Carroll, Gordon Daly, Darren Higgins, Dr Billy MagFhloinn, Cormac Ó Comhraí, Joe Queally and the late Dermot Moran.

In searching for memory, many private collections in family homes were also revealed. For access to private collections thanks go to Mary Galvin, John S. Kelly, Michael O'Gorman, Micheál O'Connell (Querrin), the late P.J. Clancy, the late Michael 'Marshall' McMahon, Fr Brendan Quinlivan, the late Jimmy Gleeson, Phil McGrath, Teasie McCormack, the Griffin family (Ballyea), Oliver McDonagh and to my great and enduring departed friend Catherine Talty.

To my father, Dan, for once taking a young boy to see an old man. To my mother, Annamae, for nurturing a deep interest in my townland, and to all my family, thanks for everything. *Ar deireadh gabhaim buíochas domhna do mo chlann. Dara, as a cuid áilleacht neamhghnách agus tacaíocht gan deireadh, mo mhac oidhreachta Dallán Camilo agus Seód Nell Áine, ar son cabhrú an solas a thabhairt i gconaí.*

Tomás Mac Conmara, 2019

A NOTE ON MEMORY

This book presents the stories and memories of a fading generation. They offer, in their memory, the brief fragments that make up the story of our past. The reality that almost all the people who contributed to this book have since passed away is a timely and powerful reminder of the need to reorient ourselves to the depths of our memory, culture and tradition. In a country so long defined by its oral tradition, these memories provide clues not only to the meanings of historical experience such as the War of Independence, but also about the relationships between past and present and between memory and personal identity.

A deeply layered landscape of memory exists, containing elements which impact on the way we remember both as individuals and communities. Commemorations, songs and monuments are all sites of memory that shape and affect the stories we recall, particularly at a public level. The same monument, song or commemoration may have functioned in the past as a painful reminder of loss to a family bereaved, and at the same time serve as a symbol of principle and patriotism for the broader community. These sites of memory are all the more powerful due to their relationship to the local oral tradition and their historical relevance to the local community. They are rooted in the concrete details of local areas, embedded in both landscape and consciousness. They are reference points, serving as coordinates of identity, reminding locals of what was achieved in their area, and reminding people from outside those areas of what the locals achieved. The agreed or acceptable nature of many such sites of memory should equally inform of the important distinction between what is publicly commemorated and that which is privately remembered. That gap is bridged in this book.

Some academics will challenge memory as a reliable source for history and are sometimes on solid ground in that criticism. The memory of humans is often subjective, biased and open to change over time. However, the reality that all other accounts were, in fact, also written by people should also be noted. In relation to the War of Independence, almost all the primary information was taken from subjective accounts of people placing their opinions on record. Contemporary police and press reports, as well as later accounts given by former IRA men, inevitably contain the subjectivities that come with the transmission of one's thoughts to record.

The stories offered in this book reflect the historical consciousness of the people of Co. Clare. While, regrettably, it has not been possible to reference all of the recordings I have undertaken over many years, and accepting that there are still many more stories to be recorded, the book nevertheless presents the widest sample to date of such local memory. In some cases, aspects of the story may be challenged by contradictory historical accounts. In other cases, dimensions will be revealed that were absent from the historical narrative to date. In all cases, the memory remains important as a unique sample of the oral tradition that was inherited from the Irish revolutionary period. The stories reflect the way in which local people inherited and understood such a defining episode in their country's past. For the narrators, theirs was a local experience that formed part of a national story. Each community had its stories and each family its tradition. All had their silences.

A NOTE ON TRANSCRIPTION

With the voice and accent so central to the potency of the message, transcription results in an unavoidable reduction in power. The challenge for transcription is to retain as much of the original effect from the moment of telling. To represent emotion in text is a challenge, as are the intonations and inflections that characterise vernacular speech. This is particularly crucial when transcribing the memories of the generation reflected in this book, those who carried in their movements, language, intonations and very being, an older way of life. Pauses, verbal emphases and gestures are all critical parts of communication and are not fully appreciable in transcript form.

It is difficult to convey personal actions or reactions, the tone of voice, smiles or laughs in a written transcript. Often, in interviews, where a voluble expression of attitude or opinion was not forthcoming, the expression and body language took over the narration. In transcribing memory that was mostly communicated in a very informal manner, it has been necessary to clarify on occasion who or what is being referred to. The tendency in rural Ireland to refer to people by their surname is also addressed with the inclusion of their first name, where known. In almost all cases, I was the interviewer for each recording. Interviews I conducted for other archives are denoted in the endnotes. Where oral material referred to was recorded by another interviewer, this is also specified in the endnotes. Pauses by the narrator are denoted by three short dashes (---). Within the stories quoted, editorial insertions that help clarify what is being referred to are included within square brackets [ ]. Square brackets are also used to record visual clues like body language as well as the raising of voices or emphases of words. Editorial deletions within the transcript are denoted by an ellipsis (…). Only words that have no bearing on the meaning have been removed, when to do so was to help the readability of the text. These include 'false starts' and fillers like 'ums' and 'ahs'. So-called 'crutch phrases' like 'you know' are left in, as often they carry a meaning in the delivery of the narrator. Double quotation marks are used to denote the quoting of a second person within a piece of memory.

Often, Irish language words are embedded in stories predominantly narrated in English. In addition, certain phrases, colloquialisms and manners of expression are used which are not detectable or understandable to all and require clarification. For example, in 2009 ninety-two-year-old Micheál O'Connell used the phrase 'they were givin' the Tans a fair scutchin', to describe the fact that the local IRA had been violently engaging the British forces. Knowledge of the term, actually relevant to an old agricultural practice, was critical to understanding his assertion.[1] I have made every effort to ensure the true meaning of the interviewee has been conveyed to the reader.

INTRODUCTION

On 13 December 1920, at 3026 Washington Boulevard, Chicago, in the United States of America, Molly Moroney finished writing a four-page letter to a relation in Co. Clare. She sealed the letter carefully and addressed it to Dunógan in west Clare, from where it was delivered to the townland of Clounlaheen. There, the recipient of the letter, Mary Moroney, herself a returned emigrant from America, was married to Molly's brother, Joseph. Contact with the home country was important for Irish emigrants and Molly was determined to ensure she maintained a connection.

Equally, she wanted to receive an update on the situation in her native country. Ireland was then in the grip of one of the most violent and turbulent periods in its history. The War of Independence had raged for almost two years and it seemed to those hearing reports in America that the violence was relentless. As Molly's letter was making its gradual way from America to Clare, less than ten miles from its destination, two young IRA Volunteers were captured in a remote house in west Clare by British forces. As the letter drew closer to west Clare, news broke in that area on 22 December that IRA Volunteers Willie Shanahan and Michael McNamara had been brutally murdered.[1]

This was part of a nationwide trend. In the weeks before Molly wrote, Ireland had experienced an unprecedented period of violence. Bloody Sunday, the elimination of the Cairo Gang and the murders of Claremen Peadar Clancy and Conor Mac Clúin (popularly known as Conor Clune), together with Dick McKee, all took place in the city of Dublin.[2] Just two days before the letter was written, Black and Tans and Auxiliaries burned large parts of

Cork city and murdered the two Delaney brothers, Cornelius and Jeremiah, in their home at Dublin Hill on the city's northside. The Black and Tans had been in Ireland for almost nine months and the force of ex-British servicemen had already begun to burn an indelible mark on the psyche of the Irish people, at home and abroad.

From America, Molly described the Black and Tans as 'the jail bird renegades that are killing innocent people' and characterised what was happening in Ireland then as 'the worst conflict since Cromwell's time'.[3] With the co-operation of the Royal Irish Constabulary (RIC), the crown forces escalated their suppression of republican activity in Ireland. Between the letter's writing and reading, as it made its slow journey to Ireland, the republican attacks and vicious British reprisals that characterised the war significantly intensified. In America, Molly was witness to an increasingly strong sentiment amongst ex-patriots, angered at the apparent brutalisation of their people by British forces. A growing movement in that country now saw complete devolution and separation as the ultimate answer to the conflict in Ireland.[4] The notion of an Irish Republic, previously whispered in covert Fenian circles, was now part of the everyday parlance of most Irish Americans.[5]

Molly's correspondence is part of a private collection of letters sent from America to west Clare to which I was given access. They powerfully convey the feelings in that country:

> I am sorry to hear that poor dear Erin is in such a terrible upset condition. We had a very touching sermon in our church yesterday about the conditions in Ireland. It made almost everybody in the church shed tears. This morning the papers are full of the burning of Cork and of course some of the papers are British papers but I

always get the *Irish World*, it is only a weekly paper. I get it by mail and it tells all the true news about Ireland. We have Miss [Muriel] MacSwiney here now, till Spring ... There are also four men here, the RIC. They resigned over there and are now living in NY.⁶ They are going to Washington today. We have a meeting of the Friends of Irish Freedom here every two weeks. Almost every Irish person in Chicago belongs to it ... We have also lots of Sinn Féin dances. A dollar a ticket. The last Sinn Féin dance, there was 2,000 people attended.⁷

Towards the end of her letter, Molly declared that 'Someday I may probably see the hills of Clare again', before asserting that 'I think if I was there I could get rid of a couple of dozen Black and Tans!' Before finishing, Molly wrote caringly about her four-year-old niece: 'I am sending a little present to the baby, just a little reminder. I know she is not a baby anymore. I guess she must be almost big enough to go to school probably.'⁸

The recipient of the gift was Mary Moroney's daughter, Catherine, who in December 1920 was beginning to form her own views and impressions of the world. The world, too, was making an impression on her. In her townland and in the area around her, strangely uniformed men of violence called the Black and Tans were spoken about in hushed tones. On a few occasions, from under her mother's protective arm, she saw them menacingly crowded together, a striking image that would endure.

The life of that little girl paralleled the birth and growth of the Irish Republic. Born on 4 April 1916, she was a month old when Pádraig Mac Piarais, Tom Clarke and Tomás MacDonagh were lined up and executed in Kilmainham Gaol in Dublin, the first of sixteen leaders to be sent to perpetual memory by the British authorities. She was just a year old when an unknown man with a strange name was introduced to the county in the east Clare by-election of July 1917. She was seven years old when her mother returned from Ennis, where she had witnessed the violent arrest of that same man, Éamon de Valera, by Free State forces under the shadow of the Daniel O'Connell monument in the town, during the Civil War (1922–23). A year after that war had ended, from her home in Clounlaheen, she watched as her townland was illuminated with blazing bonfires in a welcoming embrace to anti-Treaty republicans released from jail. She noticed, too, that they were not welcomed by all and began to understand the divisions within Irish politics and communities. At thirteen years of age, in 1929, she slowly travelled on a pony and trap with her mother to the same spot where de Valera had been arrested, where she witnessed huge crowds attend the hundredth anniversary of Catholic Emancipation and 'the Liberator' who achieved it. The invocation of history was a recurrent theme for Catherine, and her emerging interest and commitment to the past formed a permanent part of her character.

As Catherine grew to adulthood, she witnessed the transformations that her country underwent. She lived through the economic turmoil of the 1930s and saw the increasing role of the state in Irish rural life during the Second World War or 'the Emergency' as she knew it then. The horse lost its footing to mechanised machines and local trades began to weaken and fade from view. Electric light that hung from the ceiling arrived, while the thatch over the roof departed. The sound of motorised cars became more frequent, as did the sight of planes crossing the sky. In the 1940s she saw more republicans jailed for their continued conviction in the Fenian ideal. One of these men later became her husband.[9] The reaction seemed different now: no bonfires.

Later still she saw commemorations, monuments installed, heard songs sung and people talk about the history she had seen through a child's eyes. She bore witness to the repeated attempts to both remember and forget as different people saw the past differently, while others didn't want to see it at all. In the 1950s and 1960s she saw further generations stand up and make their contribution to Irish independence. She attended funerals, heard some men praised and others criticised. From the 1970s she witnessed, through understanding eyes, the north of her country implode in violence and counter-violence; a story continued. Through all those years, certain categories of memory remained constant. Through the mist of memory, images which flashed before her childhood eyes rested in her consciousness and were only brought forward in the old way, within the ancient art of meaningful conversation.

Ninety-six years after Molly Moroney enquired about her four-year-old niece, that little girl offered her testimony of that period to me, in the same house where Molly's letter arrived in late 1920. In one of many interviews, I invited Catherine Talty to recall her memories of the Black and Tans. For a moment, the four-year-old girl mentioned in the letter returned to tell her story. Across her conservatory, overlooking her native Clounlaheen, I ventured the question and waited. I then listened intensely, fading away as, for a profound moment within memory's fold, the past became more real than the present:

> I can remember ... You know Miltown Malbay? You know the garage there at the square? That house was taken over by the Black and Tans ... That was a barrack in those days and of course they were stationed there. I remember going to Miltown on the horse and sidecar. My mother and I. I don't know who was driving, I suppose my uncle, a stepbrother of my father's. Hynes's yard, we'd pull in there and the horse would be untackled. Walking up the street in front of Lynch's

pub, you know. And looking across and seeing the Tans and of course having heard so much about the Tans! I can still feel the thrill of terror if you like. Now my mother wasn't one to get excited or make anything about it, like. But oh, I could remember them. My mother never said a word but shur I had heard so much about them! But I can still see them and to this day. I suppose for the rest of my life, I hated a uniform. 'Twould give you that quiver of fear.[10]

This interview took place in 2011 and was part of a series of in-depth oral history recordings I undertook with Catherine between 2008 and 2016. I have attempted since a young age to document and record memory and oral tradition associated with the revolutionary period, in the strong view that their inclusion in the mosaic of historical sources enables the presentation of a much deeper and perhaps truer version of the past. This book represents the notion that to understand a war which occurred and was felt at such an inherently local level, the historian must go back down to the level of the parish, village and townland. The historian must metaphorically get down on his or her hands and knees to find the fragments of memory and history where it occurred, and assemble from those remains a deeper understanding of the past. Surely the tradition and memory of people from places referred to in official records are worth including? In my view, without their input, history is incomplete. In these local places, as will be shown, can be found the echoes of events only listed in archival records. Throughout the revolutionary period, the contours of the mountains, the valleys, the haggarts, the streams and the bridges, even the very nature of the soil underfoot, were fully understood by local people and used to their advantage. In a time when the oral tradition was more robust, this intensity of knowledge was passed from generation to generation with the same ease as breathing.

Like their people before them, the older generation at the centre of this research, who grew up in the aftermath of this period, knew the fields, the roads, the houses and the names of their past. With little difficulty, they can weave the endless connections and tracings that infuse our history with greater meaning.

For Jimmy Gleeson, whose family ran a well-known pub in Coore in west Clare, oral tradition as a source of knowledge of the past was self-evident. 'We had the greatest bunch of historians coming into that place there outside.'[11] In Claremount, in the east of the county, Seán Kiely declared that it was:

> In the cuairdí houses at night – when the neighbours would have their work done for the day.[12] They'd congregate and they'd be talking and tracing about things that happened in the past. That's how I picked up on what had happened in the past.[13]

The book offers a unique insight into the War of Independence. Presented thematically, this is not a history of Clare's role in the conflict. Instead it is an oral history of experience and an exposition of memory, presenting for the first time in public what has been privately remembered for almost 100 years.

'The Time of the Tans'

The Anglo-Irish War of Independence was a guerrilla war launched against the British government and its forces in Ireland. Its official start date is generally given as 21 January 1919, following Dáil Éireann's declaration of independence, and it ended with a truce in July 1921.[14] Nationally, at least 1,400 people were killed in the country during the war, with some historians placing the figure much higher.[15] The subsequent negotiations led to the Anglo-Irish Treaty, which ended British rule in the southern part of Ireland and established the Irish Free State. The Treaty led to a split within the republican movement and the Irish Civil War of June 1922 to May 1923. In Co. Clare at least 135 people, between republicans, civilians and British forces, were killed from 1918 to 1924.[16]

Nationally, the IRA was organised on a territorial basis with a brigade being the highest formation. Division areas were only introduced following the Truce in July 1921. A brigade consisted of between four and seven battalions, and a battalion of any number of companies up to ten.[17] In Clare, both the IRA and Cumann na mBan, a republican women's paramilitary organisation founded in 1914, were structured according to East, Mid and West Clare Brigade areas.[18] Flying columns were established late in the war, predominantly enlisting men from local areas and generally working within county boundaries.[19] Almost each village in Clare provided a company of varying degrees of strength, resulting in a diffusion of activity across the county, which generated memory rooted in these areas.

As a historical landmark, the War of Independence carries significant emotion, pride, anger and bitterness, and has perhaps only in recent years loosened its grip on the Irish psyche, although in certain cases this has remained palpable. For the generation that grew up in its shadow, it remained an anchor for their memory. This was forcefully illustrated in several interviews. For example, in a recording with Kathleen Nash from Scariff in east Clare, who was born in 1909, the interviewee's initial comments declared that she 'was going to school [in] the time of the Tans'.[20] Kathleen was determined from the start of the interview, which aimed to explore her life story, to make clear her position in the chronology of Irish history. She passed away in April 2011.

Kathleen's generation are all but gone now. It has been my

privilege to spend time in their company and to be enfolded for a moment in their memory. What were once vivid and frightening experiences for them had, over time, become distant memories, separated from experience by the unstoppable movement of time. Little was required, however, to evoke them. Like turf nudged in an open hearth fire, a carefully placed question or prompt would bring forth an immediate clash of recollection and a memory long silent would emerge from its place of waiting seclusion. Eyes would widen as memory ignited. The countenance altered visibly as the body took on part of the narration. The natural order of time was now reversed and once again, for a brief moment, the Black and Tans were back in Ireland.

1

'THE CRIMINALS OF ENGLAND'

STORIES OF MEMORY

THE BLACK AND TANS IN MEMORY
Since the Easter Rising of 1916, demands for Irish independence had taken on a progressively more determined form. When it became apparent that the declared political will of the Irish people was insufficient to move British democrats, the likelihood of violence increased, and shots fired in mid-January 1919 in south Tipperary sounded the commencement of the Irish War of Independence. By January 1920 the increasing violence in Ireland had left fifty-five dead and a further seventy-four wounded.[1] When the RIC was forced to concede that the escalating IRA campaign was beyond their control, the British government decided to reinforce them by raising a mobile police strike force.

From January 1920 posters were placed in London, Liverpool, Glasgow and many other British cities. Potential recruits were asked to 'face a rough and dangerous task' in Ireland. From then until December 1921, over 10,000 men, predominantly demobbed British servicemen who had fought in the Great War, joined the force in England, Scotland and even Ireland. So keen was the British government to send their new force into action that sufficient uniforms were unavailable. Some wore military khaki with the belt and cap of the RIC, while more donned the dark pants of the police and the khaki jackets of the military. An appropriate ensemble perhaps for a unit that was neither police nor military but some ill-defined hybrid coloured in black and tan. It was to be this dichotomy of colours that gave the force its enduring name, the Black and Tans. These men should not be confused with the Auxiliary Division, ex-officers who arrived in November 1920 to further bolster the RIC and Black and Tans.

Historians have shown that while the suggestion that criminals were hired for the Black and Tans can be hard to prove, the fact that recruiting agents were less than thorough in their enlistment practices for the force is certain.[2] The basic requirement of military experience was important. Those trained skills and an undeniable culture of hatred towards the Irish in Britain, as well as the implicit directive to use any means necessary to suppress republicanism in all its forms, were a deadly combination.[3] After a cursory training at the depot at the Phoenix Park in Dublin, the Black and Tans were sent out into the country in March 1920. Although in Ireland for only just over a year and a half, they left a haunting legacy in their wake and imprinted their actions on the psyche of the Irish nation. The animosity felt towards the Black and Tans during the Irish War of Independence is well illustrated by one historian, who noted the presentation of two notices posted at the time. One notice appealed for British recruits, encouraging readers to 'Join the Army and see the world'. A second notice was soon placed beside it, which read: 'Join the Black and Tans and see the next!'[4]

In recent years new perspectives have been disclosed on the Black and Tans, including the fact that a considerable number of Irish men joined the force.[5] Historians have also clarified the culpability of other elements of the British crown forces in Ireland in relation to many deaths in the period, which had initially been attributed to the Black and Tans.[6] However, while these clarifications are welcome, the correct attribution of blame to the military and not police in some cases does nothing to minimise the intent, inclination or reality of Black and Tan violence. That British soldiers, Auxiliaries and the RIC were also culpable simply draws attention to the reality that the actions of the Black and Tans were inseparable from the broader British establishment which dispatched, directed and paid for the activities of all their imperial forces.

While a distinction is evident in social memory between the RIC and the force recruited in January 1920 to support them, my research shows a consistent categorisation of the entire British forces during the War of Independence as Black and Tans or simply 'Tans'. Two considerations are important. Firstly, while the categorisations can be technically inaccurate, I have found that the collective description 'Tans' does not indicate an inability to distinguish. Instead, it is often a recognition of the divided nature of the war, which saw the British on one side and the IRA on the other. For many, the Black and Tans, RIC, Auxiliaries and even British Army could acceptably be labelled as 'Tans'. One west Clare contributor asserted, 'shur they were all on the one side anyway', while in north Clare, another noted 'they were all Tans. They were all on the British side.'[7] In the same way, their counterparts in the republican movement were referred to interchangeably as 'Sinn Féiners' and 'the IRA', despite the technical distinction.

'The criminals of England'

In 1938, when thousands of schoolchildren combed the country for knowledge as part of the Irish Folklore Commission's Schools' Folklore Scheme, the memory of that force was still raw. From stories she heard in her local area, thirteen-year-old Mary Fitzgerald in Miltown Girls' School understood the Black and Tans as 'English soldiers' who were 'let free in Ireland and could do what they liked'.⁸ Her schoolmate, Máire Ní Bhrian, characterised the force as 'demons roaring and shouting around the streets'.⁹ A Miltown Boys' School, fourteen-year-old Joe Woulfe's impression of the force was equally clear. After visiting several older people to hear about the period, he was able to decisively conclude asserted that 'The Black and Tans caused all the trouble.'¹⁰ In a possible reflection of the local community's perspective almost two decades after their departure, Teresa Kelly, aged thirteen, exclaimed in her contribution, 'Thank God we have none of those British scoundrels in our quiet and peaceful country today.'¹¹

The popular belief that the Black and Tans were recruited from the lunatic asylums and jails of England has been registered by many historians.¹² This contention hardened in social memory over time. One Irish emigrant recorded in Chicago in 2010 had a firmly fixed view of how the force was assembled:

> You see what happened in England, they opened up all the jails and they armed all them jailers and sent 'em over to Ireland. The Irish had no guns so they had to fight 'em back so the Irish had to fight 'em and get their guns off 'em ... they fought 'em with pitchforks.¹³

While Tom Brennan's description may be somewhat simplistic, it carries an impression of the force that has lingered in memory. The belief that the men had been liberated from jail was one that was commonly held at the time. On 3 November 1920 Labour Party Member of Parliament Thomas Cape asked at a sitting of the House of Commons whether 'condemned criminals have been released on promising to serve in what is known as the Black-and-Tans?' The suggestion was rejected by the then under-secretary of state, Sir John Baird of the Conservative Party, as being without foundation.[14]

Although recent research has largely challenged the notion that the force was comprised of released prisoners and lunatics, negative attitudes amongst the Irish population about the new recruits formed quickly, and it is apparent that many members of the contemporary British forces, too, were less than impressed by them. Private J. P. Swindlehurst of the 1st Battalion, Lancashire Fusiliers, commented on arriving in Dublin that 'The Black and Tans ... seem to be all out of work demobbed officers and men who can't settle down'.[15] Major General Douglas Wimberley similarly commented that the Black and Tans were 'of a type who would not or could not settle down in civil life, and some of whom were no more or less than real thugs'.[16] One British Army officer stationed in Ireland communicated to Field Marshal Sir Henry Wilson during the war that 'we are importing crowds of undisciplined men who are just terrorising the country'.[17]

If the behaviour of the force was objectionable to some members of the British imperial forces, it was searing its way into the consciousness of many communities across Ireland. This is perhaps summarised most forcefully by an east Clare interviewee who declared in 2010 that, 'They were never Black and Tans. They were the fuckin' Black and Tans!'[18] In 2008 Flan O'Brien from Ballymalone in Tuamgraney reflected towards the end of an interview that had contained much commentary on the Black and Tans:

> I often say, do you know. Isn't a fright when you think of 'em, the Tans, you know? To say that they came in there through people's

homes and ransacked 'em and burned 'em if they met anyone who was fighting for their freedom.[19]

For P.J. Clancy in north Clare, it was the arrival of the Black and Tans that set off the powder keg:

> 'Twas all right until the trouble started, do you know. They [RIC] were just doing their business away like you know. But when the trouble started and they got involved with the Black and Tans, that made an awful difference. Some of 'em [RIC] turned over and became great men with the IRA and more of 'em then were nearly as bad as any Black and Tans.[20]

In a long series of interviews with Clancy, whose parents both joined the struggle for Irish freedom, his feelings towards the Black and Tans were made clear. I asked P.J. to discuss any distinction that may have been made between the Black and Tans, RIC and broader British imperial forces. Like many interviewees, he affirmed that, for the people who suffered, the exact composition of the force was irrelevant and that their actions were deemed inseparable from British imperial activity throughout Ireland and across the world:

> Anything we heard about 'em was very bad, do you know … like from several stories that we heard of do you know; you could make no distinction between 'em do you know. They both [Black and Tans and RIC] did awful deeds. The more I read about them, and the more I read about what they did all over the world, we'll say in their time, the more I hate 'em! It has come to a time that if I met something that has come from a shop or made in what they call the UK I wouldn't eat it! It has built up because you are reading about it[,] what they

did, not here alone but the world over. Out in India even, you might have heard the story about where they mowed down 369?[21]

In Ennistymon, ninety-year-old Maureen Connole remembered that when the revolutionary period was discussed, an atmosphere of fear was foregrounded, as was the brutish behaviour of the British forces:

> Repeatedly we'd hear about it. And I would hear my mother. She was always terrified of anybody in uniform because they came so often. They just burst in the door. They poisoned our dogs, I knew that. I knew that uncle Tom was shot and burnt. It was frightening to hear about it.[22]

Over in east Clare, Peggy Hogan had gleaned from local oral tradition an intense feeling of disgust at the behaviour of the Black and Tans in her native Feakle:

> Tim Clune met up [with] the Tans when they were in Ireland and to just punish him they put him sitting down in a lug [hollow in the surface] in the road to sing a song for 'em. And he sang a song that was very much against 'em and 'twas surprise that he wasn't shot! ... What did they say, [singing] "a bunch of Peelers went out one night on duty and patrolio. They met a guard upon the road and took him to be a strollero. Meg, meg, meg, let go of my leg or I'll puck you with my hornsio." They were the Tans and he sang that song and they threatened to shoot him. On the main road in Annagh, Feakle. In the entrance to his own house in Drumminnanav.

When asked to further characterise the experience of that time from accounts she had heard, Peggy was emphatic:

Terrorised! Terrorised. Shur the neighbouring woman who was made drink thirteen cups of tea. All one after another. Baby Noonan, Annagneal. Oh that happened! He just, if there was a vulgar lad in it, he'd just penalise you, crucify you!²³

Joe 'Jack' Sexton from Mullagh was ninety-one when he offered a rounded summary, which highlighted the brutal and abnormal nature of what was the War of Independence:

> The Tans burned everything! 1921 … They tried do you see [to free Ireland]. So they called 'em the Volunteers and the women were Cumann na mBan. Women joined you know and did what they could. The fight went on. Dirt on both sides, of course, was given … the Rineen ambush was in September 1920. The boys [IRA] killed lorries of Black and Tans and they had no one injured. The British called for a truce and the truce was signed. Oh, ya, Priests joined it. Priests joined it. In May 1921, our two curates, Fr Gaynor and Fr McKenna was [*sic*] arrested. They were high up in the ranks of the IRA … they got six months in jail.²⁴

Michael Howard was five when the Black and Tans were first seen in his native west Clare. He argued that the feelings of animosity towards English rule and support towards republicans in West Clare were strong, but explained that much of this was a result of their behaviour: 'Everyone was IRA that time, do you see, because the Tans were goin' around lootin' and shootin' … they were notorious blackguards in the European war and they brought 'em over to Ireland to frighten the IRA.'²⁵

Like Tom Brennan, Kathleen Nash declared when interviewed two months after her hundredth birthday that, 'They [Black and Tans] were only let out of jail in England and brought over to Ireland.'²⁶ Joe Sexton was equally emphatic when he affirmed:

> Shur they were drunk half the time. England had no army to send to Ireland so she had criminals in jail, some for murder and some for bad deeds and she made an agreement with them that if they came to Ireland and fought … they'd get their freedom.²⁷

Martin Walsh, who was two years old when the force arrived in Ireland, told me bluntly: 'They were a shower of rowdies. They were the criminals of England, the Black and Tans that was let loose on Ireland for to plunder and rob all they had and no one to control 'em.' ²⁸ For Seán O'Halloran, whose uncle was a member of the 5th Battalion Mid Clare IRA Brigade, the impression of the force was equally clear:

> 'Twasn't very nice anyway you wouldn't be repeating it, like. They were supposed to be the dregs of society. Of course they did a lot of atrocities, like. To us anyway that time, you'd class 'em as wild animals, when we started talking about it first. That was the feeling you'd get.²⁹

When invited to speak about the force his father, Seán, fought against, John Murnane from Newmarket-on-Fergus laid the blame for their introduction with Winston Churchill:

> That's Churchill. The name Churchill around here wasn't liked at all. He sent in animals. He took 'em out of the prisons and sent 'em over here. And sent over officers from the regular army to lead 'em or look after 'em. They were ruthless.³⁰

Catherine Talty, who was six years of age when the British forces withdrew from Clare, noted that 'people [were] in dire fear of the Black and Tans'.[31] Mary Murrihy who was born two years after Talty, in 1918, recalled: 'my father was letting 'em [sheltering IRA]. Oh, he was dead on 'em [Black and Tans], he was dead on 'em. He hated 'em! He hated 'em with all his heart!'[32] Ninety-two-year-old Micheál O'Connell offered the following explanation, after I asked him to characterise the period based on the impressions he formed from speaking to people who lived through it, referring to the Tans as the 'British Army':

> They were tough times. Your life was in your fist! 'Twas tough enough on the likes of a man, who had a wife and family, a young lad five or six years goin' off to school and you wouldn't know, the British Army could come along the road and just blaze the young lads and went off. Would it bother 'em? [Wouldn't] Bother 'em one fuckin' bit![33]

Anthony Malone was a key member of the Mid Clare IRA. As a member of its 4th Battalion, he was a participant in the Rineen ambush of September 1920.[34] I asked his son, Billy, to reflect on the contention that comrades of the Black and Tans and RIC had also been killed:

> They would have sort of felt that they were unwarranted [reprisals]. You know from the point of view of the Tans who had buddies killed, the locals here didn't look at it like that. They felt they got what they deserved and if they weren't in Ireland, nothing would have happened to them, you know. So they thought that the reprisals were very unfair and that they picked on innocent people on a whim. And the Tans had a very bad reputation, that they could get drunk and shoot someone, just for no reason. As they told it, they were a bit bitter telling it. I'd say there was a bit of hatred towards the Tans.[35]

Nora Canavan from Monreal, outside Ennistymon in north Clare, was fourteen when the Black and Tans left Ireland in 1922. At the age of 104 when I invited her to describe the force, she breathed deeply and reflected, before recalling:

> Oh, the Black and Tans, that was the worst. Oh, you couldn't have a spark of light. The windows would have to be covered over. The curtains were no good. And if they saw a spark of light they'd bang a shot in through that window. And they'd arrive into you on the morning before ... I remember we were in bed, children, when they'd arrive searching the house. You'd be supposed to have some of the Volunteers in the house. But shur no one ever stayed. They were too near the [Monreal] ambush where 'twas held. The ambush was very near us, you know, there back at the cross.[36]

The men who haunted Ireland's memory for so long were not criminals or lunatics released from jails and set free on Ireland. Instead many were war heroes of the British Empire. This in no way dilutes the narrative. Rather it draws attention to the organised and official nature of the terror they were responsible for and how this was connected intimately to those directing it. In addition, given their record in Ireland over the fifteen months they were active in the country, it is important to note that if the Black and Tans were not criminals when they arrived into Ireland, they certainly were when they left.

Indelible Memories – Children Remember

Rudolph Feilding, the 9th Earl of Denbigh, fought as a British artillery lieutenant at the Battle of Tell El Kebir in 1882, during the Anglo-Egyptian war. There he aimed his horse artillery gun on a retreating train of Egyptian rebels, which led to the death of hundreds of Egyptians and helped bring about their ultimate surrender. Throughout his life, Feilding was central to British imperial activities and was colonel commandant of the Honourable Artillery Company from 1902 until 1933.[37] In February 1921, while the Irish War of Independence raged, Denbigh was moved to write to the press and convey his feelings. The man who had seen much of the violence perpetrated within the shadow of the British Empire and who, as a commander of that Empire, had discharged much of it, was prophetic about the impact the violence of the time would have on future Anglo-Irish relations. His comments were repeated in the British House of Commons:

> What hope is there of peace in Ireland when the whole of Ireland is in this condition and every child goes to bed at night in terror, hearing shots and seeing murders? These ineffaceable and indelible memories will make them enemies of our country for the whole of their lives.[38]

The endurance of the acrimony predicted by Denbigh was particularly evident among many interviewees who were children during the War of Independence. In 2008 I interviewed 105-year-old Margaret Hoey, who disclosed a lingering animosity that underlined the emotion of the period. In November 1920, just three months before Denbigh's declaration, Margaret had stood as a sixteen-year-old girl in Scariff churchyard as four young men were lowered into their graves, following their murder by crown forces. In 2008, when I asked her to reflect on the people who may have supported British rule in Ireland and who may have been opposed to the struggle for freedom, Margaret became appreciably agitated, before reaching deep into her memory and archived emotion:

Oh, everyone wasn't in favour! They wanted England all the time in the place. Indeed, we owe England nothing! I'd like to see 'em trampled on! They were no bargain for Ireland![39]

This section largely focuses on a series of people who were old enough when I recorded them to have directly remembered the period as children. This presents a unique opportunity to gain a sense of the experience, fear and emotion of living through such a violent and dangerous time.

'Ah so many is the time I walked this road!'

On 12 April 2009 I drove with 105-year-old Paddy Gleeson to the place of his youth in east Clare. I had recorded Paddy on many occasions in his home in O'Callaghan's Mills, at commemorations and at Raheen Hospital, where he spent his final days before he died in November 2010 as Ireland's oldest man. A year earlier, a digital recorder sat between us as his every reaction to the milestones of his mind unfolded. In this instance, I wanted to return Paddy physically to the places of the stories I had heard. As we drove slowly between the villages of Tuamgraney and Bodyke, each landmark seemed a touchstone for some deeply felt nostalgia:

> Are we goin' to Coolawn? I'd be delighted to see it! Ah the love of the Lord, is that the Evicted field? ... Is it the Cathsaoireach? Well the lord of mercy on 'em all, that's where all the poor people went in my time. Ah so many is the time I walked this road![40]

All the landmarks mentioned sparked vivid recollections, but were only an overture to the main act of Paddy's memory. As he peered out the window of my car, he searched and searched for 'the tree I went up'. Ninety years previously, in late 1920, as Paddy walked that very road as a young boy, he stopped dead and listened. An ominous sound in the distance had reached his ears as he returned home with a bag of messages:

> My aunt sent me on 19 December for some groceries to Bodyke, tea and sugar. I was coming on down with my little parcel. A lovely fine night around seven o'clock. And when I was comin' to Coolreagh cross, Hogans' was only 500 or 600 yards away, I heard the lorries and the tear-away at Hogans' ... I heard the running up Coolreagh Road. I was mistaken. I thought it was the Tans coming but it was everyone hooking for home! I looked around and I saw nowhere to go and there was a big tree and up I went. I went up on the tree with my messages. Sat down above and hung up my messages and the Black and Tans were all around and raiding Hogans' and raiding everywhere and I was a witness to the whole lot of it and still I stayed above on my tree sittin' down smiling away for myself. Well the gobeen was no fool. I wasn't a gobeen at all! They were quare times but the people, they were wonderful. They took it well. I heard them going in the finish between half ten and eleven and I hit on and there was staighle [steps forming an entrance through a ditch] going in to Hogans'. In I went.[41]

'Terrible devils'

In Carrigoran House Nursing Home in late 2008 and early 2009, I undertook two recordings with Margaret Hoey, who was born 105 years earlier, in 1904. Margaret offered her testimony on the War of Independence and the Black and Tans:

> By God shur, 'twas a crime in itself for two or three brothers to be living together. They tormented them, burned their houses over their heads. We often saw the houses burning. Oh, they were

terrible devils, terrible devils. Of course the Volunteers at the time were cutting holes in the road, tormenting the Tans, like, travelling. But the Tans never filled them. They'd go around to collect up the local men to fill the hole. Go to the bogs maybe, where people were working in the bog, collecting the turf. Oh, they tormented the people.

The impact on local communities, particularly those with active IRA companies was severe, an impact Margaret witnessed first-hand:

All the local lads were joined the Volunteers [IRA] and the Tans were after them, burning their houses and beating them up and the wrong people were often beaten too! Of course the roads were cut. They'd know where the Volunteers were. They'd go round and pick up the locals to fill 'em. They wouldn't lift the shovel themselves![42]

As an almost adult observer, Margaret was able to give a rounded assessment on the period, and in particular the challenges for families of young men active in the IRA. I asked Margaret if it was hard on the families of local IRA men:

Course it was! There were people, families who had their sons 'on the run'. They were worried. Terribly worried. They [British] knew the houses to burn, but they were getting plenty information [*sic*], from people who didn't like the local Volunteers, or didn't understand it at all. They were satisfied with England! People went to the police or the Peelers as we used to call 'em. Oh, they were getting plenty information … Of course, people that had some of their family in the police force, they were blamed.[43]

'Milk'

Place, smell and sound can instantly transport one's mind to an experience long gone but stamped indelibly on the memory. For Mae Tuohy from Feakle in east Clare, who was born on 24 May 1916, the word 'milk' acted as a memory trigger for more than nine decades. When I invited her in 2011 to recall her memories of the war, Mae immediately framed them around her own experience of hearing Black and Tans in thick English accents demanding milk from her mother when she was a child. In the townland of Kilbarron, made famous by the wise woman of Clare, Biddy Early, Mae was able to point to the spot where, ninety years previously, a Black and Tan stood:

> I remember 'em passing up and down here ... the only memory I have is that my mother was out milking the cows and she was coming in around that corner at that window there [pointing to her front window]. The lorry came and stopped there. And, em, the Black and Tan came in and he looked for --- I never forget the way he said "milk", "milk" you know. To me it sounded like that, anyway. So she brought out the bucket of milk and left it up on the window and brought out a cup or something. They drank the bucket of milk and went away about their business.[44]

Mae also explained that, during the period, a large tree was felled directly adjacent to her house, which is situated on the back road between Feakle and Tulla. The local IRA had cut the tree down to impede the movement of the British forces in the area. The road was used frequently by the Oxford and Buckinghamshire Regiment, stationed at the nearby Tulla Workhouse. As the occupant of the house closest to the tree felling, Mae's father, John Powell, an agricultural labourer, was questioned about his possible involvement. With tools in his house that could have easily brought down the tree, he was a strong suspect. 'Them trees there now.' Mae pointed out her front window, which had functioned to illuminate the carefully arranged tea, cakes and biscuits which preceded each recording undertaken at her house over many years. With that signal, Mae oriented me to the memory she was about to disclose:

> Then the incident about the cutting of the tree. You know that my father had all kinds of implements, saws, hatchets, you name it, he had it. We had a place out at the back, which is my back kitchen now. We used to call it the dairy, because we used to have pans of milk in it and there was a kind of, em, tables and pans on the table. [The place] for putting the saws and stuff, that was in under the table. But only for they had dust on them, they'd shoot first and ask questions later.[45]

On 6 October 1920 the local IRA company in Feakle ambushed a patrol of RIC near the graveyard outside the village. Tensions had been growing between republicans and the police in the weeks beforehand. Sergeant Francis Doherty from Leitrim and Constable William Stanley from Cork were both shot dead in the action. Soon after the ambush, local people fled to the outskirts of Feakle for fear of reprisals. In Kilbarron, four-year-old Mae (then Mae Powell) watched innocently as old women nervously assembled in her home, less than two miles from where the ambush occurred:

> I remember the people saying that Feakle was going to be burned … There were several people who came down and stayed here all day and all night like. I remember 'em being in a back room … I do remember 'em and I can see one woman on her knees with the shawl around her head. A lot of the older people wore shawls then … They

were inside in that room, kneeling down in [a] circle, praying hard that their houses wouldn't be burned.[46]

As Mae listened quietly to the sound of prayers in hushed unison, IRA Volunteers were preparing to occupy houses in Feakle which they expected would be attacked. While they were making their way towards the village with reinforcements from the surrounding area, they observed the burning of houses in the distance and realised they had been forestalled.[47]

'I used to clean the guns long ago after ambushes'

Michael Howard spent his almost ninety-seven years before he passed away in September 2011 in the small townland of Tarmon, four miles east of Kilrush town. Born in 1915, by the age of five Michael had become intimately aware of the War of Independence, the IRA and ambushes. His home in Tarmon was regularly used as a safe house for local republicans, a connection emphasised by Michael in every recording I undertook with him:

> I used to clean the guns long ago after ambushes you know. There'd be about forty or fifty guns up against the pallets and covered with hay so they could put the guns in through the hay ... I used to be cleaning them, Mausers and Enfields and them all.[48]

The family's sympathy did not go unnoticed and the house was singled out for frequent raids by crown forces. For Michael it meant a childhood full of often frightening disturbances:

> They raided here about four in the morning. I was inside of a feather bed that time ... They came into the room I was sleeping in, on a feather bed. I got a butt of a rifle and drove me out of bed onto the

> floor ... to see was there anything in the bed, do you know. There used to be meetings here and there would be a fella out on the road watching Knockerra Hill to see would the lights of the lorry be coming. There was a big crowd of 'em [IRA] here one night and they [Black and Tans] came along. The IRA lads only went down the haggard. They raided the house and went off again.[49]

In his winter years Michael was determined to underline the importance of the lesser-known figures in the freedom struggle. For example, he was emphatic about the role played by local scouts, such as Paddy Mescall, for the republican movement. Michael remembered how Mescall would often spend hours on the lookout at Knockerra church, wherein he would sound the church bell to warn of impending Black and Tan raids. Even the most dedicated and vigilant scouts could not always be on the lookout, however, and on a number of occasions, the forces of the crown would only alert the Howards of their arrival with a loud and sudden bang on the front door:

> The Tans arrived outside of the house. Not knowing they were coming, my father [Patrick Howard] had a brace of bullets and he gave them to me. I had turned-down stockings that time; they were all the go that time when I was a young lad. I put them inside the stockings and I went out. I put them into a hole in the cow shed and I suppose I put them in so far, I tried after but I couldn't get them out of it [laughs].[50]

Many such items were hurriedly concealed in the height of a violent war and have since rested in peace. In December 2013 Mick Ryan, whose father, Jackie, was an active member of the 3rd Battalion of the IRA's East Clare Brigade, remembered finding two hand grenades in an old wall at the back of his wife Noreen's homeplace in Clonlara. During the War of Independence, Noreen's grandparents, Michael Ryan and his wife, Nora, opened up their home as a safe house to IRA men 'on the run'. Their daughters were active members of Cumann na mBan and their sons joined the republican movement as Volunteers and dispatchers. When Mick Ryan showed the grenades to Noreen's father, Dan, who had been one of those dispatchers, the immediate response was 'We couldn't find them!' Such had been the determination to conceal, that the weapons had sometimes been secreted even out of the reach of the local IRA themselves.[51]

'To Hell with the Pope'

Kathleen Nash was born outside the east Clare town of Scariff on 2 August 1909. She recalled her memories in an interview conducted at Mount St Carmel Nursing Home, Roscrea, Co. Tipperary, shortly after turning 100 years old. The emotional power of a memory, which spoke of a violent and frightening time, was evident in Kathleen's voice. Once the purpose of the meeting (to gather memories reflecting her life story) was established, Kathleen immediately found a context within which to place that life. Her temporal reference point was clear. Before I had a chance to announce the details of the interview for the record, Kathleen declared:

> I was goin' to school, the time of the Tans. We'd meet a load of 'em going to school and we'd be afraid they'd shoot us! They shot the four boys [Scariff Martyrs][52] ... They didn't ever come into our house. They came into a house when you turn in the cross at John Minogue's all right. Mick Minogue, he was after gettin' a new suit and they took his suit! They took the suit. That's right.

Kathleen's oldest brother, Pat, was a member of the local IRA. He knew the four Scariff Martyrs personally and attended their funeral. Kathleen was proud of her older brother and of his role in the republican movement. While she was an eleven-year-old observing, he was participating.

However, for those observing, there was much to see. At school in Cooleen Bridge, on the road between Scariff and Feakle, Kathleen sat and fixed her eyes on her teacher, Thomas Jones, known to all as 'The Master'. In the Ireland of the early 1920s, the local schoolmaster was second only to the priest in the local social hierarchy. A figure of power. A sudden thud at the door and the entry of large, uniformed men with thick English accents changed this impression for a time. In the sight of his pupils, the power of Master Jones was swept away by men of violence who wished to assert *their* power over the local population. The following transcription can only attempt to convey the level of emotion involved in Kathleen's narration of that brief moment of transformation:

> I was in Cooleen Bridge at the time. Oh, the teacher. The Black and Tans came in one day to the school and they wrote 'To Hell with the Pope' on the blackboard and they made the Master write it down and he didn't want to write it. He didn't want to write it down. They were going to hit him. He had to write it, to write it down. Oh! Master Jones. Thomas Jones. They went away then after a while … He was very angry. Lord help us![53]

'I can remember my mother running as quick as lightning'

In the War of Independence, Tomás Killeen from Coore was a twenty-five-year-old captain in the 4th Battalion of the West Clare IRA Brigade. His friend, nineteen-year-old Dan Crawford from Shanavogh in the same parish, was a member of Killeen's Coore Company. The two men fought side by side in the Irish War of Independence and went on the run together when being sought by the crown forces. When traversing the west Clare countryside, they found a warm embrace and welcome at the Hayes' homestead, which provided a safe house for the local IRA in Shanaway East near Miltown Malbay. The men were also welcomed at the home during the Civil War, when they took the anti-Treaty side.[54] Mary Murrihy was born in that home in 1918 and, at the age of ninety-one, recalled her personal feeling of pride to have met men who were involved. Mary also illuminates the potential for men capable of extreme violence to have the capacity for remarkable tenderness:

> They [Black and Tans] came searching for some lad and searched every bit of the house and the lad wasn't in it at all that they were lookin' for. And he used [to] be there! He was Killeen, and Crawford ... I remember Dan Crawford and I can remember Tomás Killeen. I had a sore finger and the only one I'd let dress it was, was Tomás Killeen! I can remember them comin' and stayin' the night and stealing back home. What they went through ... torture![55]

Mary's childhood memories present just flashing images of the period when her home was often the scene of immense panic and fear, like one occasion when Killeen was in her home and the Black and Tans were heard coming:

> I can remember my mother running as quick as lightning, givin' 'em [IRA] whatever word came. Of course whoever came in, that was their job. "The Tans, quick quick" ... send 'em off, quick as he could. I can remember Tomás Killeen at that time.[56]

50   THE TIME OF THE TANS

At 104, Nora Canavan was able to communicate the level of intensity that the period represented, even without words. A deep and emotion-filled intake of breath was sufficient to convey the feelings conjured by a reflection on the Black and Tans:

> I think the Volunteers weren't around very much. They were in more backward places, quieter places, like. Of course the Tans passed every morning and every evening. Oh God I remember an evening we had a mission in Clouna. My sister and myself and another girl, we were on the road going to the mission and they came. They started banging shots up in the mountain where the [Monreal] ambush was.[57] Oh, I remember, we were scared of our living life. So they took no notice of us, anyway, but they were afraid for themselves but they were banging the shots but oh --- the life was frightened out of us.[58]

'He crashed over all the fields and valleys and everything!'

> I remember about the Rineen ambush. I remember the evening 'twas over of course. I remember a man comin' in there maybe about five o'clock or whatever time it was. He was all dirt and he was every way worse than each other I thought. But he kind of washed himself anyway. 'Twas comin' back from the Rineen ambush he was. He was there and he crashed over all the fields and valleys and everything![59]

Paddy McGough was just five years of age when he was suddenly shaken from his childhood wonderings by a loud crashing sound at the door of his house in Kylea, Inagh, in north Clare. Startled, he saw the dishevelled figure of IRA Volunteer Jamsie Meaney rush into his house in an evident panic. In the same kitchen in 2011, Paddy recalled Meaney's hurried arrival. Meaney had crossed the mountainside townlands of Moughna and Cloonanaha, frantically racing through approximately seven miles of bushes, fields and rough terrain before arriving at the home of Michael McGough in Kylea. Meaney was one of sixty Volunteers who had participated in the ambush on British forces that led to the death of six members of Black and Tans/RIC between Miltown Malbay and Ennistymon.[60] Meaney's arrival at McGoughs' had been hastened by British soldiers, who had arrived on the ambush scene and engaged the IRA in a rearguard action, which forced them across the mountain. Over ninety-one years later, sitting in the same home, the story of Rineen had lost little of its potency for Paddy since it was brought to his door on the evening of 22 September 1920.[61]

'Extra brave'

In Clare, as across the country, stories often centre on the heroic IRA figure in memory at the expense of many lesser-known men and women. Martin Devitt joined the Irish Republican Brotherhood (IRB) with John Joe 'Tosser' Neylon in 1915. From then until his death in 1920, Devitt was one of the most active republicans in the Clare area. He was a draper's assistant and was also, at the age of twenty-five, the vice O/C of the Mid Clare IRA Brigade. Before the Black and Tans arrived in Ireland, Devitt had taken the war to the existing crown forces in the county, the RIC. On 24 February 1920 he was fatally wounded during an engagement with an RIC patrol at Crowe's Bridge. Devitt was one of the most significant IRA figures to be killed during the Irish War of Independence in Clare and is remembered in memorial, song and story. For P.J. Clancy, his position in the folklore of the period was secure:

> Martin Devitt was extra brave now. I always heard now. Shur at Crowe's Bridge now, he told 'em to put up their hands and one of 'em

had a girl with him and he pushed the girl in front of him right away and Devitt put down his head then. He wouldn't fire on her. Devitt put up his head and yer man had his gun aimed at that spot [where Devitt was positioned].[62]

In the aftermath of the incident, the local IRA unit attempted to conceal the body of Devitt from British authorities. It was felt that the death of such a significant republican figure would be a boost for the crown forces. Devitt was taken and buried under a reek of turf in a nearby bog. Evidently, however, a member of the party involved in secreting the republican leader's remains informed the British authorities, as his body was discovered soon after and taken:

> Well the people from that area then, Paddy Harvey [P.J.'s neighbour] was telling me, brought him as far as their house in Monanana and the Clouna crowd took over from there and he was buried in Priest Rynne's bog now ... one of the ones that carried him spied on him. Paddy Harvey was telling me that he saw the lorries the following morning, coming out the Clouna road above to collect the body. Ah Paddy would be small that time, very young but he actually saw 'em, he said.[63]

For Nora Canavan, who was twelve years old when the death of Martin Devitt echoed across the north Clare landscape, the aftermath was indelibly imprinted on her memory. While her reference to a coffin is likely to be confused with the expected way a body would be carried, her recollection of Martin Devitt's lifeless body being taken across the land remains a powerful connection to a profoundly important moment in the period:

> I remember a poor fella [Martin Devitt], to see them carrying the coffin across the hills and they left it in an old shed where cattle used to be. Out in the night then, they took him away and they buried him. They went up apast the house and I remember the man we had workin' for us, he'd come in and he said, 'Well the finest funeral I ever saw,' he said, 'is gone up the road.' Oh that was dreadful. And they buried him in a bank of turf in Clouna and the following morning, the Black and Tans came and took the coffin out of that bank of turf. Well they say someone got thousands for telling the Tans. Ah 'twas very sad. Oh, I can think of that coffin goin' across the land, you know. I saw it ya and my aunt was home from England. Oh, she thought she'd never get back in time! She was so upset by it. We were all out looking at it.[64]

Matthew Birmingham grew up in Moyasta with the knowledge that three of his uncles had been members of the broader police force which Devitt and his comrades had challenged. Two of his uncles had been members of the Dublin Metropolitan Police, while a third was an RIC constable stationed in Kerry, where, during an engagement with the IRA, a bullet grazed his windpipe. Matthew's family connections may have given him a more neutral opinion on the period. Back when he was nearly five years old, however, his understanding of that time was one of a child's wonder intermingled with inherited fear:

> I remember the Tans to be around. The Black and Tans. They were brought over here from England to do the work the RIC wouldn't do. If they had to shoot someone maybe the RIC wouldn't do it but these would do it! They were said to be released from mental hospitals and places. I have a recollection of my next-door neighbour Cornie Kelleher. He had a beast up on the road some day and didn't

they collide with him. So a whole load of 'em came out to investigate. I remember I went out of the front door but I remember I was told to come in! A charabanc [motor vehicle] came down and nine or ten [Black and Tans], shur they were only soldiers or men to me. I remember my mother shouting out at me to come in!⁶⁵

I interviewed Matthew on several occasions at his home in Moyasta. In a further recording, he spoke once more about his childhood observations of the Tans:

They landed down and jumped out of the truck and off over … I was afraid of 'em of course because there was every kind of a bad story.⁶⁶

At the age of ninety-seven, Matthew had a more reasoned view on the force, tempered perhaps by his uncle's association with the police, who worked closely with the Black and Tans: 'Oh of course, they were dangerous men. Some of them. Not all. Some of 'em were lunatics of course. They got the dirty work to do … they were sent over here to do what the RIC refused to.'⁶⁷

'I was in the cot and they came into the room'
Kevin Nugent from Clonusker, on the outskirts of Scariff in east Clare, told me in 2010 how his mother often recalled the Black and Tans raiding their house during the War of Independence. Ninety-year-old Nugent explained how during one of these raids, while the Black and Tans were breaking furniture and intimidating those in the house, he was a nine-month-old baby lying in a cradle next to the family's open hearth fire. At one point, a Black and Tan almost knocked the infant Kevin into the fire – he was saved by his vigilant mother, who, although frightened, had refused to move far from her new son. The little infant had only

been glimpsed by his uncle, twenty-six-year-old IRA Volunteer Joe Nugent, the target of the Black and Tans. Joe was an active member of the East Clare IRA and was 'on the run' when the Black and Tans arrived at the home of his older brother, Tom, the father of Kevin.

At the same time as the raid on Nugents', in the west Clare parish of Labasheeda a two-year-old baby boy was similarly disturbed from his infant wonder by a Black and Tan raid on his home in Clonkerry East.[68] As with the infant Kevin Nugent, the force that entered John O'Connell's home was looking for his uncle, twenty-nine-year-old Jamie Corbett, adjutant of the 1st Battalion, West Clare IRA Brigade.[69] Sitting across from me, beside his turf-fuelled, open-hearth fire in the same house some ninety-two years later, John O'Connell reflected:

> The Black and Tan war was on at the time. The Black and Tans came into the room one night, searching. They were searching all Clonkerry at the time … They were looking for my uncle. He was in the Volunteers. But he wasn't to be had that night! My father and mother was here … Ah they were a rough crowd and mighty strong alcohol with 'em. Ah they were dreaded shur. They were dreaded by the people at the time like and that would hang on, like [in memory]. I was in the cot and they came into the room shur where I was.'Twas lookin' for Jamie they were of course. He could be anyplace the same night. What frightened my father altogether was the smell of the whiskey out of 'em. You'd smell it off 'em coming in the door shur! They'd be dangerous with that bloody thing, do you know. They could make a mistake or anything, do you know … and my grandfather and grandmother were down there in that room. My father and mother didn't hear 'em one night until they were inside in the room with 'em because the old man let 'em in, my

grandfather [shows interviewer the door through which the Black and Tans entered the house].⁷⁰

John O'Connell was born on Thursday 11 September 1919. Back then the Black and Tans were at best a burgeoning notion in the mind of Winston Churchill, then British secretary of state for war. John would be six months old before the force that later dominated the memory of Ireland would arrive in Ireland. Like Kevin Nugent in east Clare, in the charged years of the War of Independence, John was nurtured by his mother. Bridget O'Connell (née Corbett) was thirty-nine years old in 1921. It was the involvement in the IRA of her younger brother, Jamie, that drew such attention from the Black and Tans to Clonkerry East. In 2012 O'Connell explained how, despite his mother's loyal support and accommodation of her brother and his comrades, the strain was severe:

> 'Twas the way my mother was pure sick of 'em for a finish. She didn't give a damn what happened to them. When they were over in that aul dugout they were going over and heather here and shur clothes used to be often getting wet and she'd be cooking food for 'em. There used to be several telling her she should look for a pension. She was well entitled but she said she wouldn't. She wouldn't want to hear no more about 'em.⁷¹

Michael 'Hookey' Farrell was almost three years old when the Black and Tans came into his home in Tintrim, Whitegate, in east Clare. He was left with only a flashing memory of the moment he was faced with forces of the British Empire, in what should have been the comfort and security of his bed:

> I remember the aul Tans alright, coming into the room to us. I do

barely. They came up and they had my mother ordered coming up a dozen of duck eggs and a dozen of hen eggs, for to have it ready when they were done. 'How many of ye is here?' The aul lad came in. 'One, two, three, four.' He started countin'. There was nine of us, eight of us in the bed. He didn't ask us any questions or anything. He only said, 'Ye're all right. We won't touch ye. Ye can go asleep.'[72]

'Hookey' didn't go to sleep. Neither did any of his siblings. The door closed and Michael huddled closer to his brothers and sisters in a shivering hope they would not return. He discovered many years later that, on the same day, his neighbour was taken by the same group:

> Poor Paul Kelly and his brother. They were training a young horse and they had to come across our place and the Tans was below. They said to them, "One of ye come up and the other one stay there." So Paul came up and they said, "Come on, come on, get into that lorry." Fucked him into the lorry and told him to stay there until they were finished here in Tintrim. Brought him off to Scariff and kept him there, all night filling trenches and he had to walk home.[73]

The charged years of the War of Independence carried an air of volatility and uncertainty. For a period of over two years, violence lingered. For the general public there were two sides. Although increasingly cautious, the crown forces were deliberately open in their activities and movements. For them, it was important to demonstrate force. For their counterpart, the IRA, to conceal was to survive. From within the shadows of their own landscape, they were able to execute a guerrilla war that frustrated an empire built on conventional military campaigns. It was rare to see the army of the Irish Republic openly display their movements. Martin Walsh, a native of Kilmihil, who, after returning from London, married in Creevagh in Mullagh, was given one such rare opportunity when returning from school as a child:

> There was and I remember they to be drillin' and I a young lad goin' to school. I didn't know. There was a grove out near Teermanagh Cross [near Miltown Malbay]. Trees at each side [of] Matt Kelly's. 'Twas a landlord place. And there was a big grove there on the road runnin' under all these trees. And I was comin' home one evenin', dark, and the IRA they were drillin' there and I never knew what drillin' was like or what were they doin'! And when I came near 'em, I saw 'em lined up and they stopped drillin' when they saw me and they beckoned me on. And I went and passed away and that was the first thing I saw about IRA.[74]

Born in 1909, Timmy Ryan from Kilmihil had a clear and vivid memory of seeing the Black and Tans pass his house in Corgrigg, three miles from the west Clare village of Kilmihil:

> Ya, I remember them. They never raided us. Oh, I remember seeing them in Kilmihil and I remember seeing them passing in lorries. They'd be standing up on the lorry, standing up and watching always … I often see 'em in the lorries. A load of men going and the back of the lorry would be open and any of them that would be wounded would be sitting on a chair or something like that going to the hospital. But the Black and Tans, they hadn't much to do around Kilmihil. Watching around public houses and things like that but they weren't as rough as they were in different places.[75]

The War of Independence emerged from the shadow of the First World War. Timmy Ryan was old enough to remember local men from his parish who returned from that war, where they had served with the British Army. Some returned broken, others wounded, while some who had come back on furlough decided to desert and remained in the area. All returned to a more politically charged Ireland than they had left. A young Timmy would observe the men as they walked past his house on their way home to Kilmihil:

> You used to meet a lot of 'em coming the road. After coming out of the trenches you'd be allowed seven days off. You'd see 'em walking. I remember seeing 'em walking past there. Someone of them kind of wounded. Paddy Butler, Buddy Nevins was on the run. He wouldn't go back … I remember the ambulance going then with a horse. The bowdy [*sic*] car. We were afraid of it. It used to be bringing people to the hospital, with sickness or one thing or another. Christ it used to frighten us!

Palkie McNamara (sometimes spelled Mac Conmara), who was born on 15 March 1916, met soldiers in his childhood too. This time, however, they were not natives of his land. Instead, they were the Welsh Guards, temporarily camped in the town of Scariff in east Clare, near the old national school on the Connaught Road, close to Palkie's house. Here, Palkie offers a rare fond memory of the British forces. Notably, it was not the Black and Tans, however, whom Palkie warmly remembered:

> In 1920 there was a soldier's camp in our field. The Welsh Guards were there. And there was curfew law at the time, martial law. You had to be in before dark you know. They were in a tent anyway, in a camp. I was missing for some time anyway. I went into the canteen and I got tea and biscuits! [laughs] My mother found me there.[76]

'I was taken off that road by the Tans'

The memory of the revolutionary period is deepened by its inextricable connection to the place in which it originates and in which it has endured over the last century. A sense of place and identity are critical to experience, memory and understanding in an Irish context. Daniel Corkery, in his 1965 introduction to Micheál Ó Súilleabháin's *Where Mountainy Men Have Sown*, powerfully articulated the emotive force of history and connected it vividly to the local and the lived. In reflecting on Ó Súilleabháin's recollections of the War of Independence in west Cork, Corkery remarked that: 'The tensions that still stir in our depths are not due to the discussions of historians but the remembrance of very living local instances: the grabbing of territories, the laments of poets, the desecration of holy places, previous attempts at insurrection.'[77]

A taped interview conducted in 1988 in Raheen Day Care Centre in Tuamgraney was uncovered during this research. The recording is forcefully instructive with regard to the intensity of knowledge and emotional connection associated with place in the Irish psyche. This is particularly so when the interview in question is focused on a time of such high trauma and emotion as the War of Independence. The interviewee, Tommy Bolton, was a former IRA Volunteer in the Caherhurley Company of the East Clare Brigade, in which he acted as a scout. Born in 1900, he was interviewed by a local historian, John S. Kelly, and the parish priest of Tuamgraney, Canon Paddy O'Brien. For Bolton's generation, the connection between place and people was assured and for many the townland, the smallest geographical division of territory in Ireland, was the primary unit of identity. In the townland, their consciousness formed and their understanding of the world began. Close to the end of the tape, Tommy Bolton can be heard sitting forward in a chair beside his bed at Raheen Hospital, as if to allow more amplification in his voice. He was going back to his townland to relate one last defence of his place and wanted to make sure he was communicating the story with sufficient power. His story took him back a number of decades, to a time when change was coming to his native Ballydonaghane in the mountains overlooking the rural village of Bodyke. Forestry was beginning its gradual takeover and the *botharín* (small road) into Tommy's old family home was under threat of planting. Tommy's reaction, illustrated below, is deepened by his placing of that simple road in the broader history of his family, of his townland and of his country. In animated tones, he explained:

> I had a few words with the forester and a few sharp words too! I got into a bit of a temper the same evening ... I said, "Do you know sir, you have a nerve and to send in machinery there! That's a private road," I said. "I was taken off that road by the [Black and] Tans around about the country in early morning and I digging the surface of that myself and my uncle ... and you're tellin' me you're takin' it over as a forestry road! Well you're not," says I, "while I'm in it! You can be quite sure of it," says I.[78]

Tommy's robust defence of his small road was based not only on its importance to his family, but on its place in his memory and in the memory of the Irish people. For Tommy's generation, the Irish War of Independence, or 'the time of the Tans', was a key landmark of memory. For him to be captured and taken off that road by Black and Tans created an emotional connection that transcended any notion of land, money or change. It was a permanent mark on his consciousness, evoking both the heightened emotions of fear and trauma and the retrospective pride in a people who, from their own townlands, made a determined stand against an empire. Tommy Bolton died two years later, on 29 December 1992. At the time of writing, in the townland of Ballydonaghane, the small road that Tommy fought to retain is gazed upon by a forest at either side – but there it remains.

The foundation of my own interest in older people and their memories was firmly located in my native townland of Ballymalone. There, from the age of eight, I would visit the neighbour closest to our home on an almost daily basis. A native of Corbehagh in Kilanena, Jim McNamara was born in 1908 and moved to Ballymalone sometime in the 1930s, later marrying Sarah, the daughter of the man he came to work for. In all his ninety-nine years, Jim never read a book or wrote more than his name. He never left Co. Clare, save day trips to Limerick or parts of Galway close to his native parish. Yet, he remains a profound example of the deep wisdom that came from a largely undistracted life, one rooted in the local and in the patterns of seasons and time.

Jim was a child when the Black and Tans came. As a young teenager, I would often ask him the question: 'Do you remember the Black and Tans?' Jim, drawing on his pipe, would patiently answer as if it was the first time I had asked. In one teenage folklore journal entry, dated 13 March 1996, I recorded his answer:

> The Tans? Oh, by God than I do, Thomas *a stór*. I remember 'em alright. I remember 'em to come into the room one morning shur, above at home. I was inside in bed with a few more of 'em [siblings]. Three or four of us would be in the one bed that time. They burst in the door, shoutin' and roarin' I remember. Christ man, they were right mad-lookin', the hoors. There was some road up the way a bit cut by the IRA and they wanted it filled. They dragged my brothers out anyway. Jack was there and Tom I'd say. They were a bit older than

me. I was left there in the bed lookin' on shur. I was no good to 'em. I was too small I suppose. Ah, they had done terrible rack alright, the Tans.⁷⁹

Jim died in January 2007, as he reached towards his hundredth birthday. To have met with such a profound example of heritage conducive to transmittance so young in life, and in such an isolated location, exposed me to local memory of the Black and Tans and almost by osmosis developed in me an understanding of its importance. The shift then, from passive recipient to active collector, was an easy transition.

'They struck my grandfather' – The Experience of the Old

For those who had not seen much of the world, the experience had become imprinted, a memory that would endure as their youth eventually surrendered to age. For those who throughout the troubled years were already in the wintertime of their lives, however, the violence was seen through knowing eyes.

John Corbett was born in 1842 in the west Clare village of Labasheeda. When he was just three years of age, he witnessed through a child's eyes his country submerge into the depths of what many around him referred to as *An Gorta Mór* or The Great Hunger (1845–52). At a local level, it was remembered mostly in silence. Not far from where he was raised, however, one interviewee told me of how her grandfather remembered 'seeing a woman with a child in her arms and she bending down to pick up leaves and eating them, she was that hungry'.⁸⁰ The calamity which led to the death of over one million Irish people was caused as much by the British imperial system as by the potato blight. John would see much of the British system in his long life. Famine, land wars, evictions and repeated attempts by Ireland to devolve itself from British rule formed a backdrop to his life.

In 1921, eight decades after his country's worst human disaster, John was an eighty-one-year-old man when he was woken in the middle of the night by the sound of a familiar knock on the sash window at the back of their home in Clonkerry East. It was the height of the War of Independence and John Corbett would arise from his bed with only his tired joints complaining. After welcoming the weary IRA Volunteers into this home, he would place a heavy coat around his shoulders, settle his cap on his head, lift the latch on the door and move out into the darkness of the night. Inside, his two-year-old grandson John slept soundly. In 2012 that grandson was a ninety-four-year-old man himself when I recorded him at the same house, bringing a direct line of memory from the Irish Famine to 2012:

> They [IRA] used to come off and on my mother used to say in the summer morning in the break of day. There was a back window in there. There was a casement sash window [hinged at the sides] that you could open and there was a bed there in the back room, 'twas always idle. And they'd sleep mad there. The grandfather when he'd hear them coming, he'd get up out of bed and he'd go away out around the hills, to see was there anything happening.[81]

The story of John Corbett and his grandson, John O'Connell, is a powerful illustration of the way we can reach deep into the recesses of our nation's history, through the memory and tradition of our older people. Not only does the testimony recorded take us back to the childhood of the interviewee, but by eliciting oral tradition about their forebears, we can engineer glimpses of memory which journey even further into our country's past. For many, who in their winter years watched knowingly as the ancient conflict took on new and bitter dimensions in the War of Independence, yet another chapter in an old story was unfolding. Our understanding of that story is made all the richer when those evanescent fragments of experience are assembled and become part of its narration.

In the charged years of the War of Independence the majority of active IRA Volunteers were young men in their early to mid-twenties. The average age of the fathers of a cohort of Volunteers' that I examined was sixty-two. For many of these men, the activism of their sons brought severe consequences. An animated Gerome Griffin told me in 2005 how his elderly grandfather was forced to stand on a flag floor in his bare feet for over an hour by the Black and Tans led by a member of the RIC, after refusing to give information regarding the whereabouts of his son, Seán, the father of Gerome:

> They called for him one time, the time 'on the run'. This [RIC] man, back there in Lisheen was helping the Tans. He went up one day. My grandfather was there on his own and he wanted to know where was my father. And, ah, my grandmother died at the age of sixty-five from cancer so he was on his own. Ah, he wanted to know where he was and the grandfather wouldn't tell him. He [Seán Griffin] couldn't go near the house. He couldn't go home that time or they'd catch him. There was an aul flag floor that time and he had the gun pointed at my grandfather and he put him standing on the floor barefooted and he made him stand there for over an hour. The father often thought that was what gave him rheumatic after. The freezin' he got standing on the flag floor![82]

Michael O'Gorman is an intensely knowledgeable historian from Scariff in east Clare. Oral tradition handed down in his family was inherited by receptive ears. Amongst the many stories carefully preserved within his family tradition was the evening that his grandfather and grand-uncle were severely beaten by the Black and Tans. The two men from the town of Scariff were returning from a day's fishing when they were confronted by a mixed force of military and police. One of the men, Patrick Harte, Michael O'Gorman's maternal grandfather, was a former British soldier:

> There was a Captain Rigby here who was commander of the Black and Tans here in Scariff.[83] He hated my grandfather, do you now. He'd have stupid questions, you know, "How can you, as an ex-British Army officer, how can you find your way of being associated with an illegal organisation like the IRA?" My grandfather would say, "I'm not!" He was kind of tellin' porkies! But if they could prove it and it was a time they didn't need proof for much! Those guys were a law unto themselves. But the first chance they got of him, himself and his brother-in-law Micho Young. They were coming in from Lough O'Grady one evening. They were out fishin' and they used to use what they called a creel. 'Twas illegal as regards fishin' ... There was a crowd of the British below on the Feakle road ... They had a commander, a Captain Rigby. Oh, a monumental ass, if ever there was one! When they searched the lads, they discovered the creel ... They struck my grandfather anyway with the butt of a rifle and they smashed his jaw and they hit Micho into the side of the head and he was forever after stone deaf.

The severity with which Micho Young and Patrick Harte were beaten by the British forces was evident to Michael in both the stories he heard about the incident and the physical legacy of the assault. He remembered with remarkable detail how, with each telling, the viciousness of the beating was underlined. As a child, he would listen intently as the story was relayed of how his grandfather, Patrick Harte, was being beaten on the ground and how Micho Young bravely tried to intervene:

> They hammered him and kicked him while he was on the ground but Micho tried to help him so they struck Micho with a butt of a rifle and Micho fell. One of 'em stood on his arm. He stood on his arm and another one stood on his back and they got the butt of the rifle and they smashed his arm, again and again and again with the butt of the rifle. When I was a little lad, I used to spend a lot of time with my grand-uncle [Micho Young]. He had a bit of land. I used to think I was helping him anyway [laughs]. I used to notice his arm, even when the sleeve wasn't up. 'Twas like a sickle [an agricultural tool with a curved blade]. The doctors were never able to get his arm straightened out. They were able to save it all right, but they couldn't get it straight so his arm was bent over like a sickle and he had very limited movement of it.[84]

The paternal grandfather of well-known traditional singer Seamus O'Donnell would regularly get republican newspapers and read them to his neighbours in Currakyle, Caher, in a house known locally as 'The House of Commons'. Late one night during the War of Independence the Black and Tans came:

> They took my grandad out in his shirt in the middle of the night. They took him out in his shirt and put him up agin the wall and here was no pyjamas that time! They hit his toes, reddened his toes with the butt of the rifle, choppin' 'em down. They did the same thing to my other grandfather over in Turkenagh. Oh, they did. They ate every bit they had in the house and they sent them next door then for more bread. They ate all the bread.[85]

The Murder of Charles Lynch

By October 1920 the conflict had escalated to dramatic levels within Co. Clare. In all areas of the county, significant violence had been inflicted by both the IRA and crown forces. Travel was restricted and, for those who did travel, danger was everywhere. For two British soldiers to leave their company and travel throughout the countryside, while inebriated, would seem unwise in this environment. Nevertheless, that is what occurred on 21 October, when Lance-Corporal Alexander McPherson and Corporal Norman Buchanan from the 2nd Battalion of the Royal Scots began burgling houses in the Breaffa North area outside Miltown Malbay. Having stolen from several houses that they purportedly were searching for arms, they arrived at the home of seventy-five-year-old Charles Lynch at approximately 5 p.m. Lynch's son, Ned, an active member of G Company, 4th Battalion of the IRA's Mid Clare Brigade, was also there. Over three decades later, in a statement made in December 1955, Ned Lynch recalled how he immediately confronted the soldiers:

> The taller of the two men [McPherson] said they were raiding for arms and tried to push past me ... He carried what I first took to be a revolver, but on closer scrutiny noticed that it was only a glass one painted black, which I knew had been looted sometime previously from Blake's pub in Miltown ... I hit [him] a heavy punch on the right arm causing him to drop the 'shot of malt' as the toy gun was known to us locally, and it broke in pieces on the doorstep. Just as this happened, one of the neighbours arrived. He accused the soldiers of having stolen a £10 note from him, whereupon the bigger soldier tried to break away. I tripped him and brought him to the ground. We searched him thoroughly, but though we recovered other articles which he had looted, we failed to find the £10 note. The second

soldier [Buchanan], who was less truculent, was also searched, but he offered no resistance. He asked my brother if there was any other way back to the military post and, on being shown it, he made off.[86]

Lynch had been a participant in the Rineen ambush less than a month earlier. An experienced republican, he knew it was prudent to leave his home after the confrontation, as inevitably he would be sought out by the British forces. Although intimately aware of the often brutal nature of British reprisals, he could not have predicted the consequences of his earlier action as he departed his family home that evening. When McPherson did return, Charles Lynch was standing at the front of his family home. McPherson immediately took aim and shot dead the seventy-five-year-old.[87] In the British House of Commons six months later, Hamar Greenwood, the chief secretary for Ireland, claimed that Lynch was accidentally caught in the line of fire. Almost two decades later, a child was born to the Lynch family and was named after his grandfather who was murdered in 1920. Young Charlie Lynch grew up to inherit the story of his grandfather and of his family's connection to the War of Independence. In the 1950s he and his brother would march around their kitchen in Miltown Malbay with a rifle reputed to have been used in the Rineen ambush.[88] Charlie Lynch outlined his family's story, beginning with his childhood military drilling:

> We had an aul shotgun in the house that was supposed to be used in the Rineen ambush. My mother was mad to get rid of it! [laughs] Because when we'd get a chance, we'd be going around the floor with it on our shoulder. She had a horror of all those things and maybe she had a reason to have it!

It was evident from family tradition that although others were involved, his uncle Ned was the central character in the family's connection to Ireland's freedom struggle:

> The main man was Ned Lynch, my uncle, who at a young age went to England … He came back in I think around 1916 … He was involved over in England to a certain extent. I think he joined the IRB in London. He knew Michael Collins, when Collins was over there and he also knew Sam Maguire … It led on then to 1920 and he was a man 'on the run'. My father was John Lynch and he worked at home on the land here. He wasn't as involved but they'd be sympathetic. They'd be strong IRA people, like. But Ned was always 'on the run'. I suppose he nearly broke the aul woman's heart. She used to say, when she'd open the door, "Would it be a British soldier or an RIC man outside?" Anyway, they [the British forces] used to target the house quite a bit.

As with many young IRA Volunteers, the lure to the family home was strong. Despite the clear danger this entailed, 'on the run' republicans would often risk both their own and their family's safety to return home, if only briefly. Charlie spoke about one such homecoming to Breaffa North:

> He came home here one evening and he'd always call in the night. She'd [Ned Lynch's mother Katie] know when to get the bit of food ready for him. He was just sitting down inside in the house when the two doors opened together, the back door and the front. Of course it was a planned thing. The RIC and there was a few Tans with them as well. He was there and he was caught unawares. 'Twas in the height of the winter and they were all indoors. They took him out, I'd imagine to shoot him. But luckily enough, the old woman, she was

tough and she was brave. I remember her. I was about eight or nine when she died. She was a woman of her period and time, like, you know. She was very tough. She knew once they went outside the door … they had their faces covered which was a sign that they weren't goin' to bring him to the barracks. They were going to deal with him there and then! She kicked up a bit of a scene … of course one of 'em was a fella who had a small bit of principle about him. He got a small bit worried when he saw her getting so upset about it. My father used to tell me he said, "I'm not going to hold this woman, she's in a very bad state." So there was another fella there and he said, "Here hold this fella and I'll hold her" … While they were exchanging, and yer man loosened his grip on Ned, he knocked yer man over the low wall outside and he got away. He was lucky but 'twas pitch dark like. Just back there a small bit we were building a shed and the stones were out on the road and when he was running, he fell over the stones and the shots went out over him. He escaped down to a house in Caherush [Quilty] … My father came to the door when the old woman was struggling with yer man and the other fella, the second RIC fella turned around and fired at him and he missed him and he hit the jam of the door. But if he made any move he was going to be shot definitely. But he knew that they hadn't got him [Ned]. He went upstairs to a room that was up there and he could see the outline of the people and he knew they didn't have Ned with them.

Sitting in the same house where in October 1920 a rough knock on the door opened up a deeply traumatic episode in his family's history, Charlie Lynch spoke openly to me about this profound and harrowing landmark:

When the grandfather was shot out there. He wasn't involved at all. He just happened to be in the wrong place at the wrong time. 'Twas just the fact that he was half deaf and he didn't hear the tender at all. The old woman was with him … The three boys were gone. My father and Ned and Jimmy were gone because they were expecting them [crown forces] to come out. But I remember my father saying that "Shur there is no fear of the old man, they won't do anything to him." It was something that kind of never left him [John Lynch] and even Ned. They felt guilty about it always because their activities in confronting the two boys, that it led directly to the father being shot. That was one thing my father never much spoke about and he didn't want you to talk about it. My father was very upset about it and he never really wanted to talk about it.[89]

When Charles Lynch was struck by the bullet discharged from the rifle of Lance Corporal Alexander McPherson, his sixty-five-year-old wife, Katie, was the first to reach his side.[90] He died with his wife kneeling over him. When Katie rose to her feet, she had to face the world without her husband and continue to care for her three sons, one of whom was a direct target for the British forces. The impact of her husband's murder took its toll on Katie, but it was a burden she endured. In 2014 Charlie Lynch remembered his grandmother:

> She was a tough cookie. She was a small bit strange after that in the head … And another thing too. There were these courts set up afterwards where people looked for compensation for stuff, do you know. All our hay and whatever they had in the sheds outside or whatever, that was burnt during 1921, I suppose. There was a committee there in town and they were set up to take statements from people who lost property and they'd get compensation. But I heard the old woman went in. They asked her repeatedly to know would she, because they had lost a lot of property, not to mention the

old man. But she said she would. She went in anyway to the meeting and she stood up and she said she didn't want any English money and she turned around and walked out! I heard that now from my father.[91]

Children observe. Little occurs in their surroundings that does not register somewhere in their consciousness, an image or a sound that is remembered but may wait years to be fully understood. Young children could easily detect the sense of fear and impending violence during the War of Independence. It was unavoidable in the raids, arrests and attacks that many of them encountered or witnessed. It was discernible, too, in the behaviour and visual clues of their parents and grandparents. The hushed whispers, the fearful looks, the missing uncles, the anxious grandmothers and sombre grandfathers all reinforced a sense of the abnormal. In a war predominately fought between men in their twenties and thirties, the episode would enfold every age in an all-consuming experience. When that story came to be written, however, much of their experience was marginalised or ignored. Only through memory and oral tradition like the above, can we retrieve these stories and experiences and, in doing so, dramatically deepen our understanding.

2

'RUN FOR IT'

STORIES OF EXPERIENCE

CLOSE ESCAPES

By 1921 Martin 'Neighbour' McNamara had been in many violent situations. In France he witnessed man's destructive nature when he fought in the Great War, from which many did not return. Those who did carried memories of death and destruction at an almost incomprehensible level deep in their consciousness. As a senior member of the East Clare IRA Brigade's 5th Battalion, he also found himself in many intense positions. In 1921, for example, at the height of the War of Independence, he stood inside the door of a safe house in Kilkishen in east Clare. He had just made out the shape of a Crossley tender through the window and heard the unmistakable, purposeful footsteps of thick-leathered boots approaching the door. He forced his breathing to regulate, retrieved his Webley revolver from his pocket and put his back to the pillar located in an area behind the doorway. The revolver was loaded and had the useful feature of a chamber that could be broken for fast reloading, although McNamara knew that there would likely be no time for reloading on this occasion. As the footsteps became louder, he said an Act of Contrition in an internal whisper, blessed himself and waited.

There are many stories of death and violence relating to the War of Independence. There are perhaps more of near misses.

Momentary incidents of memory, which result in an IRA Volunteer leaving through the back door as the crown forces enter the front, or the clever concealment of a brace of bullets in the turned-up stocking of a six-year-old, away from the observant eyes of searching Black and Tans. Paddy Clancy from Kilkishen, whose uncle, Joe Clancy, was a former British soldier and IRA officer, heard many such stories. In 2010 he relayed to me this story, told to him by Martin 'Neighbour' McNamara, his uncle's comrade and friend. McNamara spoke to Paddy in the 1950s about how close he came on one occasion to ending another man's life, but for the realisation that to do so would mean the end of his own. Critical to the story was the practice of leaving hurleys in the Hehir household, close to Kilkishen Gaelic Athletic Association (GAA) field, so that they could be used in rotation by young hurlers from the area. Hehirs' was also a safe house for the local IRA. As Paddy explained, on one occasion a young local man, John 'Jack' Cunneen, realised just before leaving for St Flannan's College in Ennis, that he had left his hurley at Hehirs' and could not return to the well-known bastion of hurling without it:

> The story, the way it goes. The following morning, Jack Cunneen … he had been in the hurling field the night before … Jack Cunneen was going back to Flannan's. He came out and his hurley was left above in Hehirs', never knowing that when he arrived above at Gleesons [near Hehirs'], there were two tenders and they [Tans] collared him above at the gate: "What are you doing there?" "I lost my hurley." "What has that got to do with you being in there? Why were you in there?" "I left my hurley here last night" … They kept him and they surrounded the house [Hehirs'].

Inside the house at that time was Martin 'Neighbour' McNamara, one of the most wanted men in east Clare. Importantly, Paddy explained that the layout of Hehirs' at the time was such that when you entered the kitchen area, a significant portion of the room was concealed behind a peculiarly positioned doorway:

> The 'Neighbour' [McNamara] looked out and he couldn't believe his eyes when he saw a tender outside. He told me himself, he went back to the pillar and took out his revolver … stood behind the door and said an Act of Contrition to himself, blessed himself and all of a sudden the door opened and someone [Black and Tan] looked in.

Paddy recalled how the 'Neighbour' McNamara explained that he was left with a dramatic decision, which he had to make in milliseconds. Many years later, McNamara confided in Paddy:

> "Paddy Clancy, when you see a man's head one foot from you and all I had to do was pull the trigger and that man is dead, but where would I be three minutes later? I'd be dead too." He said, "Someone up there, someone up there [referring to God]. He [Black and Tan] just opened the door and just looked in there and I was standing there with my revolver there but someone up there or else he was a good citizen … he closed that door and went out, went away." He didn't know was it that man or the Lord up there that took him away.[1]

A similar story is relayed about Seán Murnane, a senior officer in the East Clare IRA Brigade from Newmarket-on-Fergus. His son, John, spoke in 2012 about how it was the decision of an officer that let him live:

> They raided here, this house. This house was thatched, you know, before it was slated. 'Twas a single storey house. And they came to the

front door. The officer came to the front door and he just happened to be a good man, you know. He saw my father's toes behind the door. If he was one of the bad fellas, I wouldn't be here now. They'd have killed him straight away. And the officer said, "Go on, clear off. We have to go," he says, "he's not here."²

'He saw the soldiers coming up the *botharín*'

In November 2014 ninety-eight-year-old Johnny Doyle passed away in his native Broadford. Doyle was born in 1916 and by the time the Black and Tans arrived into his parish, he was observing the world around him. Back then his father, Edward, was an active member of the local IRA. As a consequence, their house in Lissane was the focus of considerable attention from crown forces. In October 2011, sitting in that same house, Johnny affirmed, ''Twas raided three times! By British soldiers.' Involvement in the IRA required a need for constant awareness. Even the most mundane of decisions had to be carefully considered. A knock on a door could signal danger and a seemingly innocent invitation could summon misfortune. At the age of ninety-six, Johnny Doyle explained:

> My father was outside in the workshop one day. I think he was making a horse-car or something. Mr Bentley would send out for my father.³ So he sent on the note to the house here and 'twas into my mother the note came. So she took it out to my father and he said, "Ah to Hell with him, I haven't time to go there now, I want to finish this job" … My mother convinced him anyway. He had to only go across the field to go into Hurlerstown House and she said, "You don't know what he might want you for." My father was 'on the run' that time so the way he had to go was up our own hill and into the wood and once he was in the wood then he couldn't be spotted

so well. He was above behind a beech tree in the wood when he saw the soldiers coming up the *bothar̄ín*. They were looking for him! They didn't get him that time.

In 1920 Edward Doyle was a thirty-eight-year-old man living in the townland of Kilseily with his wife, Bridgid, and their children. Johnny spoke to me about the eventual arrest of his father and explained that his older siblings were with him when he was caught. He speaks of an explicit threat made – that his father would never return:

> They got him the third time and that was one Sunday after Mass. He was at Mass, himself and Katy and Paddy, they were the two oldest. They put him into the lorry and took him away and the two children were crying and all they said to 'em was "He's going but he won't come back." But you see Michael Collins signed the Treaty and he was let back.[4]

'"Twas God done it'

The townland of Ballymalone overlooks the village of Tuamgraney in east Clare. There, in 2008, I spoke with one of the last of the older generation in that townland. The story of Flan O'Brien takes the reader to his townland and home at the height of the War of Independence. In the house, at the time, were his parents, John and Johanna, and four of his older siblings. There were also two local IRA Volunteers, John Dillon and Michael Hogan, who were being sheltered in houses all across the townland of Ballymalone and the surrounding area.[5] With wanted men in the house vigilance was important, and when a group of Black and Tans were heard approaching, the situation looked perilous. In that same house, Flan explained that 'My father told me the whole lot of it there by that fire years ago, years before he died.' The story enfolds momentary life or death decisions, when the instinct to run for the two wanted rebels was the most dangerous impulse of all:

> Shur I can tell you about my father, the Lord have mercy on him. Bride, John Pa, Nora and Palkie. They were the four eldest of my family here. The Tans came in above in Corragnoe. Down across the mountain, there was seven of 'em in it ... and 'twas God done it, do you see Thomas Mac! Wasn't John Dillon here and [Michael] Hogan in Coolreagh beyond. 'Twas God done it, aren't I telling you! This house would be in dust the same day. This would all be gone up in smoke! They [Dillon and Hogan] were gone as it happens and there is an aul sod ditch there beyond. Denis Brien, the Lord have mercy on him, planted trees in it after, twenty feet high! 'Twas only a sod ditch that time. And didn't John Dillon go to go above across it [the field beyond the ditch] and the whole way in front of him was an open rae [large field] ... You could see down the whole way to Whitegate and the Shannon.

Presented with an expanse of countryside in front and the footsteps of Black and Tans behind, the compulsion for Dillon and Hogan to make a run for it must have been almost overwhelming. As Flan explains, however, for a seasoned republican like John Dillon, the more prudent reaction was to remain calm and nearby:

> According to my father, anyway, there's two doors in this house, one there and one here. They're the same to this day. And didn't one of the Tans go out the back door the same way as John Dillon was after goin'. Out and up on the ditch with him. Dillon and Hogan were cute, do you see. If they kept going, they'd be shot in the back! They

went down 130 yards down by the butt of the sad ditch, do you see, and lay in below as close as you like into the ditch. And the two boys [Tans] went up on the ditch. Their sight was good enough all right. They could see all the way to Whitegate but they couldn't see the two lads below [laughs]. They [Dillon and Hogan] could have them two Tans shot back into our field but they had their intelligence too and they knew there'd be more than the two of 'em going around together, do you see. There was five more of 'em in it. If they shot them two Tans shur the house would go up in smoke, children an all shur! They came back then after having a good look beyond and up the stairs here. Bride, John Pa, Nora and Palkie were there. I was born in 1927. All was quiet that time. Anyway, upstairs and there was only the four children up there … they came down there and she [Flan's mother] put down seven duck eggs. That time we had twelve or fourteen ducks out there in the house. Put down seven duck eggs for 'em and gave 'em plenty to eat, this seven men.[6]

The Black and Tans refused to leave without some return for their efforts and a number of local men, including my own grand-uncle Tom Hill, were forcibly removed and taken to be interrogated in Killaloe:

They took the two Thomas Hills anyway then; they weren't married at all. They left my father. They went down to Tomgarney [*sic*] then and they took Joe Noonan. Joe was a great singer, you know, Kathleen's father and a great violin player [laughs]. They took 'em down to Killaloe boy and Joe Noonan sung the whole way down for 'em in this aul thing, whatever they were travelling in. They interrogated 'em below about their movements like and what they were doing. Feckin' Black and Tans! Brought up back anyway, the two Thomas Hills. Shur Thomas Hill that time told my father.[7]

Joe Noonan, referred to by Flan, was an officer in the Tuamgraney Company of the 4th Battalion, East Clare IRA Brigade. His daughter, Annie, who was interviewed for this research at her home in Croom, Co. Limerick, told me how, after her father was arrested by Auxiliaries and Black and Tans, he 'sang the whole way down to Killaloe'. It appears that Joe began to sing as he was being transported with others towards Killaloe. Annie affirmed that this singing (in addition to giving a false name) led to his subsequent release.[8] Although a young man of twenty-five, Joe was a veteran republican and knew that something was required to release the tension of the occasion (see pp. 176–7 for more on Noonan's arrest). In other parts of east Clare I was also relayed the belief that the crown forces felt 'it would be a pity to shoot such a good singer'.[9]

Many years after the Black and Tans had left Ireland, Bridget 'Baba' Durack, who ran a pub in the village of Tuamgraney, would suspend all work when she heard Joe Noonan break into song:

> There were some great singers used to come into the pub. Joe Noonan was a wonderful singer. His favourite song was *Christmas Eve in London*. You'd stand up in the middle of the street to listen to him! The Black and Tans brought him to Killaloe one time to shoot him. When they got to Killaloe, he had sung all the way from Tuamgraney to Killaloe. He sang all the way. They thought that he was such a good man they told him get out and run![10]

When Thomas (better known as Tom) Hill, my twenty-one-year-old grand-uncle who was arrested in the same sweep that caught Noonan, was finally released after his interrogation by the Black and Tans, he was also told to run. In 2017 Tom's niece recalled his response in an often-told story against the backdrop of open-hearth fires in his locality:

Tom was taken away by the Black and Tans and of course, my mother was worried about him. One of the Tans had said to her that he'd be fine but she was still worried sick because they knew what the Black and Tans were capable of. They were after raiding the home place and smashed everything to pieces. Tom was there of course and he was taken. Tom Hill was always a very cool man. He had a great wit and was liked by everyone in the area. Very sociable. But for years after, it was always told. One of the other men who was arrested told it. I think it was Joe Noonan. They let Tom out of the lorry or tender or whatever and they said, "You better run for it boy!" Of course, they'd probably shoot him dead if he ran. Tom was very quick and he looked at 'em, then he looked at the ground and he said, "Era this a bit slippy there, I could fall if I ran and ye wouldn't want me to get hurt would ye?" and he walked away for himself. That was always told around Ballymalone and they used to get a great kick out of tellin' it![11]

In Feakle, I was told by 101-year-old John Michael Tobin about how his mother's observations helped to divert local IRA men from a path that would lead directly into a Black and Tan trap. His mother, who was a member of Cumann na mBan, had taken the precaution of sending John Michael to the parish of Ogonnelloe, where he stayed with relatives for three weeks to avoid trouble. 'I was sent down to Ogonnelloe to get me out of the way [laughs]. I was below for three weeks. I was below lookin' out at the Shannon. My mother got an IRA pension … she helped the IRA that time.' John Michael explained:

> I remember the Black and Tans. Shur they were in Feakle station the Black and Tans … Era shur they arrested a lot of men and pucked 'em and belted 'em and kept 'em in prison. There was a break down in it for a finish. I remember there was a great welcome for 'em [IRA] when

they came home. There was dances given in their honour. I remember 'em [Tans] going around the country. Feakle was their headquarters and they'd come around anywhere there was young men and belt the sugar out of 'em. They did that for certain. I remember 'em a bit above the house and they waitin', thinkin' the lads might come up the road and they did too only that John Tuohy, he was a young lad keepin' an eye for the Tans coming and he came into our house. He asked my mother did she see any of the lads but she said, "I didn't but I see the Tans above at the turn of the road."[12]

With indiscriminate firing a regular feature of Black and Tan activity, there were many occasions when shots fired from a distance would threaten the lives of ordinary people. In west Clare Morgie O'Connell spoke of one incident when crown forces searching for local republicans discharged shots:

They were always mentioned. They only came around here a few times. They came the morning of Peadar Clancy's Mass.[13] They came around here one day. I suppose they were looking for [Jimmy] O'Dea, he was the Commandant that time. They searched his house and they didn't find him. They went out the road then and they discharged a few shots. A man named Murty McMahon, he lived a quarter of a mile in from the road. McMahon's door was open. The kitchen door was open and they discharged those shots, I suppose to frighten O'Dea. To let him know they were there anyway. The shot went in Murty McMahon's door and broke the ware in Murty McMahon's dresser. So that was a fair warning to the people around here![14]

As the War of Independence raged around her, seventy-year old widow Ellen Moloney sat at her home in Kilroughil in the southeast Clare parish of Bridgetown. Ellen had grown up hearing stories of her uncle, Michael Devitt, who in the 1830s had led a group of agrarian rebels against the injustice of local landlords. Michael Devitt was a young man who threw all his energy into fighting against all forms of British rule in his native land. For this, he was transported as a convict to Australia, where he spent the rest of his life.[15] Now, Ellen's son, as a young man, had thrust himself into the depths of the same ancient conflict. Jim Moloney was then a twenty-eight-year-old member of the East Clare IRA Brigade's 3rd Battalion. As one of the more active men from his area, Moloney was very much wanted by the crown forces and had been 'on the run' for some time. His returns home to visit his elderly mother became less and less frequent, but he would try on occasion to make the dangerous journey to Kilroughil.

Jim's daughter, Maeve Hayes, was raised in Killaloe. In her home, a decommissioned Webley revolver is a proud family heirloom. A carefully inscribed caption reveals that the gun belonged to Jim Moloney, who passed away in August 1974. Maeve told me how on one occasion during the War of Independence, when her father was making his way towards his mother's home, he heard an ominous noise approaching:

> My father was collecting the rates that time and he was just heading in home in Kilroughil and he heard the lorries coming.[16] All he could do was drop down inside the ditch. The Tans went up to the house and they raided it. They smashed the whole place up and broke everything. There was just my old grandmother above in the house. They had *súgán*s in the house that time and didn't my father have his gun hidden in the *súgán*.[17] When she saw the Tans come in, my grandmother sat down on the chair with the gun hidden in the *súgán* and pretended to the Tans that she was an invalid. When they were gone for a finish and my father could come back, he took the gun out

and he hid it in the wall of an aul shed outside and it was there we found it years and years later.[18]

'He put the two good heels he had to work'

Jimmy Hanrahan from the townland of Cloghaunsavaun in Kilballyowen, at the end of the Loop Head Peninsula, spent most of his life in Ennis. When interviewed in 2012, Hanrahan demonstrated forcefully that Cloghaunsavaun had never left him. His native place was a Gaeltacht area until the mid-twentieth century and although Jimmy was not raised exclusively through Irish, he spoke it fluently until he died only months after I recorded him. Amidst recollections of tradition, folk belief and the history of his native area, Jimmy was able to offer stories of the revolutionary period and of how one local man used his athletic ability to escape the Black and Tans:

> There was a man in Carrigaholt, 'Shang' was his name. Big tall man, great runner in his time. A fine summer's night, he had a few pints in the village. He went back from Carrigaholt, back west. He went back the road and he crossed a trench. 'Twas in the summer time, in the month of July. There was a field of hay, trammed [cut, dried and stacked for fodder]. He was a fine runner now. He went through fields anyway, north of the road, the third field up from the road … He was a fine big strong man. He could shift the whole tram of hay. He had sufficient strength in his hands. He did shift it a bit anyway we're told and, ah, settled himself down for the night there, you know. He got a bit of heat there and he was goin' to go to sleep there. But by God, low and behold he woke up sometime during the night anyway and he heard noise. Jazus, I think 'twas about two o'clock in the morning, he heard noise. 'Twas a bright moonlit night when he stuck his head out through the hay and whatever way he

saw the lorry. He looked back down towards the road and there was the lorry, the Tans! So he put the two good heels he had to work! Ha! They wouldn't catch him if he kept running to Ennis! [laughs][19]

The man referred to in the story was John Scanlon, who was a thirty-year-old former member of the Shanghai Municipal Police. His service in Shanghai from 1912 to 1915 earned him the nickname 'Shang'. The British-controlled force policed the Shanghai International Settlement until 1943, when it was agreed by treaty that China would take control of the area once the city was retaken from the Japanese. Scanlon's brother-in-law, Patrick Keating, was fatally wounded in an attack on Kildysart Barracks on 7 August 1923, during the Civil War.

Jimmy's father, James, was not as fortunate as 'Shang' Scanlon. When the Black and Tans drove in to the Loop Head Peninsula they saw him working on a water pump across from his home. They stopped. Having been made aware that there was a story relating to his father from the period, I prompted Jimmy with the simple question, 'Did your father ever encounter the Tans?'

[Laughs] Jazus you are hitting the right nail now, you know, and I would have forgotten it. My father was arrested by the Tans ... 'Tisn't a very good story. 'Twas the month of May, early on in May. He was across the road teaming water. He had [a] trough there, a cement trough. They had one of the hand pumps for it, I think. My mother often said it, the Lord have mercy on her, [that] she saw the lorry stopping you now. She ran out. She saw the lorry stopping and they went over to him and told him "get ready", they wanted him. Ah, so my mother came out. This is what I heard from her. Very upset and she wanted to put a clean shirt and a clean pants on him. So they wouldn't let her near him. They brought him to Carrigaholt barracks.

> Oh, of course they queried him upside down and downside up. They wanted to know if there was anybody "on the run" back there, they wanted to clear that up. He never said a word there to anybody.

At the time of his arrest, Jimmy's father was a fifty-three-year-old farmer who had been raised through Irish on the Loop Head Peninsula. Jimmy's mother, Mary, was forty-four years of age when her husband was taken from her side by the Black and Tans. In 2012, when Jimmy was asked if his mother ever offered her feelings on the force, his response was clear, if circumspect:

> Well she did, I suppose ... without using the adjectives that she used [laughs]. I'm not going to use them now into your bloody transmitter [laughs]. They got anything and everything but a blessing! [laughs] They wouldn't let her put a clean shirt on him and he ringing wet outside after working on the water!

'When they went out she fainted'

High above the village of Kilfenora, in the townland of Tullaha, the McCormack house was a safe place for republicans during the War of Independence. Nationally known men like Ernie O'Malley and Liam Mellows both stayed at the house, as did several local republicans. From the McCormack home came one of the best-known female republicans of the period, Katie McCormack. For years before the Black and Tans arrived in Ireland, Katie and her family had turned their face against the British Empire. However, for the period of the war, the occupants of the house remained affiliated with the republican movement, rather than directly involved. Strategically, this aided in the maintenance of security on their hilltop setting. Teasie McCormack heard many stories from her mother-in-law, Norah 'Lala' McCormack:

The people here weren't involved, 'twas a safe house, you see. But they [Black and Tans] did come in. And ah, the officer … There was a box, like a biscuit tin left on the table beyond, and he tipped it with his bayonet or whatever … and he said, "What's in that?" "Oh, those are sweets for my sister-in-law." And when they went out she [Norah] fainted. Because if she opened it, 'twas ammunition was in it. And 'twas Katie McCormack had it left in it. Katie McCormack was a very famous woman from here.[20] She lived for a while in Ennistymon. She had a pub there and she used to have the [IRA] meetings there. But I think she lost the licence on account of holding the meetings there.[21]

Born on 4 April 1916, Catherine Talty was one of those rare people who from a very young age developed an intense interest in the history of her place. At her home in Clounlaheen, Catherine would listen intently as discussions were held around their open-hearth fire about subjects ranging from farming to emigration and from Biddy Early to Brian Boru. Catherine also listened when stories were told of the Tans and of the IRA who fought against them:

I know of course that they'd have been 'on the run'. Shur goodness sake tonight even, those that were in the IRA. Shur they were 'on the run' and they even stayed in Kerry and various places. Brought back stories. I remember one of them telling a story how he was in a house in Kerry and they knew that the RIC were coming with soldiers and it seems there was a bed, well the space of a bed in the wall. Okay, there was this shutter and when you opened the shutter, the frame of the bed and the mattress and the clothes were spread out but you closed it up and closed the door, you didn't know there was a bed there! This man, he was from this area and the woman of the house anyway caught him and shoved him in and closed the door on him. They came in and they searched the house. Never opened the door and there he was [laughs] ... he was one of the Coore [IRA company] men anyway.²²

In Scariff, the home of Paddy Harte was raided repeatedly by British forces. His grandson explained that the crown forces were so regular with their raids that his grandfather would prepare for them:

My grandfather [Patrick Harte], I never knew him but the thing about it is that I heard so many things about him ... He had been in the British Army. He [also] had been a gun instructor to the local IRA. He was fairly good with guns and stuff like that and he could teach military drill and discipline ... so then again the stories of the beating that he used to get from the Black and Tans, shur they were always here! He used to have this joke you know [laughs]. He'd say to my grandmother, he'd look at the clock and 'twould be coming on, we'd say, seven o'clock in the evening and he'd say, "God, Kay, put on the kettle. They'll be here any minute now" and he'd be nearly right a lot of the time you know!²³

One such occasion, when the British forces arrived as expected at the home of Michael's grandparents, was firmly rooted in his family tradition:

I remember my grandmother [Kate Harte] telling me here one time that one day, erra a big party of military and police arrived. The military wouldn't really know where a place would be, so the local constabulary were really the eyes and ears of the establishment ... they knew where everybody lived. So Sergeant Brennan would have been the local police sergeant at the time. So he was the man that brought 'em down here ... this particular day he came and he sat there on the table. It was over there by the window. 'Twas a long table and he went over and sat on the table. The boys [British forces] went up the stairs and out the back and everywhere. After a long time anyway they reported that they found nothing. So Brennan said, "Okay so, lads, we'll go away." So they went out there and they lined up on the road … So Brennan went to follow them out and he got there as far as the door and he looked back and he says to my grandfather, "Find someplace else to hide that rifle!" he says. "That's the last time I'm goin' to sit on that table for you." He knew about the hooks under the table.[24]

'Don't ever stand now in the times you have'

Deep in the west Clare parish of Coolmeen, John O'Connell lived all ninety-four years of his life in the townland of Clonkerry East. From there he learned much of his parish history and that of the surrounding area. In a series of interviews at his home, John told me many stories that illuminate the west Clare landscape in 'the time of the Tans'. One story told by him surrounds the unfortunate Thomas Browne from Effernan, who, in travelling to buy ball bearings and other items to help repair bicycles, encountered two curious Black and Tans, evidently concerned about the steel balls carried by Browne. As O'Connell explains, despite his best efforts to avoid trouble, Browne landed in it:

> I will, I'll give it to you. Thomas Browne of Effernan shur. Thomas Browne was the general tradesman. He was a shoemaker as well. His father was a shoemaker also. Thomas used to carry on several jobs, repairing bicycles, gramophones, several things. The house that they had in Effernan was a bit tidy [small], do you see, for all the work that was going to be carrying on, so didn't he take a house in Kildysart. That was all right. No one stopped him doing that. He

wasn't long in Kildysart and he ran out of materials. If anyone came to do anything with a boot or a shoe, he hadn't even a bit of leather. But in any case he decided that he'd go to Ennis. That time shur if you were caught going, you'd be afraid to walk from here to the road! Browne anyway got his bicycle here in Effernan and he hadn't a mile to travel to Kildysart. He went up and he went into the [RIC] barrack. The sergeant said to him, "You shouldn't come in here today for anything! You know the times you have. You could be caught and termed as a spy. Will you go out!" But anyway Browne says, "I came in here for a permit for to go to Ennis with a bicycle." Well, he says, "No one ever asked me for a permit but as long as you came in I'll give you a bit of writing." So he sat down to the table and wrote down: "I, John Feeney, Sergeant of the RIC barracks, Kildysart, without any further authority, give permission to Thomas Browne of Effernan to carry with him his pedal cycle to and from the town of Ennis on this eighth day of May, 1922".

The short piece of literature obtained from the RIC sergeant emboldened Browne to make the journey towards the town of Ennis:

He went into Ennis, got everything he wanted. No one ever asked him anything and he was ready to go home and he was walking past Baker's[25] ... He was a Raleigh Agent and didn't he pull up looking at Raleighs in Baker's window and didn't two of the boys [Black and Tans] come behind him and landed him over to the barracks. He had his pockets full of ball bearings do you know and pieces of bicycles. He was trying to bring everything he could ... Didn't they land him into a big day room and peeled off everything he had and scattered everything he had on the floor. When they came to the ball bearings they said, "What are them?" Browne said they were ball bearings and they were doubting him. There was a man writing above at a desk and he said, "Them are ball bearings. Go ahead, they are nothing to do with ye." The minute he said that they went off, the two went off and left everything scattered. "Gather up your stuff there," the man said from the bench. And he said, "Where did they get you or what were you doing?" Browne told him. "Ah," he said, "don't ever stand now in the times you have. No one can say a word to you if you keep walking." Tom Browne told me that story himself. I think he showed me the letter.[26]

John O'Connell also relayed a story concerning Paddy Clancy, a republican from the Coolmeen area of west Clare, four miles northeast of Labasheeda. Brigadier Clancy of Derryguiha was the commander of the 1st Battalion of the West Clare IRA Brigade and was involved in a number of incidents over the revolutionary period before taking the republican side in the Irish Civil War. John's story illustrates the network of support in place for wanted IRA Volunteers like Clancy:

> Clancy in Coolmeen came home of a Saturday evening … He went over to Coolmeen Mass the following morning. The priest, when he was settling up the altar and he saw Clancy and he said, "If anyone wants communion now before Mass they can have it." So Clancy and some few of the Volunteers were there and they all received. 'Twas a confraternity Sunday. Before half Mass was over, the church was surrounded by the Black and Tans. But Clancy had two scouts out if he hadn't three. There is hills around Coolmeen, you know. There's hills at the west of it, there's hills the south and there's hills over this side of the mountain … the man that was back there, didn't he see the rifles … 'Twas a grand fine morning and didn't he see the sun shining on the rifles. They had them up on their shoulders. He went into the

chapel and went up to Clancy and ordered him out. Clancy went out through the sacristy and over the mountain. The boys [Tans] came along then and they surrounded the chapel. They blocked the doors. There are three doors in Coolmeen chapel and they blocked two of 'em. They wouldn't let anyone out so they all had to pass 'em out because they had a policeman with them. They all filed out past 'em and no Clancy in it![27]

Returning to east Clare, the stories of two famous IRA Volunteers, Joe Clancy and Martin 'Neighbour' McNamara, are greatly assisted by the oral tradition offered to the record by Paddy Clancy in 2010. Paddy had heard many stories from the period, both from his uncles, Joe and Paddy Clancy, who were involved, and from McNamara, who, as already mentioned, he got to know later in life. When I asked if he had heard much tradition on the period, Paddy declared, 'I heard it all by the fireside aul stock', before offering several examples of incidents when Joe Clancy and 'Neighbour' narrowly evaded the attempts of the crown forces to capture their two former colleagues in the British armed forces:

Joe was a wanted man and the Neighbour [Martin] Mac. They were like that [close friends]. The famous Neighbour. Great, great man. They were through the war in France [First World War]. The two of them went together. That's where the Neighbour got his name, in France. Joe called him the Neighbour and the gang kept calling him the Neighbour. "Here is my neighbour back home!" When they came back, they joined up here [IRA] and they were wanted men. Very much wanted … there's no doubt about that … The Neighbour, a wanted man and after the [Glenwood] ambush they kept very much out of Kilkishen.[28] Paddy Clancy, my uncle, told me that he got up at a quarter past seven one morning above in the aul house and when he looked across the *bothárin* [small road] ... there he saw a leg above on a stump like that and it polished. Seven of them [Tans] were there at that stage. At that stage, Clancy's aul house at that time was thatched and there was no back door but great tradesmen they were, they had an escape window that you'd never know was on a hinge. The very minute you were out and down the road. They were camped above ... inside there in Cullaun. In there in the Craggs. That was the camp that everyone of 'em would sleep. Wet or dry, that was the escape patch. The bloody Tans knew bloody well you know but dare they go in? They'd never come out do you know! Oh, Jazus, no way would they chance it.[29]

A further story of a close escape recorded in the Kilkishen area relates to an evening when Joe Clancy, Martin 'Neighbour' McNamara and Paddy Clancy decided that it was perhaps safe enough to venture into the village for a drink:

Sometime after the [Glenwood] ambush, things were cooling down. Joe and the Neighbour and Paddy Clancy and ... They used to have scouts at that time ... But anyway they got no scare so they said they'd go down here to Jacks [public house] down here for a pint. They came out the door above and when they came down they would never, ever, ever talk when they were walking. That was a rule with them and Paddy Clancy told me that the boys [Tans] were in front and Joe or the Neighbour heard a click ... the bolt of a rifle. Like that Clancy said "go" and thank God the gate was behind 'em and there was no way the boys would follow them. They found out afterwards that there was seven of 'em in it ... they had lined along, three at this side in Plunkett's drive and there were four in O'Brien's field. In another twenty or thirty yards, that was it. They were dead. No doubt about it.[30]

In his Bureau of Military History (BMH) witness statement, Joe Clancy himself refers to an incident when lorries of RIC and military arrived into Kilkishen, leading to a frantic escape across several miles of countryside, encouraged by the continued automatic fire which followed closely behind.[31]

'They weren't battle hardened'

In the west of the county, Michael 'Marshall' McMahon remembered hearing about one incident when it was the crown forces who had a close escape, although, on explanation, McMahon claimed that the men who escaped were perhaps not in as much danger as they may have thought:

> There wasn't much activity in this area in the War of Independence. Road cutting and the burning of the boat below at the pier and I think they burned the barracks in Labasheeda.[32] You know goin' into the corcass [low-lying land adjacent to a river or lake] above in Clonderlaw, Dinny Shannon, Sini Haugh, Mick Kennedy and Paddy Clancy, didn't they fire on two policemen and missed them, but they didn't want to hit 'em! How could you miss 'em? ... they couldn't find it in their heart to shoot 'em. They weren't battle hardened at all and like I say. They [police] were people who they didn't know at all or done nothing to 'em ... one of the policemen he was so frightened that he ran down across over to Ailroe and Sino Neylon's father was digging his garden and he asked him for a cup of water. He ran the whole way to the barracks in Kildysart with fear. But one of the fellas that escaped was the fella that Bill Haugh shot inside in Kilrush.[33]

The same incident was referred to in a later interview I undertook in Cranny with the interviewee claiming the order for the action came from Jimmy O'Dea, O/C of the 1st Battalion, and that the incident occurred in April 1919:

> 'Twas the police in Kildysart that the people here would have a grievance, do you see ... eventually he got two men to do it. They had no experience of guns and the policemen escaped. The sergeant threw himself into a dike when they fired on 'em and a young policeman from Limerick ran with his life and he never stopped until he went down to the barracks again and signed the book and resigned there and then!³⁴

One of the men referred to by both Michael and Morgie was Detective Constable John O'Hanlon (listed as 'Hanlon' in the RIC General Register), who was later shot dead by Bill Haugh, a senior officer in the West Clare IRA, on 21 August 1920. Haugh followed O'Hanlon into Walsh's pub in Moore Street, Kilrush and shot him in the head. A native of Kerry, O'Hanlon was married with two children. He had been targeted by the IRA for some time due to his apparently overzealous detective work in pursuit of republicans.³⁵ One interviewee characterised O'Hanlon as 'a very busy man and he was watching everything'.³⁶ In 2008, when ninety-eight-year-old Jack Dunleavy was driven towards Moore Street during a recording of his memories around Kilrush, he began to discuss the killing of O'Hanlon (who he mistakenly refers to as 'Hanley'):

> This is Vandeleur Street. 'Tis over this way that Haugh shot Hanley ... He [Haugh] pretended he wanted to go back to America and at that time you had to get permission from the RIC. He was out to kill Hanley ... he met him up the street and arranged ... He left his name and address on the table ... that's how he got Hanley to sign

the paper and while Hanley was signing it and drinking a naggin of whiskey, he went around and blew his brains out and ran off. That's how they found it was Haugh because the paper with Haugh's name and address was on the table. They went up to Monmore and burned his house. But he didn't go up that way, he came up this way. He left the bike and went up two fields across the land and he was above in the Cutt Hill, Gerry Grogan's place. Another field and he was in Monmore! He became a commandant in the Free State army afterwards, Commandant Bill Haugh.[37]

'I still suffer'

There is no question that the IRA Volunteers who did fall into the hands of the crown forces were left with enduring memories. For many more, it meant death. Catherine Talty knew many men who had fought against the Black and Tans, some of whom carried the wounds of those encounters over the decades that followed. In moments when her attention was drawn from her immersion in the popular literary series of the day, the Penny Dreadfuls, she would listen carefully as, on occasion, the experience of those days would be recalled:

> One of the IRA was a first cousin of my father's. And that same man, when they arrested him I suppose, [he was] taken to the barrack in Connolly. I suppose they tried to get information out of him. He was that kind. He'd go very silent. They beat [him] up and he was never in the better of it [afterwards]. His nickname was 'Casey' Moroney. He was a Michael Moroney ... It seems they hurt his back or something but he never spoke about it. He was here night after night and it wouldn't be spoken about at all. But the odd night when he was here with my father only, it would all be discussed, from all sides ... then, of course, the Penny Dreadfuls took precedence [laughs].[38]

Like 'Casey' Moroney, Coolmeen's Patrick McMahon was taken to a military barracks and beaten by Black and Tans during this period. In a diary I was allowed to read, McMahon later wrote how he continued to suffer both physically and mentally decades after the incident: 'I still suffer, all owing to the beating which I received from the military at Miltown Malbay Barracks.'[39]

The physical and emotional scars lingered for those affected. Even children who lived through the period were left with lifelong impressions, based on what they had experienced and been told, which in their winter years had lost none of their potency. In an oral history project in Dublin, undertaken in the 1980s, eighty-six-year-old Billy Dunleavy characterised the Black and Tans as 'criminals', 'gangsters' and a 'gang of bastards'.[40] But for all too many, there were no near misses. The ubiquitous violence and death that characterised the War of Independence made narrow escapes all the more intense and memorable.

'The skies of Clare reddened night after night' – Burnings

> Shur my God, listen to me. The Black and Tans arrived to McDonnells and they put Mrs McDonnell and the daughter out with the only thing they had on 'em in bed. We heard knocking at the door at 1 a.m. They had Mrs McDonnell and the daughter. The daughter was a nun after. The daughter told us not to light no light. My grandfather was alive and he told them to light the fire. "Well surely," says he, "ye'll allow me to put down a bit of a fire in this cold weather?" I remember him arguing that point. "Can't ye put down a fire for the poor old woman?" The daughter told us, "Ye can do that but don't light any light." So the next thing was I was above at the window looking over and I heard hand grenades and bombs being thrown at the house and

big blaze and the house went up ... The daughter told me that she had brought a suitcase of clothes as far as the door and they shoved her out without it. We heard 'em going. They had the house on fire this time. My aunt slipped over and pulled the trunk of clothes out of the fire. I went over and I knew the back kitchen and there was a pig after being killed a day or two before and I saved the barrel of bacon and a few other things, a few chairs and the churn the farmer had. That was all. The wind was blowing towards Tuamgraney.[41]

Paddy Gleeson was 100 years of age when he narrated his experience of watching his neighbour's house being destroyed by British forces. That was on 3 December 1920 and Paddy Gleeson was then fifteen years old, as he watched the house of IRA Volunteer Paddy McDonnell in Kielta, Tuamgraney, being burned to the ground by British Auxiliaries and Black and Tans.[42] McDonnells' had been raided on at least four previous occasions, on 3, 17 and 22 October, as well as 22 November 1920.[43]

It is challenging to convey the sense of devastation and inescapable fear that is evoked when a fire has ripped its way through a building, beyond the point where any intervention can be made. Time after time the scene was the same, with only the landscape changing. Houses that had stood for generations were destroyed by anger and hate. Another son 'on the run'. Another mother crying. Another sister managing. Another house destroyed. Another memory firmly planted. Across the county, the angry flames of fire and the wisps of smoke drew the eyes of those affected to attention. Countless families would helplessly stand at a safe distance, not from the radiant heat of the flames, but from the Black and Tans whose animated shapes were illuminated by the fires. Fixed on their own devastation, suffering families and neighbours could only watch painfully as the flames licked the thatch that covered most houses and engulfed their homes, twisting and melting their worldly possessions into nothing.

For hundreds of families in Clare and across the country, this was the spectacle they faced in mid-1920 when homes and buildings were burned on a regular basis. The attack on McDonnells' was part of an escalation of reprisals on the part of British forces. Between July and November 1920, large-scale burnings took place in towns including Thurles, Templemore and Upperchurch in Co. Tipperary, Limerick city, Trim, Mallow, Balbriggan, Boyle, Listowel, Tralee, Ballymote, Tubbercurry and Granard.[44] Florence O'Donoghue, the former head of intelligence in the Cork No. 1 IRA Brigade, documented that in one month the 'forces of law and order' had burned and partially destroyed twenty-four towns.[45] Even Colonel George O'Callaghan Westropp, the former lieutenant colonel in the Clare Artillery and a landlord whose father had infamously overseen the Bodyke evictions in 1887 in east Clare, had his hayshed and cattle shed burned down by members of the self-professed 'Anti-Sinn Féin gang' in response to O'Callaghan publishing letters in the press condemning Black and Tan atrocities.[46]

After British forces descended on the towns of Miltown, Lahinch and Ennistymon on the night of 22 September 1920 with their vehicles loaded with petrol, an indelible mark was left on those communities. Ernie O'Malley later described the area as resembling 'an Iroquois raid on an American frontier settlement in the middle of the seventeenth century'.[47] The West Clare IRA commandant, Bill Haugh, recorded that 'over twenty miles of countryside smoked and smouldered for days afterwards'.[48] A letter written by Máire O'Dwyer on 29 September 1920 perhaps illustrates more powerfully the intensity of the occasion for one observer. O'Dwyer witnessed the reprisals first-hand in Lahinch, which she conveyed to her sister, Nora, a medical student in Dublin. Chillingly, she recorded that 'above all the din could be plainly heard the hellish laughter and shouts of revenge from the raiders':

> You never saw anything so sad as the sights on the sandhills that morning Nora, groups of men and women, some of them over seventy years, practically naked, cold, wet, worn-looking and terrified, huddled in groups on the wet grass. I met two mothers with babies not yet three weeks old, little boys partly naked, leading horses that had gone mad in their stables with the heat … distracted people running in all directions, looking for their friends with the awful thought haunting them that that burned corpse might be some relative of their own. Oh! It was awful.[49]

The burning of homes has lingered powerfully within the oral tradition of this time. In the late 1930s one child in an east Clare school recorded testimony that:

> Several burnings took place in the time of the Black and Tans. When a house would be put on fire by one of them, all the neighbours would gather and try and quench it. Some neighbours would try and pull out what was inside and others would bring water. Very often the house was burned because all the old houses were thatched and once the thatch took fire there was no chance of stopping it. In very few cases houses were saved. The only chance of its escape was if there was an abundance of water near. I remember to see a great fire once, its object being a cock of hay.[50]

'I saw Savage's house burning'

Micheál Brennan and members of the East Clare flying column sat in a remote part of the East Clare mountains. Night was coming on 21 January 1921 and violence had visited the east Clare parishes of Sixmilebridge, Kilkishen and Broadford. The Glenwood ambush, one of the most significant actions in the War of Independence in Clare, had been executed by Brennan and his comrades. Participants Joe Clancy and Brennan both recorded the reprisals that began soon after their departure from the ambush scene. As the senior officers who led the ambush 'retreated back into the hills', flames began to illuminate the darkening countryside. Brennan claimed that from their position up on the mountain, they could count thirty-six houses on fire in the surrounding countryside.[51] It was only possible for Brennan and his comrades to see the houses that were on fire. All the other homes were ominously dark, their lights extinguished in a bid to avoid attention.

In the darkness of that landscape in the townland of Lissane, a five-year-old boy was picked up by his mother and elevated towards a skylight in their home. The child, too, could see the flames in the distance. Ninety-one years later, Johnny Doyle remembered:

> I saw Savage's house burning. There's a skylight upstairs and my mother held me up to the skylight to see Savage's house burning. Well Savages' and Broughtons' were burnt that night anyway. I think there was a third house burned … Ah you'd only see the blaze; the night was dark, do you know.[52]

Johnny was witnessing the aftermath of the Glenwood ambush. Six members of the Black and Tans and RIC had been killed, while a further two had escaped. There were no casualties on the IRA side and they captured eight rifles, six revolvers and a quantity of ammunition. The father of J.P. Guinnane from Kilkishen was going to school when the Glenwood ambush began:

They were sent home from school anyway. So they had hurleys anyway. They were doing some hurling in school. They were going home down near Fitzs ... aul Fitz came out and he said, "If the Tans catch ye with them hurleys, they'll whale the life out of ye. Leave 'em in there in the house," which they did. But shur that night they were all burned!

J.P.'s grandfather also witnessed the scenes following the action, which included observing a fleeing Black and Tan:

They were thinning turnips down in Belvoir and he came down Halloran's avenue with his hands up, took off his coat, left it after him and a grand watch inside in it. He hid under a bridge down in Belvoir, down where you come out near Pollagh there and aul Wilson Lynch took him into the Bridge [Sixmilebridge] when it got dark. He was one of the men that escaped.[53]

For local people in the area surrounding Glenwood, the reprisals are as much a part of the story as the ambush. The severity of the response was foregrounded:

Oh Christ, they burned before 'em shur ... I'll go back to my father again. Madgie's was burned outside there. Madgie Mac, abroad near Dan's there. A big, long, thatched house. They were all young and they went down to see the burning ... Jazus, dogs and banbhs [piglets] and everything roarin'! Everything burned ... They were saying afterwards if the Tans came back, they'd be all shot ... They could hear the banbhs roar and the dogs, the aul dog. 'Twas a terror shur.

Once again, humour finds its way into the most abject of situations. J.P. recalled with bemusement the way in which one elderly man, whose house had been burned to the ground by the crown forces, was able to distract himself from the situation:

> Old Mac was there ... Sonny's father. Himself and the wife, they came up to the cross, up to my grandfather. They were sitting inside in the hob. Jimmo Mac came. He'd be their son. He'd be kind of involved in it [IRA]. He came in anyway at some hour of the night. They were there in the corner and Jazus, the house and all burned. And the aul father said to him, "Have you aer a bit for the pipe?" That was all that was botherin' him! [laughs][54]

'It isn't worth burning it'

When 104-year-old Nora Canavan recalled the events that followed the Monreal ambush of December 1920, the angry flames of fire at her neighbour's house returned to her mind. The Black and Tans were next door to her home. Nora was twelve years old:

> The terrible shooting and the burning of the hay. Oh, dear that was bad. And shur we were lucky that time that the house wasn't burned. Oh, and they were trying to save the hay for the cattle and the more they were saving it, the more it went up. Ah 'twas bad ... Oh shur a lot of people's houses were burned.[55]

In a separate interview Nora once again spoke feelingly:

> There was only just two or three [Black and Tans]. On to some other place then. I remember people next door [Mees] and they had all that was in their house cleared out. And there was a fort at the back of it and they had all the furniture everything they had put into it. They were preparing for the fire. And, ah, one of the soldiers looked

around and said, "Curse it, it isn't worth burning it." They didn't burn it. Well 'twas an old thatched house but that's what they said ... I remember the evening of the [Monreal] ambush, when the burning was going on. There was an old sergeant with them from Ennistymon ... They burned the hay, three reeks of hay. I can remember that.[56]

In Inagh, the McGough family similarly were prepared to watch their house go up in flames when they were told the Black and Tans were coming. The late Paddy McGough remembered being five years of age and watching his mother hurriedly assemble belongings, before frantically taking him by the hand and leading him forcefully out of their home:

> Remember seeing the Black and Tans? I suppose 'twas 1920. My uncle [Patrick McGough] was in the IRA. He was in with the Miltown brigade or whatever the hell they were called. So a message came, was it a dispatch they used call it? That the house was going to be burned. So we were all evacuated, my mother and father and my grandfather. Well I'm not sure if my grandfather was there. We were sent up the road to the neighbours and we had to sleep. There was an aul bed made in the kitchen for us, my mother and father and myself. Stayed there until the following day. Then we came back home again shur and that was that.[57]

At 105, Margaret Hoey too could see the flames in her memory. When I enquired about the Black and Tans and local burnings, she was able to recall two incidents where flames reached angrily for the sky close to her home:

> I did, I did. You'd see smoke and flames. Only two that I remember. I could see it from our own yards, in the distance. Oh, they knew the

houses to burn ... Neighbours and families took them. They were better, far better houses built for them, after. Far better houses.⁵⁸

'They have left us the walls'

In Clonloum in O'Callaghan's Mills, the home of Tom and Pat 'Thade' McGrath was repeatedly raided by British forces. Both Tom and his older brother, Pat, were active members of the East Clare IRA Brigade and had drawn the attention of the authorities to their townland and home. For example, in January 1921 a police car passing through Clonloum was ambushed and fired on by the local IRA, including the McGraths.⁵⁹ Tom, a member of the All-Ireland-winning hurling team of 1914, later went on to become a Free State officer and then a colonel in the Irish Army. Pat took the anti-Treaty side in the Civil War and later left the country for a period. In 2014 I interviewed two of Tom's daughters, Phil and Kitty, in Dublin, where they were raised. However, the connection with Co. Clare was strong and both were aware of certain stories surrounding their family home in O'Callaghan's Mills. Phil explained:

> One day it was raided by the Black and Tans. They surrounded it and somebody thought they saw Daddy or Uncle Thade [Pat] and they shot through, but it was one of their own they shot. Aunt Lil and a cousin of hers, Maggie Moloney, were in the house. They brought down a mattress and they put him on it and fixed his wound. The officer who was in charge said that the house would not be searched again. The next day it was burnt to the ground!⁶⁰

Emotionally, Kitty added to the story by acknowledging the neighbourly support shown to the McGraths. She also recalled two rocking chairs in their childhood home in Portobello, which for many years acted as an *aide-memoire* to that event:

I remember him telling me. There were two beautiful rocking chairs in our house in Portobello. He told me that he sat in the ditch and watched the house burn and when he was able to get in he grabbed the two rocking chairs. The only thing that was saved were the two rocking chairs.[61]

In 1921, soon after the burning of his family home, thirty-three-year-old Pat 'Thade' McGrath wrote the following letter. It was addressed to his younger sister, Kit, a twenty-six-year-old nurse who was then living in Canada. The letter provides a powerful insight into the determined mindset of a rural IRA Volunteer, but also suggests the disruption and hardship such activism often caused. Below is a slightly abridged version of the letter, which has been carefully preserved by his niece, Phil:

Dear Kit,

I hear the sound of the lorries, perhaps tis on a visit to ourselves they are. They cannot do much more to us – they have left us the walls. We heard of the atrocities of Belgium committed by the G[ermans]. Did we believe that it could be committed by men under military command? I have seen it – the excesses would make your skin creep. I suppose war is war but why can't they recognise it as such. Fancy treating our prisoners as criminals – the best of Ireland's sons – brains and brawn – but we will get even with them yet. I don't think you will ever see one of us again or even hear from us as we mean to die fighting if needs require it. Tis a hard lot to say you cannot rest or sleep in your own home … Ireland needs all her sons at present. Tis a glorious fight – though you don't think so, we are winning and when the crowning day comes though we may not be there yet I hope and expect we will, you will be proud of the Two [Tom and Pat] who never failed her in her hour of need. Don't be one

bit alarmed about the two of us. If we die, we die in a good cause …
We may enjoy each other's society yet when our oppressors are gone
to the wall.

Your outlaw brother

To H[EL]L with England

I must say my prayers.⁶²

Mick Ryan, whose father, Jackie 'Bishop' Ryan, was commandant of the 3rd Battalion, East Clare IRA Brigade, outlined the impact that this involvement had on his family throughout the war. On one occasion, Mick explained that his father's sister, Mary, was home from America, to where she had emigrated many years before. Her holiday in Ireland was a turbulent one:

> One of them was at home one time, Mary, herself and her three kids. The day before she was to go back, my father came to see them. He was 'on the run' at the time. He couldn't stay around. He was above in the room and who arrived only the Tans! She said her three kids were above in the room. They were American citizens and they couldn't go in. She stood at the door and wouldn't let them in. That's all that saved him.⁶³

The bravery of Mary Ryan was not enough to save her family home in the long run. In fact, the homes of both Jackie 'Bishop' Ryan's parents and his wife's parents were burned out during the War of Independence. When asked about the effect this had on the families, Jackie's son Mick affirmed, relating to his mother's childhood home, that:

> It had an awful effect on them. Shur they [the Larkin family] had cattle then and they had no fodder for them. They burned the hay

and burned the house ... Paddy Larkin was there and my mother was there. Eddie Larkin was there. Her parents were there too. Ah there was a gang of them in it.

Equally, Mick's paternal grandparents were present when their home in Clonconry in Kilbane was burned by British forces. Mick explained in 2013 that 'it wasn't fully burned. They saved a couple of rooms. They had fairly good outhouses and they slept in the outhouses.' For Mick Ryan, despite such hardship, his father's parents were supportive of their son, and he reasoned that 'They wanted to get the British out of Ireland.'[64]

'A SECONDARY OPINION' – WOMEN AT WAR

The Black and Tans! [raises voice] raided my aunt's house where my mother was in bed at three o'clock in the morning. And I was due to be born three days later ... she got a stroke of paralysis and she lost the power of all her left side. So I never saw my mother walk ...[65]

In a conflict that depended on the support of families and communities, it was inevitable that women of all categories would be drawn into the experience. Both women who were active members of Cumann na mBan and women who had no technical involvement would play roles in the conflict. All of these women have one thing in common: their relative exclusion from the historical narrative of the period for many decades after its conclusion. Using the Military Service Pension records, as well as my own documentation of the names of Cumann na mBan members, I learned that there were at least 400 members of Cumann na mBan across Clare.[66] While the latter may exceed the numbers actively involved, it does not account for non-Cumann na mBan women who often played an equivalent role, and so the figure can be considered a relatively effective reference point.

In the early 1950s forty-three contributors from Clare made statements to the BMH. While not all contributors were former IRA members, no woman was interviewed in Clare as part of the project. Nationally, only ten per cent of the 1,773 statements to the BMH were made by women.[67] Despite almost 100 memorials and monuments to the revolutionary period across Clare, until 2016 only one Clare Cumann na mBan figure has been memorialised. This occurred in 2010, when a plaque was erected over the grave of Nan Hogan.[68] Before 2010 only one monument in the county recognised the contribution of Cumann na mBan: the East Clare Memorial Park in Tuamgraney, officially unveiled in 1952, explicitly recognised 'the patriotism of the East Clare Brigade of the IRA and the members of Cumann na mBan'.[69]

For female participants who later left their native place to marry, their stories were often left behind. This is borne out in a private collection of papers that I was allowed to examine. In the collection, Mollie Lenihan, a former Cumann na mBan member from Kilkishen in east Clare, resignedly declared the following, while attempting to contact members of Cumann na mBan regarding pension applications: 'It is too bad there is so much bother in getting addresses, there are so few of the girls living in their own parish now, it seems hard to get them.'[70] The latter is further illustrated in a separate letter written to a contact in O'Brien's Bridge in search of the addresses of twenty-two former members of Cumann na mBan who had left that parish.[71] Increasingly domesticated and restrictive roles in the new State inevitably affected how the women were viewed in memory and also the way they spoke about their former lives. For many women, motherhood overtook revolution.

It was the election of Éamon de Valera in July 1917 to the east Clare constituency, left vacant by the death in the First World War of the sitting MP Willie Redmond, which stimulated what historian Kevin J. Browne referred to as 'a mad rush' to join Sinn Féin or its 'kindred organisations', including Cumann na mBan.[72] The inscription of a registration form at the Old Ground Hotel in Ennis during that election campaign with the word 'rebel' by Countess Markievicz, in response to a question about her 'trade or occupation', firmly set the tone for the role of women in the republican struggle.[73] The election was the first opportunity since the organisation was founded three years previously for Cumann na mBan in the county to play a direct role in the struggle.[74] The organisation in Clare played an increasingly open and confrontational role in an election campaign that they could not vote in. For Madeline Kileen from the town of Ennis, the period was reflective of a growing realignment of public opinion, one that left her father, Jack, on the wrong side. Jack Kileen joined the British Army at the age of seventeen and fought in the First World War. He returned to Ennis in June 1917 at the height of a new political energy:

> When he came home then, you see, there was terrible animosity towards these people that were in the British Army by the Cumann na mBan and all these people you know. They were going up the street one day, himself and this other fella who was also home from the war. They spotted about forty of these women coming down towards them. They had pitchforks, sticks, every kind of an implement, he said, and they were charging down the street and didn't they put their eyes on the two and they knew they had been over in the British Army. They charged down the street after them shouting and screaming. When they got to the square, they separated, the two men and they went their own way and of course they didn't catch up with

them. But he said if they had, I don't know where we'd be. Oh, there was terrible animosity in every direction.[75]

While membership levels may have been relatively high, participation in Cumann na mBan was not uniform in Clare. Those women who did join the organisation often actually found themselves isolated within community life. The nephew of one member from Kilkishen in east Clare revealed that during the War of Independence only one local person would speak publicly to his aunt, Winnie Clancy:

> Winnie, the sister, she was Cumann na mBan. That's another girl that suffered. She told me herself the Clancys were so wanted there was only one woman, only one in Kilkishen that would talk to her. All the rest were terrified if they were seen talking to Winnie Clancy, they'd be marked as well.[76]

'I never saw my mother walk'

Beyond social isolation, the impact on women republicans was far more severe and lasting in certain cases. In early 2010, in a project involving the Clare oral history group Cuimhneamh an Chláir, the National University of Ireland Galway and the Irish Immigrant Support Group in Chicago, I arranged an interview with a Clare exile in Chicago. Keen to foreground his family's connection to the independence struggle, Tom Brennan, who was born in Sixmilebridge towards the end of the War of Independence, first put forward his connection to a well-known IRA family from Meelick:

> Brennan's Cross was a great big house. That's where my cousins Micheál Brennan, Austin and Patrick were from. They were the ones

who were the real rebels! My father was involved in it too. That's why they raided the house of my aunt in Cratloe and 'twas a house that was in the woods. That's why they raided the house or went to the house. They were looking for my dad.

Tom, who emigrated in 1955, explained why he was born in 27 William Street, Limerick, in a nursing home. The activity of the Brennans and IRA Volunteers like Tom's father attracted considerable violence to those around them. For Tom's mother, Elizabeth, a native of Woodcock Hill between Cratloe and Meelick in southeast Clare, her relationship drew her deep into the troubles and would have enduring consequences. Sitting at his home in Chicago, Tom emotionally explained that towards the end of the war, three days before he was due to be born, the house in which his mother was sleeping was raided by the British forces. He described how this changed her life irreversibly:

> There was six in the family and I was the only one born in a nursing home. And this was because the Black and Tans, the Black and Tans [interviewee raises voice] raided my aunt's house where my mother was in bed at three o'clock in the morning. And I was due to be born three days later. So they flashed the flashlight and she got a stroke of paralysis and she lost the power of all her left side. So I never saw my mother walk, but she could get around with the aid of a chair.[77]

Despite the painful and lasting impact of the period on his mother, Tom spoke glowingly about her involvement, prior to her debilitating experience:

> My mother, she used to have to take dispatches from Sixmilebridge. She had a bicycle but the way she took the dispatches was in her hair.

She had some head of hair too! And ah, 'twas in her hair and she'd be told, "Oh, you have to get that down now to Micheál Brennan" and she'd have to cycle through Limerick and go through some backways and give it to him because they'd be arranging for [him] to go out that night. They'd know where there was a lorry coming. They'd have an ambush ... But she had to go with them dispatches in her hair. She might have to cycle twelve miles, maybe two or three times a week or whatever ... she wasn't scared, she was a brave woman. Always happy, always smiling, always laughing.[78]

An obituary that hung proudly on Tom's wall in Chicago was read to the record at Tom's request. The obituary reinforced Tom's view of his mother:

Another link in the country's struggle for independence has been severed by the death this week in an Ennis hospital of Miss Elizabeth M. Brennan of Limerick Road, Sixmilebridge, a member of the Moran family from Woodcock Hill. She was, according to her comrades, one of the most daring Cumann na mBan officers during the War of Independence. Actively in touch with the boys of the famous East Clare Flying Column, she was regarded as one of the cleverest Volunteers to outwit the Black and Tans and Auxies and her escapades during this period are now recorded in the great chapter of Irish history.[79]

Increasingly, as the war became more violent, it was challenging for IRA units to maintain communication with each other. In this context, the role of female republicans took on a heightened importance. Time after time, women were dispatched to travel dangerous roads carrying communications that often planned actions against those likely to stop and search them. In southeast

Clare, a large network of republican sympathisers existed. Threaded throughout the countryside, they formed part of a chain of resistance. They were connected often by young women, who would depart on their bicycles and begin a sequence of communications which would end in the planning of an ambush or IRA action. Mick Ryan, whose mother carried dispatches, outlined the laborious and intricate network involved, as well as the dangerous and tense nature of the activity:

> They used to carry dispatches from that area [Kilbane] on to Ballyboucher. They used to carry the dispatches from Larkin's over there. Ned Larkin was the intelligence officer. When he'd get a dispatch, he'd have to have it delivered over there. The Ryans were supposed to deliver it to an old house down here at the back of Nihil's in Sallybank, just above Truagh church. Dan Ryan and his party would collect it there, take it on to Ballycar, over to Donnellan's. They'd have to go from there, down over the hill down into Meelick or Cratloe with it. One dispatch never arrived in Cratloe and there was fierce noise over it. They quizzed up everyone along the line to know what happened. So when they quizzed up Dan Ryan here, he said when they went to collect the dispatch, it wasn't there ... They were nearly going to be shot.[80]

At the age of ninety-one, standing for over two hours in his workshop in Tulla, Pat O'Halloran explained to me further how women played a role in supporting the IRA:

> There was an aul aunt of mine and she was the Reverend Mother in St John's Hospital in Limerick and she used to get the tip from the reliable RIC men, when they'd come in by the way. She'd maybe be injecting their ears or whatever and he'd pass on the hint and the lads

[IRA] would be gone just ahead of 'em. Oh, she was administering. She was a qualified nurse and a nun, like. They'd be whispering to her that such a thing was going to happen. The lads would be gone then ten minutes or maybe half an hour before the place would be raided.[81]

'Her house and her time were always at the disposal of the boys'

For Teasie McCormack in north Clare, exposure to the social memory of Clare's War of Independence commenced after she married Mickey McCormack and moved to Tullaha, Kilfenora, in the late 1950s. Teasie would often hear tales of one family figure in particular, Katie McCormack. As already mentioned, Katie McCormack was a committed republican. She took the anti-Treaty side in the Irish Civil War and was involved in at least two hunger strikes. When asked to reflect on her aunt-in-law, Teasie summarised that 'she was [a] very strong-willed person, very strong-willed. Not married. Fearless and didn't take fools [laughs] – what's the saying? – kindly'.[82] An obituary published in early January 1944, following her death, demonstrated the esteem in which Katie McCormack from the townland of Tullaha was held by her former comrades:

> The coffin was draped with the tri-colour and a guard of honour of members of the Old IRA … The large concourse at the funeral paid fitting tribute to a life devoted to Ireland's Freedom. A loyal member of Cumann na mBan, her house and her time were always at the disposal of the boys 'on the run'. In the early days of the Sinn Féin movement, frequent visitors at her house in Ennistymon were Ernest Blythe, Eamon Waldron and Liam Mellows.[83]

Mothers of IRA men, although not technically members of Cumann na mBan, would not escape the conflict. Tom Brennan related a story regarding the mother of the three Brennan brothers from Meelick, senior IRA Volunteers in the East Clare Brigade:[84]

> Micheál Brennan. He got the Volunteer force. He had 'em from Sixmilebridge. He had 'em from Broadford. All them areas around there. They were looking for him. He was the head one of the three. So there was ten thousand pound on his head. His mother was a small woman and they had a great big house but they had an open fireplace. She used to sit on an aul box in front of the fire. Apparently the three sons were gone out of the house about an hour in the morning. I don't know where they were goin' but they had rifles anyway. The Black and Tans or the officers came to the house. She let 'em in. They said, "Where are your three sons?" She said, "My three sons? 'Twas so long since I saw 'em, I wouldn't know 'em!" "Well," they said, "we're going to check the house out to see if there are any guns here." So they went upstairs they went to all the rooms … so they left and she was sitting on a box on ammunition! That time, the ladies wore very long clothes and she was small anyway and the clothes were hitting down to the floor.[85]

Although the price on the head of Micheál Brennan may have been slightly overvalued in the above, there is no doubting that he was one of the most wanted men in Clare. It is also certain that his home in Meelick was raided on several occasions.

The story of Brennan's mother is characteristic of the narrative surrounding Cumann na mBan, where an evocation of defiance typically intersects with the conveyance of fear. Mary Brennan was at that stage a fifty-seven-year-old widow. A native of Limerick, she experienced much attention from the crown forces due to her sons' intense involvement. In September 1917, when her three sons were on hunger strike in Mountjoy prison, she wrote to the governor affirming that 'if my boys are dead by return, I'll leave their deaths at your door'.[86] In Tom's story, Mary had seen her sons earlier that day, and she would see them intermittently as they dared to come home to Meelick. However, for the majority of that period her sons were 'on the run'. Her claim that she wouldn't recognise them is both tongue-in-cheek and ironic. In 2014 Phil McGrath, whose father, Tom, fought alongside Micheál Brennan, remembered speaking with the latter in May 1968 at a reunion at Knappogue Castle for the East Clare IRA Brigade. During their conversation, Brennan revealed that on one occasion, he didn't notice his own mother on the streets of Limerick as he walked past her:

> I met him at Knappogue. He was a very quiet man but "Phil," he said, "I just went around with thoughts in my head and I remember passing my mother in Limerick one day and she said, 'Micheál,'," and he said, "I was in another world."[87]

The courage of women outside of the Cumann na mBan fold recurs in many stories. For instance, Teasie McCormack spoke about Bridget Ward, whose son, Paddy, was an active member of the Mid Clare IRA's 5th Battalion. On one occasion, Bridget was in her home in Tullaha, Kilfenora, making shirts out of flour bags, when Black and Tans forcibly entered:

> She had ten in the family and she was making shirts for the children out of flour bags which we all did [laughs] and all the old women did. She was sitting at the table and they said, "We're goin' burnin' the house." "Well ye can burn me along with it," she said and they got a reprieve. They had got a tip-off that they were going to be burnt so they had the dressers and whatever few things they had hidden

beyond in the bog nearby. Well whatever valuables people had in those times.[88]

'The whole of County Clare knew Nan Hogan'

The late Jack Hogan from Newmarket-on-Fergus was born to a father who had been in the IRA and a mother who was active in Cumann na mBan. Both his uncles were also in the IRA as were his first cousins, the aforementioned Brennan brothers.[89] While Jack grew up with a clear awareness of this family connection, the presence of one family figure dominated the narrative. Jack's aunt Annie 'Nan' Hogan was O/C of the 2nd Battalion, East Clare Cumann na mBan Brigade and one of the most active members of the organisation in the county. In June 2011, then ninety-one years old, Jack explained that ''Twas only a short time after I was born that she was arrested. I was born on 20 July 1922 and she was dead in twelve months after!'[90] Nan Hogan, who took an anti-Treaty position, was interned during the Irish Civil War. She later participated in hunger strikes during which her health failed and she died soon after her release in 1924.[91] For Jack, the position of Nan Hogan in social memory was secure and he declared that 'the whole of County Clare knew about Nan Hogan'.[92] After I put it to Jack that he seemed proud of his rebel aunt, he declared, 'I was and I was proud that she was my Godmother as well.' When asked if his father, Tom, spoke about his sister, Jack explained:

> He did, he spoke about her. We'll put it this way – he spoke about her with reverence. He did now, as if she was almighty God nearly. He did now to give him his due. My mother particularly, she was great friends with her through Cumann na mBan. She would tell you lots of stories about the time.[93]

In the Hogan family's private collection, a framed etching made in 1923 by Grace Gifford is treasured. The etching is protected by a unique pane of glass, which was taken from a cell window in Kilmainham Gaol by Gifford. Gifford, who married Joseph Mary Plunkett, one of the leaders of the Easter Rising just hours before his execution, presented an image of the chapel where their union took place in the etching she gifted to her friend Nan Hogan.

In a collection of private family documents relating to Cumann na mBan's East Clare Brigade found as part of this research, Nan Hogan's leading role is powerfully illustrated. A handwritten account by a contemporary of Hogan outlines how on one occasion, after an IRA Volunteer had been severely wounded in southeast Clare, Nan Hogan's role and, by implication, the role of Cumann na mBan became apparent.[94] On 18 November 1920 members of the East Clare IRA attacked a group of British soldiers who had been guarding a plane that crash-landed in Cratloe. Private Alfred Spackman died at the scene and Private Maurice Robins died five months later from wounds received.[95] The attack resulted in large-scale searches by military and police from both Limerick and Ennis. During these searches, Seán O'Halloran, an IRA Volunteer from east Clare, was wounded in the neck in a shootout. It was Hogan who was called on to assist in transporting the IRA Volunteer on roads that were teaming with British soldiers. Tuamgraney IRA Volunteer Joe Noonan, who was involved in the attack, remembered that on one occasion, when O'Halloran was being transported on a pony and trap, Nan Hogan's calmness became evident:

> On the way into Limerick the trap was held up by a party of military. O'Halloran pretended to be the worse of a heavy bout of drinking and as he was being questioned Nan Hogan came to the rescue saying, "He is my brother. Don't wake him. He's soused."[96]

In the handwritten account of the incident, her fellow Cumann na mBan activist Kathleen Foley (née McCormack) explained in more detail the role played by Hogan after she had been made aware of O'Halloran's injuries:

> A man took word to Nan Hogan, who promptly got her pony and trap and drove to the cottage and collected the wounded man. She took him to the house of a friendly ex-RIC [constable] as her own home was suspect by this time. The wounded man was in a very bad way by this time and he had lost a lot of blood from a wound at the back of his neck. Nan Hogan brought a doctor to the patient, who ordered him into the hospital immediately. The trouble was to get him to hospital and to arrange for a hospital that would take him. It was the custom at that time for chief mourners at a funeral to drive in a carriage, so Nan Hogan and her friend decided to hire a carriage and take the wounded man to the county home in Limerick, where they had arranged he would be taken in for treatment … In a few weeks he was on the mend.[97]

Despite the evident role played by Nan Hogan during the period according to her contemporaries, it would appear that over time her story faded, particularly outside of her family and local area. Notwithstanding Jack Hogan's contention that 'the whole of County Clare' knew about his aunt, it would be 2010 before her contribution was acknowledged publicly, when a small plaque was erected at her grave.[98] As mentioned by her godson, Nan died at a young age soon after her release from prison at the end of the Irish Civil War.[99] Her one-time friend and comrade, Kathleen Foley, poignantly explained:

> Nan Foley [Hogan's married name] was arrested the same day as Mr

de Valera at the meeting in Ennis. She was charged with obstructing the military when they were arresting Mr de Valera. She was sentenced and sent to Mountjoy to serve her sentence. She was treated as a criminal. She demanded to be treated as a political prisoner and when they refused she went on hunger strike. She became critically ill and had to be released. Shortly after, the fight was over.[100]

'She didn't say much about it' – Kathleen Foley

Towards the end of an interview in July 2013 with eighty-nine-year-old Mary Galvin from Ennis, much of the War of Independence had been discussed. Most of this had been framed by the experience of Micho Foley, the father of the interviewee and a member of the Mid Clare IRA Brigade. Micho's wife and Mary's mother was also discussed, but little was told about the gentle, retiring mother, Kathleen, who had lived with Mary until she passed away in 1982. It was known that Kathleen Foley was in Cumann na mBan, and that she received a small pension and a medal in recognition of that service. Mary explained that her aunt, Peg, who was also a member of Cumann na mBan, was far more open with her experiences than her mother. For example, while Peg informed her about carrying guns from Limerick hidden in a pony trap, her mother's recollections were limited to a memory of canvassing for de Valera in 1917. When he sat in on a recording with his mother, Kathleen's grandson, Noel, who was born in 1961, recalled the lack of any information regarding his grandmother's involvement in the revolutionary period:

> My grandmother lived with me until she died in 1982. She was here from my birth. But she never would have mentioned, never, anything. I was twenty-one when she died but from zero to twenty-one, she never mentioned anything of any description whatsoever. I can

remember the hand grenades being in the house, as a child literally being thrown in the wardrobe. Occasionally as kids rooting around, we'd find these but that was it! Apart from that, nothing, there was never any word.[101]

When searching through her memory for any clues about her mother's role, Mary Galvin recalled a box of documents carefully stored by her mother for many years:

Whatever papers mother had, she gave them to young Michael Carr [Mary's nephew] and he has all those. And there was probably a lot of stuff in that. Mother gave him all her ... whatever papers she had. I honestly don't know what she had in it.[102]

That box was later discovered in the attic of her cousin Michael. Michael was a teenager interested in history in the late 1970s. He was aware of his grandfather's role in the IRA and that his grandmother, too, had a connection. Over many years, he had built up a rapport with his grandmother and was able to create an environment of trust within which Kathleen Foley would disclose some of her past. For almost six decades, Kathleen had remained largely silent about her revolutionary activities. Now, in an exercise book, Michael took notes as he sat with his grandmother and explored her memories. The notes highlight some key landmarks in the life of Kathleen Foley, who, as the first note in the exercise book shows, was born on 24 October 1896. Living in Clonlara in southeast Clare during the War of Independence meant travelling to Limerick frequently for family errands and shopping. On trips to the city, Kathleen McCormack, as she was then, would regularly pass a British military checkpoint at Corbally Bridge.[103] At her home, names were pinned to the back of the door to indicate the members of her family who were supposedly resident. While the names rarely changed, those in the house would and often IRA Volunteers 'on the run' would be sheltered. Guns were secreted in a double ditch at the back of the home by those Volunteers, and retrieved when needed. One of the men who stayed at McCormacks' was Micho Foley, who later married Kathleen on 28 June 1922, the day the Civil War broke out.[104]

Subsequent to my interview with Mary, the collection of documents, which thirty years previously had been given to her cousin in Limerick, was located. The papers revealed that Kathleen Foley, the quiet, gentle woman her daughter had known, was one of the most senior figures in the East Clare Brigade of Cumann na mBan. For Mary, the collection illuminated aspects of her own mother's life about which she had been wholly unaware. The various accounts of Cumann na mBan activities, including a detailed narration describing Foley's own actions, powerfully convey the dangers inherent in such roles, including regularly concealing guns within her pony and trap as she passed a military checkpoint on her way in and out of Limerick. Mary's mother was deeply involved in all aspects of the revolutionary period. Her brother, Jack McCormack, was a senior member of the East Clare IRA Brigade. In her own pension application made in 1939, Kathleen outlined some of the many activities she was involved in across east Clare. By 1921 she was recognised as having such authority that she 'had charge of over 400 Cumann na mBan at the review at Glenwood'. Kathleen also commented that during the period of 1 April to 30 September 1923, 'I did not actually do the work but gave orders to my comrades as my baby was born on 30 March 1923.'[105] Mary Galvin, who at the age of ninety experienced such a profound disclosure of her mother's secret revolutionary past, was that baby.

'When I think of her bravery'

For many, the failure of monuments or history books to provide information on Cumann na mBan and the women's role in general was countered by local memory. For Patricia Donnellan in east Clare, awareness of the role played by women and stories of her Aunt Katy's involvement were disclosed in her adulthood:

> The story of Aunty Katy would have come from Aunty Katy. That wouldn't have been included in Daddy's account.[106] But I actually didn't know about the activities of Cumann na mBan until Mrs Cleary [Delia Cleary from Whitegate] beyond, who was active in the Cumann na mBan, started telling me stories about it and it was then I realised that the women were involved as well.[107]

Patricia Donnellan grew up in Mountshannon in east Clare with an awareness that her father, Thomas McNamara, was a member of the 4th Battalion of the East Clare IRA. When the Black and Tans arrived in Ireland in March 1920, McNamara was already a twenty-one-year-old republican and member of the IRA. At home, his fourteen-year-old sister Katy looked up to her brother, a hero in her eyes. Although she would not become a member of Cumann na mBan, the life of Katy McNamara would be impacted by having a brother in the IRA. Katy went on to become Sr Mary Dolores, a Catholic nun who lived most of her life in Bangladesh, where she died. In 1986 she was a retired seventy-nine-year-old when her niece visited her there. She spoke to her about her IRA brother, about the day their home was burned and about the Black and Tans who burned it:

> I never knew of the women's involvement growing up at all and 'twas only in later years, much later because Aunty Katy came home in

the fifties. So I think it was 1986 when I went out to see her in Bangladesh … She told me that in later years … He [RIC Sergeant Brennan] was eating Marietta biscuits … he was sitting and he offered her a biscuit and she said, "Keep your biscuits, you offer me biscuits and you burnt my home!" But she was very brave. When I think of her bravery!

In his own statement to the BMH, made in February 1955, Thomas McNamara recounted the day his home was burned:

> [A] neighbour of mine who had been rounded up and released brought me the news that my home and its contents had been burned by the enemy. On my return there that evening I found my father sitting on a stone outside the ruins. He told me that Sergeant Brennan was among those who took part in the burning and that the rere [*sic*] portion of the house was in flames before any of my family were actually out of it. In addition to my father and mother, four of my sisters were living there, and they all had to run out of the place in the attire which they were wearing. It was a long thatched house, built for generations, and readily took to the flames.[108]

Katy also spoke to her niece Patricia about an incident when she was locked in a stable by the Black and Tans, aware that her brother and his comrades were close by. She needed to get a message to her brother:

> The sisters were locked into a stable. The Black and Tans locked them into a stable. They were on guard. They hatched up a plan that Aunty Katy would go out to release the cows to get water. She was, I think, around twelve years of age and this was a dark night here. I often think of her, I actually even to this day, think of her setting off from

here. And she set off for the mountain road, up to the mountain and was going back off up. This was about a mile and a half up, running for all her might to warn them [IRA] that they [Tans] were below waiting for them. And heard them coming singing, they were singing when they were walking. Could you believe it?[109]

As the War of Independence wore on, greater restrictions were imposed on the civilian population, which affected men and women alike. Folklorist Michael O'Gorman documented one story that showed how some of the women were sometimes less willing to accept these impositions than their menfolk:

> I was doing an interview with Jack Farrell there some years ago and Jack told me about some family who needed to go to the market in Limerick. They needed a few bob and they had a lot of stuff. [Captain] Rigby hated the servile way that people approached him. He really did! Jack told me that this man who was looking for a piece of paper that would give him permission to go to Limerick, to leave Scariff, you know to leave the jurisdiction and go to Limerick ... He was there and he had this hat and he twisting it around and he hummin' and hawin' and Rigby told him to "get the hell out of it", you know. Jazus, yer man went home anyway and he told his wife that Rigby refused to give 'em permission. Well she came down to Scariff herself on the ass and car and she stormed into the office where Rigby was and she laid down the law and she said, "We're not goin' to starve above on the side of the hill just to keep you happy. This is our life and you better sign up that form and that's final." Jazus he signed up the form straight away and off they went. She had things to say to [her] husband I'm telling you! Well, do you know, you have to kind of compromise with women! [laughs] There was no way her husband could do what his wife was after doing. They'd put a bullet in him.[110]

'A secondary opinion'

Where it was discussed, the position of Cumann na mBan in social memory was often afforded a decidedly secondary role. This is illustrated best by Seán O'Sullivan, who was interviewed in 2012 at the age of eighty-seven. Seán was the son of the late Susan Flanagan from Lahinch, an active member of Cumann na mBan in north Clare. In early 1921 Susan was singled out for praise in Ennis court for having 'showed great courage in saving her sister' in relation to the burning of her home during the reprisals that followed the Rineen ambush in September 1920.[111] One item that the judge had no difficulty in compensating for was a Perry violin. Susan played the 'finely tuned instrument', which had been destroyed, and was awarded £15 to replace it.[112] Her ability to play the fiddle was useful later, as her son explained:

> As you know after that she had to go 'on the run' because the RIC and the military knew now of her involvement [obtaining weapons and ammunition for the IRA] so she had to go out in the country, so she spent a good deal of her time in Moher and from there she went to Gleeson's in Coore. They were very friendly with them and the one thing was that she used to play the violin and at country houses she'd be playing music for the dancing. So that's what kept her going at the time, like.[113]

According to Seán, despite her having procured and carried arms for the local IRA, as well as fundraising, his mother's role was barely recognised in discussions on the period:

> No, they would talk mainly amongst themselves. She was a secondary opinion, like, you know ... my mother, her people had a pub in Lahinch. A pub that time meant there was a bakery involved in the

pub. And the custom that time was that you'd give out free bread to the clients, do you follow? Now that pub was mainly used by the military soldiers from the hotel which was at the end of the street from that camp. The officers used a different pub, 'The Nineteenth' … Her main function was I think, as in any group of people; there'd probably be hundreds of soldiers passing through and going on to France, after their training there. There would always be some who would be alcoholic. Now she would know the ones who'd be alcoholic. And that was the weakness of the military system. They were the ones who would sell their rifles. She would know who those weak links were and ah, she would find out what they were willing to take for the rifle and she'd pass that back. And there was a contact made with a woman who owns 'The Nineteenth', O'Dwyer's, 'Mary O' she was known as. She was a noted pro-revolutionary person [laughs] and because she had money, she would give the money and that's how the circuit was completed. So the guy was paid for the rifle, but he took the rifle from his friend or from one or other men and that's the gun that ended up with the local IRA.

Seán's brother, Tomsie, spoke to folklore collector Frances Madigan about his mother's reticence in talking about the period and emphasised how it was not just a reluctance to remember, but a determination to forget:

There was a jotter, which mam had been asked to make notes in [about the War of Independence]. It was a jotter which was [the] brown paper of the war years so it must have been written in the forties or fifties … and I up in the old attic looking through stuff with a candle. I asked at teatime that night about this jotter I was after getting … So I go up and take down the jotter to her. She looks at it and flicks through the pages and she tears it and then she puts it into the open fire and I got a very, very harsh talking to about going up into the attic.[114]

Several stories present young women travelling with seditious messages hidden somewhere on their person, along what were then danger-filled roads in Co. Clare. In southeast Clare, Noreen Ryan remembered her aunt's description of being stopped and roughly searched by Black and Tans, who fortunately did not manage to find the republican communication concealed in her sock.[115] In Kilfenora, Jimmy O'Donoghue's mother, Catherine O'Brien, was in Cumann na mBan and carried dispatches 'in the sole of her shoe' for the IRA.[116] On the roads outside Kilrush, eleven-year-old Mary Howard similarly walked with extra padding inside her sock:

> When Mary O'Donnell [née Howard] would be going with dispatches to O'Donnell of Tullycrine, she'd have 'em in her shoe. They [Tans] met her a couple of times and she'd always bring a schoolbag on her back to let on she was comin' from school. They didn't know where she lived. They threw the books a couple of times, scattered 'em on the road to know would she have anything in the bag, but the dispatch was in her shoe! She was my sister.[117]

For some women who remembered the period, their youthful risks transformed into elderly worries. In Whitegate, towards the end of her life, Mary Joe Holland spoke with increasing frequency about a biscuit tin she had hidden in the family garden many decades previously:

> My aunt, Mary Joe Holland, she didn't talk very much about it. In our house there was a box, a biscuit tin box, a tin box of all IRA court files. The court. They had their own courts. All the files were

in this tin box and the morning they were raided, when the Tans arrested the boys [Scariff Martyrs] on Tuesday 16 November. That morning when they had the boys captured below they came up and searched all Nutgrove House, all our house. Mary Joe was seventeen or eighteen years of age that time. She was given it at the time on the quiet, this tin box to go out and get rid of it. She didn't talk about that then for years after, until three years before she died and it worried her. She plagued me to go out. She was trying to explain where she buried it, would I ever go out and dig it up. But shur, sixty years later, a tin box and the files were gone. She never dug it up. She left it where she put it.[118]

'They sat her down and cut her hair to the bone'

The significance of women who provided safe houses for IRA men 'on the run' should not be underestimated. As one historian suggested, 'women were easy targets for frustrated British soldiers and particularly vulnerable to attack'.[119] The British forces were guilty of malicious and violent behaviour towards women they felt were supporting the republican campaign. Tom Brennan remembered speaking to a woman in Sixmilebridge who suffered the anger of the crown forces:

> There was one woman, her husband was a blacksmith. Fennessy, Joe Fennessy. He had a blacksmith's shop in the square in Sixmilebridge. His wife, they went into there looking for something and she was there alone. They sat her down and cut her hair to the bone. Oh, that's true, she told me.[120]

For John Cleary in Kildysart, it was clear that 'the main burden and thrust of the whole thing lay with the women. Mothers and sisters, they took huge risks.'[121]

The IRA was equally capable of brutally punishing female informers. Mellie Enright in Kilmihil remembered that after the war became more bitter, women would have tar put in their hair if they continued to speak with the police. In north Clare, one interviewee was aware of a much more severe and brutal punishment:

> It was carried out in Lahinch, I was told. 'Twould be what they called a pig ring now that you'd ring a pig with. When I heard about it I went looking for one … You'd put it in and squeeze it and 'twould go into a circle do you see. When 'twas carried out in Lahinch [clamped on her buttocks], they told the lady "You can go to the RIC now to take out that." I heard that she went off on the train the following morning and was never heard of again. Whether you'd hear so many things now and some of 'em might be added to, do you know … That was one punishment but the usual one was tarred and feathered but the ring wasn't ever spoken about much … If you had anything to do with the Black and Tans or the RIC, if you even spoke to 'em, if [you] gave 'em a cup of tea, any involvement would do at times. In a lot of cases, they made off that if you gave them a cup of tea, you could be giving them information as well. So they [the IRA] took no chances.[122]

'Be as brave as if it was your wife you were talking to'

P.J. Clancy grew up with the certain knowledge that his mother, Maria Conneally, had been a member of Cumann na mBan. He was equally assured of these women's central role in the revolutionary period. In 1917, when Co. Clare took centre stage in the national story, Maria Conneally became a captain in the Lavareen Company and threw herself into the struggle, with contemporaries such as Máire O'Dwyer and Nellie Marrinan, who were leading figures in the organisation in north Clare:

Well, she joined the Cumann na mBan as far as I know in 1917 and she became a captain of the Lavareen and the Ennistymon area. She was very involved in dispatches and enemy movement and this kind of thing. She was threatened for takin' down enemy posters even, do you know … there'd be a Máire O'Dwyer in Lahinch. She'd be the head it seems …[123]

It was not long before the crown forces became aware of the activities of Maria Conneally:

There was some one of 'em that had some set on her and traced her up to the Spa [Lisdoonvarna] of a time do you know. She had to come home by the Kilfenora way in order to avoid him. He was marching up and down past the house where she was staying in Lisdoonvarna.

Involvement in the struggle for Cumann na mBan went much deeper than tearing down posters. Depending on the levels of IRA activity in the area, Cumann na mBan were drawn into much more serious levels of involvement. In July 1920 twenty-one-year-old Michael Conway, a local IRA Volunteer, was shot dead on the bridge in Ennistymon while attempting to disarm two British soldiers.[124] Over the years, P.J. heard much about this incident, including from his neighbour, Paddy Harvey, who was a child at the time:

Up from that then, there is an old ruin of a cabin where Micho Conway was waked. Micho Nestor brought him up there in an ass and car and he covered with hay. They brought him to Paddy Harvey's … they left him there, Paddy Harvey told me … He was shot shur. They brought him to Paddy Harvey's shed. Paddy was telling me himself now that when they brought him up, they had a sow [female adult pig] out and they had to put in the sow that day for fear she'd discover the body, do you know. 'Tis that night he'd have been waked then you see and he was waked below there in that cabin.¹²⁵

P.J. also learned that his mother was called upon to help deal with the aftermath:

> I remember her telling me about that she was involved in the laying out of Michael Conway in that cabin. She was that type. She was the coolest you ever met! I'd say they actually wanted to be that way to survive. If they were an excitable type, they wouldn't do.

A year later, the IRA launched an ambush immediately outside the house of Maria Conneally. Inevitably, given the geographical proximity, as well as the family's strong republican connections, it would be targeted following the incident. In the ensuing reprisals, Maria's elderly father, Tom Conneally, was badly beaten by Black and Tans:

> Her father was very involved. He just didn't live long enough to see the amount of freedom we got. He died on 11 December 1921, I think.¹²⁶ The house was raided very soon after the Monanana ambush.¹²⁷ The house was wrecked. Everything was thrown around, the same as if a bomb was thrown in it nearly. A rifle was put up, put up to her [Maria's] head. She was going to be shot but for an RIC man, kind of that she knew in town, that saved her. My grandfather then was badly tortured but he lived away until December. The ambush was July.¹²⁸

Born in 1898, Maria Conneally was twenty-two when her country was plunged deep into the struggle for its own independence.

When she died in 1994, at the age of ninety-six, she still held the same values and outlook, according to her son. Maria had married Michael 'Micho' Clancy, himself a member of the Mid Clare IRA Brigade. Despite Micho Clancy's evident involvement in republican activities between 1917 and 1923, which included a period of almost nine months' imprisonment, he was unsuccessful in achieving an IRA pension.[129] An application under the Army Pensions Act 1932 was reviewed by the Army Pensions Review Board and it was found that he 'had no disability due to Military Service'. The only official recognition Micho Clancy did receive was a Service Medal (1917–1921) in respect of his membership of Moy Company, 4th Battalion, 4th Brigade, 1st Western Division of Óglaigh na hÉireann, awarded on 12 January 1948. Before this award, Micho had made one last attempt to gain a pension and was granted an interview in Dublin. A handwritten letter amongst a large collection held by P.J. Clancy was written to Micho in the days before his interview. Steve Gallagher, who had been his O/C in the IRA, reminded Micho in the letter that 'this is your last chance'. Towards the conclusion of the letter, in a profoundly ironic attempt at encouragement, Gallagher insisted that when Micho was in front of the interview board, he should be 'as brave as if it was your wife you were talking to!'[130]

The burnt-out remains of Tom Connole's house in Ennistymon, taken in the days after his murder on 22 September 1920. (*Courtesy of Clare County Library*)

Maureen Connole photographed at her home following a recording in 2008. In 1920 her uncle, Tom, was shot and burned by British forces during reprisals for the Rineen ambush. (*Author's collection*)

Paddy McGough was five when a participant in the Rineen ambush arrived into his house after the action. In the photo he is holding a model of the monument to Rineen, which he and his father, Michael, built in 1957. (*Author's collection*)

John Whelan's home in Ennistymon after the British reprisals for Rineen. (*Courtesy of Clare County Library*)

P.J. Clancy, who spent many years researching the story of his parents, Micho and Maria Clancy, who were both involved in the republican movement. (*Courtesy of John Kelly Photography*)

A young Michael Howard with the 'turned-up stockings' he used to conceal a brace of bullets from the Black and Tans. He later hid them in a shed, where they remain. (*Courtesy of the Howard family*)

Michael returning to the shed where, ninety years earlier, he hid bullets from the Black and Tans. (*Author's collection*)

Catherine Talty from Clounlaheen in west Clare was born in April 1916 and remembered the Black and Tans in Miltown Malbay. (*Courtesy of Jackie Elger*)

Storyteller Francie Kenneally at his home in Leeds, Miltown Malbay. (*Author's collection*)

An illustration of a 'military ghost' contributed as part of the 1938 Schools' Folklore Scheme. A belief existed in Miltown Malbay that the spirit of a Black and Tan lingered. (*Courtesy of the Department of Folklore, UCD*)

Right: Batty McNamara (better known as 'Batty Mac'), a well-known character from Claremount in O'Callaghan's Mills. Batty was imprisoned for cattle driving in 1918, later arrested for occupying a landlord's house, and had many encounters with British forces where he used his natural humour to ease the tension. Batty was my grandfather. (*Author's collection*)

Below: The Murphy family from Glann, Ennistymon in happier times in 1917. Francie Murphy (standing, far right) was shot dead, allegedly by British forces, two years later at the age of fifteen. His sister, Una, pictured behind his right shoulder, spoke his name on her deathbed, forty-six years later. (*Courtesy of Flan Garvey*)

Nora Canavan was fourteen when the Black and Tans left Ireland in 1922. She was interviewed at the age of 104. (*Author's collection*)

Kathleen Nash was born in 1909 and witnessed the Black and Tans forcing her schoolmaster to write 'To Hell with the Pope' on the blackboard. (*Author's collection*)

Peggy Hogan and Mae Tuohy both had many stories about the Black and Tans. Mae was born in May 1916 and remembered the force outside her home. (*Courtesy of Press 22*)

A postcard of Seán Breen, shot dead during an IRA action in Kilmihil in April 1920. (*Courtesy of Clare Museum*)

Kilfenora republican Katie McCormack. After her hotel in Ennistymon was closed down by British authorities, Katie was forced to rebuild her life in Lisdoonvarna. (*Courtesy of Teasie McCormack*)

John O'Connell from Labasheeda was a baby in his cot when Black and Tans entered his house in search of his uncle, IRA Volunteer Jamie Corbett. (*Author's collection*)

Paddy Gleeson at Scariff churchyard on Easter Sunday 2008. (Courtesy of the *Clare Champion*)

3

'ALL THEIR OWN SONS'

STORIES OF COMMUNITY

> You had to admire all the rank and filers up and down the country – no great names, no great positions, but they worked loyally and fought and gave up everything. All the people in the country, young and old, were involved. It was the people of the country who suffered most. They stood by the men and clothed them and fed them and kept them and took great risks. And they'd hear the roar of the army lorries at night. They were the real heroes of the war.[1]

Numerically, only a small percentage of Irish people are recognised as having participated directly in the struggle for independence. I have attempted to show how that number should be dramatically increased to accommodate the many men, women and children who played brave roles indirectly, without being registered members of either the IRA or Cumann na mBan. Certainly, when the nature of the war is considered, the reality that the echoes of each action rippled across the entire community rings true. For a period of over three years, normal life was shattered for the population who lived through it, at both passive and active levels. The war itself had no precedent. Culturally, politically and militarily this was a new departure for the Irish people. The violence, fear and volatile nature of the period is evident in the stories I have recorded. Underlining this, 104-year-old Nora Canavan recalled 'the danger was everywhere', while for the late Micheál O'Connell, who was born in 1919, such was the precariousness, 'your life was in your fist'.[2]

The abnormal nature of the period is illustrated in an example from Tipperary in June 1920 provided by Michael Laffan. In it, a man was found to have beaten his own father and stolen items from his home. When the RIC failed to locate the individual, the father of the man reported the incident to the local IRA Volunteers, who arrested the man within hours. Ironically, as the IRA were hunting down the criminal, the RIC were pursuing the IRA![3]

'Oh 'twas an awful time' – The Tans' Impact on the Community

Patrick 'Brud' Skeehan was interviewed in 2010. He was born on 15 November 1915. At the age of ninety-five he explained his understanding of the Black and Tans, who left Ireland when he was just over six years old. When asked if he remembered the time of the Black and Tans, Skeehan declared emphatically, 'I do well. I do well and I have reason to remember it! The Black and Tans. Oh Jesus I did.' For 'Brud', whose father, Batt, was a district councillor and peace commissioner who ran for the Dáil in 1923 as one of two candidates of the Farmer's Party in Clare, the practical impacts on local people were the primary consideration upon reflection:

> Oh, the regulations … you had to have a sign about that width now [showing a sheet of paper] with all the names, the father, mother, workmen, tacked to the back of the door. You can see the tack marks on the door in the house below to this day. All the names of the house. If they called and checked and somebody was missing, you see, you'd have to account to know where was such a one. 'Twas in every house, the time of the Black and Tans … If you didn't know

> you'd have to give a fair indication that they were gone on business and they might call back to check. It was all about trying to track down people 'on the run', you know. There was a family off up there beyond, there's nare a house there now, Moloneys' and Ahernes', and all the young men that time used to flee there in the night ... They'd lie down behind a reek of hay because the Tans would be coming searching, you know. They'd take them then to clear the roads. All the roads were blocked at that time. Oh 'twas an awful time, an awful time, the Black and Tans.[4]

In the same parish, marks are also left on the creamery wall in the village where, in January 1921, the Auxiliaries fired shots and set the building on fire while en route towards Kilkishen, where the Glenwood ambush had just occurred. Across from Bridgetown creamery are the remains of a building that was known as 'Joe's Barn' in 1921, and was a local meeting place for the IRA, who planned defences of the creamery, a vital fulcrum for the farmers of the area.[5]

'With the snow on the road, they'd track him'
In contrast to the distant experience of conventional warfare, the War of Independence was brought to the doors of local people in a literal sense. For a communicant on the way to Mass, or a farmer foddering cattle, the sense of impending danger was sometimes overpowering. Pat O'Halloran was born in Tulla during the War of Independence and inherited many stories in his native parish. In one interview, he illustrates how the ordinary and extraordinary were in close union at this time:

> The late John Melody was a county councillor and he told me the story himself. He was goin' to Drumcharley Mass and he was cycling

over that road and there was, I suppose, maybe six inches of snow on the ground and he came on this armoured car pulled in on the side of the road. He had to get off the bike anyway to pass it and he could see in through the fogged windows of it and he could see two soldiers asleep. I suppose they had enough drank! They had two revolvers laid up on the car outside. He thought to take 'em but he thought with the snow on the road, they'd track him and bring tore [trouble] on the church.[6]

In 1920 John Melody was a forty-four-year-old living in Cloondoorney More, Kiltannon. He was an Irish speaker and was married to Charlotte Bell, whose mother was a native of Armagh and a member of the Church of Ireland. His decision to resist taking the apparently abandoned revolvers was based on a deeper desire to safeguard his community, who were then assembling at Drumcharley church. The Black and Tans regularly used the weekly Mass services as a way of targeting communities when gathered together. Pat O'Halloran recounts another occasion when the weekly liturgical ritual for Catholics was the scene of panic and fear:

> On another occasion at Knockjames church, they rounded up … as you say there were trees knocked and the road blocked around Drumcharley, where the mushroom business is now, and they rounded up the lads at Knockjames church and they got 'em to bring the stones of the wall at the mushroom factory up Knockdrumleague hill and to draw out 'God Save the King' [laughs]. Matt Clune, he was a big tall man. Jazus, Matt was a bit slow but Matt was a republican and farmer with his brother and one hoor [Black and Tan] said, "Wouldn't he be a fine man if his legs were cut off at the knees!"[7]

Fortunately for Matt Clune, the danger departed soon after the Black and Tans had sufficiently frightened the local churchgoers. However, in April 1921, just over three miles across the land from Knockjames church, a farmer apparently feeding his cattle was shot dead by a mixed force of British military and Black and Tans:

> Mick McGrath's uncle was shot up in Glendree. 'Twas the fair evening of Tulla in March or April. He was goin' with a beart [bundle carried on back] of hay and they pulled up on the road and they had a bet in one of these Crossley lorries. That was the Tans. They had a bet anyway and some one of 'em says, "I'll ping the trousers off of him." Some slang word like that or sentence … oh they shot him.[8]

The farmer referred to by Pat O'Halloran was Thomas McGrath, a forty-one-year-old married man, who was shot dead by a British soldier on 25 April. Police reports suggested that McGrath was killed at approximately 7 p.m. near a public road at Glendree, outside Feakle. At the court of inquiry two days later, it was claimed that a shot was fired at the mixed force of police and military and that McGrath was seen running away, at which point the British forces fired and killed him.[9] The man who shot McGrath was revealed to be Private Hemmings, a member of the Oxford and Buckinghamshire Regiment stationed in Tulla. Hemmings suffered no consequence for the death of McGrath.

'God, you wouldn't know the hour of the night that they'd knock on the door'
For Nora Canavan, who was born in 1908, the period impacted heavily on the local community. At her home near Monreal in Ennistymon, her family was encircled by republican and crown force activity:

They [the IRA] were all for having their own government. They wanted to clear the English away out of this country. But I know the time of the Tans, 'twas an awful time. God, you wouldn't know the hour of the night that they'd knock on the door and they'd come in and search your house. If there was a spark of light seen, the windows had to be barricaded, no light to be seen.[10]

On the morning of 18 December 1920, three tenders left Ennistymon for Ennis. Nora and her family were huddled in one room in their family home in the frightening certainty of impending trouble. Close by, a large active service unit (ASU) of the Mid Clare IRA was crouched and in position. The ambush had been originally planned for the previous evening:

'Twas a Friday night, the eighteenth of December and there was a crowd of us coming home from school and they said that they'd hold the ambush that evening; that they were ready for it but over the crowd of children that were on the road, they stopped.[11]

That evening twelve-year-old Nora had seen men on the road near Monreal and wondered what they were doing:

I did. Throwing the rocks at both sides of the road. They were making a barricade. Stopping them [the Tans] from goin' down that road. This was down a bit from the cross. Oh and we couldn't understand what was wrong at all. We came in home, "Oh, there is lads down there and they're throwing rocks out on the road." There was no word [from her parents]. They were down and out. They knew what was going to happen. We were coming from school and ah, two lads, I couldn't tell you who they were. They were strangers probably … We came in from school. I remember my father and mother. There wasn't a word out of them. And they didn't tell us anything but we knew it in the morning what was wrong. And we were all collected into one room in case there would [be] any shots come through the windows or the doors. The stone walls were the safest ... the Tans were going off to Ennis. That's the time it [ambush] started. Oh, the banging was fierce! ... And my father had to go to see the cattle and he was on his way back and he went and sheltered from a shower. And there was a bullet put through the tree where he was, over his head. Ah my! 'Twas bad, a bad time.[12]

Nora also remembered the Monanana ambush six months later, in June 1921, close to Monreal. Like the previous December, Nora and her family once again had to prepare for the worst: 'Just listening to it. Oh, what you'd have to stay inside doors and lie down. Afterwards they were showing us spots where the bullets hit between the two windows. Ah, 'twas a lovely summer's day!'[13]

In the east Clare town of Scariff during this time, local people suffered severe consequences for their support of the IRA. The town had previously been the subject of a military order, specific to 'a radius of one and a half miles from the post office of Scariff'. Consequent restrictions included the prohibition of fairs and markets, and a curfew between 8 p.m. and 5 a.m., unless a permit was obtained from the district inspector of Killaloe.[14]

On 10 April 1920 *The Clare Journal* carried a report that recorded how, in the previous week, all able-bodied men in Scariff were assembled in the town, their shirts were removed and they were horsewhipped.[15] Twenty-four-year-old butcher Jimmy O'Brien was one of many men from the town who were awoken from their slumber in the middle of the night. His son, James, explained in 2012:

One night, all the suspects in Scariff that were thought to have any involvement [with the IRA] ... were ordered out of their houses and they were lined up in the street from the Commercial Hotel to the Market house. He was telling me 'twas about four o'clock in the morning, maybe in February or around that time in the year 1921 ... They were stripped to the waist and the horse whips came out and they were horsewhipped. That came straight from the man who was there.[16]

'The Tans burned the Coolmeen jerseys'

Inevitably, the republican movement and the GAA were intertwined. Several of the 1914 Clare hurling team who won the All-Ireland final were later members of the IRA, including Tom McGrath, Brendan and William 'Dodger' Considine, Pa 'Fowler' McInerney and Ned Grace. In 1917, when Clare competed in the All-Ireland football final, republicans James 'Sham' Spellissy and Tull Considine were members of the Clare panel, as was Patrick Hennessy, who would be shot dead in April 1921 by British forces in Miltown Malbay at a place called Canada Cross.[17] That the GAA and IRA were in many ways interlinked was also shown in the treatment of the former by the British forces. For local people in the west Clare village of Coolmeen, the burning of their club jerseys in June 1921 was a grievance that has lingered in social memory:

> The Tans burned the Coolmeen jerseys at Haugh's. As we're talkin' about the GAA in Coolmeen, the Haugh's would be the centre of the GAA in Coolmeen since the founding of it ... The Tans raided the house and burnt the jerseys at Coolmeen cross. They won the county championship the following year! They were all brothers except Sonny O'Neill and my father.[18]

'Shooting cattle and shooting at geese'

The frequent disruption to agricultural activity, as well as the repeated shootings of farm animals and fowl, wounded a people whose culture and heritage was farming, more deeply perhaps than the Black and Tans understood. In the context of a war that saw over 1,400 people killed, the shooting of a dog or the taking of a horse can only be reduced in comparison. However, for the family who suffered the loss of an animal at the hands of what they perceived as foreign invaders, such grievances were amplified. For P.J. Reidy, whose father, Patrick, was a member of the IRA in Newmarket-on-Fergus, such behaviour by the Black and Tans hardened people's attitudes towards British rule:

> Ah, well things weren't bad until such time as Tans came that time and what they were doing and the way they were robbin' houses and taking anything of value and tormenting people, shooting cattle and shooting at geese or anything like that. Even in my mother's house, there was one of their geese shot. Took a cock, shot at 'em when they see 'em outside in the field.[19]

In Claremount, between the villages of O'Callaghan's Mills and Broadford, the Black and Tans fired on a local farmer for no apparent reason:

> They fired on Sonny Moloney. He ran anyway and there was some bit of oats sown and he rolled into it. They thought they had him. They didn't bother checking him. Someone said that "Sonny Moloney from Ballymacdonnell is shot", but he got away. The same day, they drove through a flock of geese belonging to Devitts and got out and took them in the lorry and took them off with them. They were ruthless. 'Twas handy meat for them.[20]

'ALL THEIR OWN SONS' 153

In Kildysart, a farmer named Keane went to great lengths to take his prize Irish Draught mare via a circuitous route to the blacksmith, to ensure she would not be seen by British forces, who had begun to commandeer horses in the area, but he was ultimately unsuccessful:

> The horse artillery. The British had horses coming. They came from Kildysart and they came hither to the forge. They surrounded it. That was in Ballygeary [Labasheeda] at the time you know. They only picked one [horse] in the finish, do you see. She was belonging to a man over near Gortglass lake [Kildysart] by the name of Keane. He was avoiding. 'Twas Kildysart that he used to be going to, to shoe the horse. He was avoiding Kildysart that day and he came back to Coolmeen here. He was avoiding them over that she might be taken off him. He was just an ordinary farmer. The blacksmith, he described it to me one time. The two horses that was at the forge, one of 'em was shoeing [having horseshoes replaced] and the other fella was outside. They [British forces] gave orders to stop both jobs until they saw the horses. The horse that was outside, they didn't take him at all. He wasn't fast enough! The one that was inside, they gave orders to Bird [William O'Connor] to shoe away. They were goin' carrying him. There was two of 'em anyway, Bird said, and one of 'em stood in and put his hand up this way [John demonstrates how they measured the height of the horse] and the other lad had his book here at the wall here and he taking down the information. So many hands you know for the horse's height, you know, and her colour, and bridle and saddle. 'Twas all wrote down. They told him that a certain day, nearly a month after, to call for this mare at Gerry O'Kerin's yard in Ennis and she was there! Shur Keane thought he'd never again see her![21]

Martin Walsh sat up to emphasise his summation, when I

asked whether the Black and Tans caused hardship for the local community:

> Oh, they did. Oh they did and they told a lot of stories about what they did. They were a shower of rowdies. They were the criminals of England the Black and Tans that was let loose on Ireland for to plunder and rob all they had and no one to control 'em. I heard all about it … They did and they took the people that they used to kill a pig for their grub and the barrel the pig would be put into. They came in and they raided the house and they took all the bacon away and left 'em starving.[22]

It was not the British forces alone who imposed themselves on the lives of local animals. When the Mid Clare Brigade planned a raid on the RIC barracks at Ruan near Ennis, various considerations were put forward. One, which may not have registered with many, was the perennial concern of overly vigilant dogs. In October 1920 sounds in the night were infrequent. When the quietness of the night was disrupted, the first to respond were the many farmers' dogs whose erstwhile slumber had been disturbed. For an IRA unit, who required the advantage of surprise, there was only one, somewhat cruel, solution:

> The local neighbours poisoned the dogs two or three days before it. Everyone had a couple of sheepdogs that time, farmers, and they'd all bark. When we were young you'd hear 'em barking a mile away when we were going on cuaird. So there was no dog in the area then.[23]

'The road was up'

A key advantage for the IRA Volunteers in the campaign in Clare was their intimate knowledge of the local landscape. In addition, the guerrilla nature of their campaign meant travelling on foot while carrying relatively light weaponry. Usually for an ambush or action, weapons would be stockpiled close to the planned location. In contrast, the crown forces used heavy cumbersome vehicles and weapons when travelling through active areas.

The rural nature of Co. Clare with its isolated villages meant that the narrow roads of the county dictated to a large extent the places British forces could go. For the IRA, it was imperative to cut off, in so far as possible, these access routes and to disrupt the travel plans of the ominous Crossley tenders. However, this cutting of roads impacted on the local people as well, in many ways. The late Gerome Griffin spoke about the disruption caused in his community of Ballyea, near Ennis:

> There was a woman [Ann Byrnes] back near our place long ago. She was tellin' Michael not long before she died … that the road was up when she was goin' to America in 1920 … The people of Ballycorish couldn't come over to go to En [Ennis] in a horse and car to meet the train to go for Queenstown [Cobh]. She had to go up to Lissycasey to go in the Kilrush road … the road was up. It meant that the republicans had a trench dug along the road. They'd [Tans] meet any neighbour there and they'd just point the gun at them and tell him hop in the lorry and gather the locals and go backfill the trench again, like. The father and them [IRA] were above near Caherea school, they dug a big trench there … They'd be hopin' they'd run into them [Tans] and maybe they could ambush them.[24]

Paddy Gleeson remembered the almost weekly scene in the east Clare village of Tuamgraney, when young men, having risen from their knees, retrieved their peak caps from their pockets and emerged from Sunday Mass to embrace their day of rest, only to be instead faced with a waiting contingent of Black and Tans:

> They used to come to Mass then in Bodyke and Tuamgraney. When you'd come out to Mass, they'd be there waiting. They used to take young fellas out to mountainy areas where the roads were blocked or cut up or bridges broken. They'd be there all day without a bit to eat.[25]

Micheál Falsey is a well-known traditional musician and fisherman from Seafield in Quilty on the west Clare coast. In January 2012 he was able to offer me an example of the way that the conflict impacted in frustrating ways for the people of the entire country. Falsey paints a picture of a local man, Peter Boyle, returning from a bog in Cree some six miles from his home. As he made his way along the road towards Tromra, across the cliff tops, he saw an ominous sight ahead. His long, arduous day working in the bog was not over yet:

> They'd talk about the Black and Tans, what they did around. There was a local man here. He was goin' to the bog for a creel of turf with a genet and cart. I knew the man well. But when he came home in the evening after a long journey, I suppose, 'twas six miles down to the bog. But the road was cut not far from his house and the Tans were waiting. They stopped him. "Empty that load of turf in there into that trench." He said, "I'm after coming a long way with that load, I'm not emptying that load." So the rifle was caught, anyway, and there was bullets hopped near his legs. He was hopping off 'em. He had to empty it then! He was Peter Boyle.[26]

Not far from Quilty, where the above incident took place, another farmer was troubled by roads that had been disrupted as he made his way with turf, trouble that was made worse by a second self-imposed journey, as explained to me by Martin Walsh:

Oh ya, that bridge. There was a bridge at the end of our avenue and 'twas broke. And there was a man; he had an awful [big] family. He had eleven and he workin' on the road. He was sellin' turf in Miltown. And they [IRA] broke the bridge so that he couldn't go to Miltown with the load of turf. He had to go three miles or four miles all around for to get to Miltown to sell the turf and the price of the load of turf was three shillings! 'Halfpenny Gallery' was his name. He was told not to sell it without three shillings. And he was getting two and eleven pence halfpenny for it and he wouldn't give it and he brought it home ... they called him 'Halfpenny Gallery' ever after [laughs].[27]

While often it was local young men who were forced to repair the roads at gunpoint, on a number of occasions more senior people in the community were obligated. John Minogue in Scariff explained that after the road was cut in the townland of Core, the local Cooleen Bridge schoolmaster, Master Jones, was forced to accompany the Black and Tans to fill it in.[28] Similarly in west Clare, Master John Brennan of Tullycrine schoolhouse was awakened by the Black and Tans at three o'clock one morning and ordered to fill in a pit which had been dug on the road near the school. In the darkness of the night, a torch illuminated a shovel and a gun side by side outside the school wall. Brennan was asked which he would prefer. He quickly and prudently responded, 'pass the shovel'.[29]

Even as a child, Mary Murrihy from Miltown Malbay could not avoid the impact of the period when roads were cut. She had to manoeuvre her way around them with her siblings:

On the Shanaway Road, I remember the lorry right well on the Shanaway road and we comin' out from school. And they cut the road ... They cut the road between the school and that house

[O'Gormans']. I can remember right well Mrs O'Loughlin tellin' us, "Be very careful, keep well in. Put your hand on the wall and keep well in." They [the IRA] cut the road for to stop the Tans. The Tans were comin' that way and they cut the road on 'em. I can remember that right well, the road cut. She was afraid we'd fall in but of course there was a grass margin and we could walk on that along by the wall.[30]

'An extraordinary situation'

All areas of community life were affected by the War of Independence. In communities across Co. Clare and Ireland, old institutions were undergoing radical change. At the beginning of the conflict, the system of courts applied the law in the name of the British state. A short time later, however, the republican movement had largely swept that system aside and established its own judiciary. For the communities affected, this transformation was all-consuming.

The late John Kelly spoke in west Clare in 2012 about his father, Patrick 'the Soldier' Kelly, a man who fought in the Boer War for the British Army, became a Sinn Féin judge and also served as a Fine Gael TD. During the War of Independence, as Sinn Féin sought to assume the machinery of justice, Patrick Kelly was invited to serve as a judge in the increasingly powerful Sinn Féin courts. His son explained that Sinn Féin 'were trying to assume the power from the British. 'Twas an extraordinary situation.' Kelly heard many stories of the period including several tense court proceedings attended by his father:

> There was court up in Craggaknock one day, between the Christy Kellys and a local family, the Curtins, over a boundary drain. Something very trivial. The Christy Kellys had allowed the Black

and Tans put their horses on their land ... Fr Charlie Culligan and a Shanahan man ... and my father, they were the three judges. I have seen the house where the court was, Tomás. It was the most isolated place you could find, but didn't the Tans hear about it! Someone spied on them and they raided the place, five or six Black and Tan lorries. Some of the people there ran, including Willie Shanahan.[31] Willie had the court papers. The Tans fired on them. They shot a Curtin man, shot him through the forehead. I'd say 'twas a lucky shot. But ah, they say Willie Shanahan went in the back door of some house and he escaping. The woman of the house said, "Willie, will you drink a cup of tea?" He said, "Not today, mam, thank you!" And out the front door and escaped down towards the sandhills! He got away, but my father, the Lord have Mercy on him, and Fr Culligan and the Shanahan man stood their ground ... Willie Shanahan was court clerk.[32]

The above incident occurred in the remote townland of Cloonagarnane, Craggaknock, on 6 December 1920, during a session of the Sinn Féin Appeals Court.[33] It was the increasing efficiency of the IRA signalling system that enabled Willie Shanahan and others to remove sensitive material from the court sitting.

After a mixed patrol of military and Black and Tans, under the charge of Lieutenant A.W. Tuffield, 2nd Battalion, Royal Scots, arrived on the scene, firing started. Thomas Curtin, a forty-three-year-old farmer from Craggaknock East, was shot in the head. The Christy Kelly referred to in the court case was a justice of the peace, who, it appears, informed the RIC about the planned court case, convened to address a dispute between Kelly and his neighbour.[34] The attending doctor's statement to the inquiry indicated that the bullet had caused a wound to Curtin 'about three to four and a half inches long. It had ripped up the skull, the coverings of the brain and the brain itself. The wound was about one inch wide.'³⁵ A second man, Michael Crotty from Kilrush, fell not far from Curtin after being wounded in the back in the same incident. Both Curtin and Crotty were taken to a nearby house, where Curtin was pronounced dead.³⁶ Many decades later, Jack Dunleavy from Kilrush would observe Crotty, who was married to the famous concertina player Elizabeth Crotty, standing at the door of his public house in the town of Kilrush. When he saw Crotty walk, he noticed an easily discernible discomfort, a legacy from the shooting at Craggaknock:

> He was a yank and he opened up there. They used to call him the 'Bully' Crotty … he was never off of that door [pointing at Crotty's pub in Kilrush]. He'd salute everyone passing up and down. He had bad kidneys. He was wounded. There was a republican court on. The IRA used to hold their courts that time and the military heard about it and they raided 'em. They all ran and the military opened fire and Crotty was wounded in the back. I don't think he ever recovered fully out of it.³⁷

John Kelly spoke at length about the local divisions that manifested during this time. Given the brutal behaviour of the crown forces, it was not surprising that a negative communal reaction was reserved for those who were seen to support the British:

> There was a Kelly family in Craggaknock and they allowed the Tans stable their horses there. You can imagine that wasn't a very popular move at the time! But there was a young fella with the Kellys and they used sell butter every week up near Annageeragh creamery. The Tans were there minding the Kellys. The young [Josie] Kelly, I'd say he was only twelve or fourteen. He came over with the workman and

two Tans came with 'em. At Looney's pub at Annageeragh, they used to sell the butter. But the local IRA got a couple of ladies to distract the Tans and the IRA seized the young lad and they brought him over along the river, the Annageeragh river and kept him, kidnapped him. They changed him around to different houses ... but he got so fond of the IRA he wished to be buried in Knocknahila, which wasn't Kellys' graveyard at all ... His wish was to be buried close to Seán Mullins, who was the local IRA leader and he *was* buried beside Seán Mullins![38] One time, it seems he was hidden down near Cooraclare and when they'd be out picking turnips or doing something in the garden, one of the old Kelly men had a very elaborate carriage and ah, when he'd be passing into Kilrush, the young fella [Josie] would lie inside in the drills. He was in no hurry home! [laughs][39]

'THE BOYS ARE OUT TONIGHT' – SAFE HOUSES

'Twas funny that time they'd be out at night time and the farmers or whoever would be around there, they'd be in bed. It could be eleven o'clock at night and the dogs would be barking if anybody came near farmhouses and they'd be in bed. The husband or wife would say, "Oh, the boys [IRA] are out tonight. The boys are out." They knew, you know. They'd get out of their bed and give 'em something to eat and let 'em stay for the night and go off in the morning.[40]

Lieutenant General A.E. Percival, the infamous British commander and intelligence officer of the Essex Regiment, was stationed in Kinsale, Co. Cork, during the War of Independence. There he became known and was deeply hated by republicans due to his zealous pursuit of IRA Volunteers and his alleged use of torture on prisoners. In this pursuit, Percival's intelligence methods were central to his effectiveness. As part of his strategy he kept a large-scale six-inch map in his office on which he marked every farm and detached house. He filled in the name and occupier and kept a note of the political sympathies of each farm or house.[41] While the British administration refused to accept that the trouble officially constituted a war, Percival was evidently aware that the army he was facing was deeply rooted in the country. He knew that for the IRA to be successful, the will and mind of a significant majority of the population had to be with them and that houses would open their doors in support.

The role of the safe house is critically important for social memory but remains untreated in any serious fashion by historians of the period. The term 'safe house' was used to describe the home of a sympathetic family, usually located in remote and isolated areas offering broad views of the surrounding countryside, where IRA Volunteers would be sheltered and fed during the War of Independence. The safe house was of immeasurable importance to the republican movement. When, in 1921, flying columns (mobile units of between fifty and one hundred men) were established, many IRA men lived 'on the run' and required considerable assistance in the countryside.

Undoubtedly, however, IRA Volunteers spent many cold hard nights exposed to the elements in remote mountainy areas of the countryside, particularly following a military action. For example, after IRA Volunteer Seán Breen was shot dead during an attack on the RIC at Kilmihil in April 1920, his mother, Catherine, wrote of the sufferings of his comrades, who were forced 'on the run' following the incident. Only days after her son was buried, she wrote to her sister in Australia, declaring: 'What a hard life his poor comrades have … there is a big price on their heads. They have to seek the lonely mountains and bogs for shelter.'[42]

While it is clear that not all doors were opened unreservedly, there is no doubt that significant numbers of homes were prepared to offer shelter to IRA Volunteers. The provision of a safe house carried significant risks for the family involved and meant very severe consequences for many. Francie Kenneally in Miltown Malbay explained the risk when I recorded him on the first of many occasions:

> You had to put up a notice in your house, do you see. How many people was in it? If they got an extra person, he might be one of the boys [IRA], do you see? 'Twas a terrible risk to let 'em into a safe house. They were known as safe houses. But 'twas a big risk. They could burn your house on the spot![43]

In 1936, while reflecting on the safe house, more than fourteen years after the war ended, one former IRA leader was clear about its value to the republican movement:

> We do not forget those other comrades of terrible but glorious days, the men and women and even children of Clare. They were our solid base. On them we depended for everything and without them we could not have existed. The skies of Clare, reddened night after night, bore eloquent testimony to the suffering and unselfish heroism of the noblest men and women of our race.[44]

The observation of reddened skies over Clare indicates the literal consequences for many IRA actions and their impact on the local population. Repeatedly, the houses and families of IRA Volunteers and those suspected of harbouring them were violently targeted by British military and police. The interim report of the American Commission on Conditions in Ireland, published in 1921, recorded 48,474 raids by British forces on private homes in

1920 alone.[45] Such occurrences are commonplace in memory and often are reduced to the most local and personal of experiences.

'She wouldn't eat a morsel of meat in case one of the Volunteers needed it'

For a period of six years the McCormack home in Tullaha, Kilfenora was used as a safe house by a variety of both local and national republicans. Teasie McCormack spoke frequently to her mother-in-law, Norah 'Lala' McCormack, about that experience:

> This house was a safe house where the Volunteers used to stay. Of course, they had good view of the countryside because we were up on the hill, so they could see the Black and Tans coming … Mickey's mother used to get out of her bed and give the bed to them. If they came in they'd see the bacon hanging up and they'd say, "The ceiling looks good tonight!" … My father-in-law Peter would have to keep a look out and maybe the Volunteers mightn't have slept for nights, so they'd let them sleep. People were badly off. I often remember Mickey's mother saying she'd love to eat a small bit of meat but she couldn't bear to think that the Volunteers might need it worse.

Peter and Norah McCormack were a young married couple with children when their house was used during the revolutionary period. Men 'on the run', republican courts martial and wounded Volunteers were all brought to the McCormacks', with the women of the house sometimes even charged with removing blood from clothes: 'They'd have to bring the bath of bloodied clothes down the back in case anyone would come and they'd be seen. That was a time now of no light, no running water, nothing.' For young children in the McCormack home, who witnessed unknown men arriving during the night, there was also danger:

The children would be warned never to say a word if they met anyone, where anybody was. "I don't know" is what they were told to say. I think they were nearly christened "I don't know" [laughs].

The house was not just a refuge for local rebels. National figures also were sheltered under the thatch of McCormacks' house in Tullaha, including one man remembered as 'thin and gaunt from being "on the run" but he was a proper gentleman':

> Ernie O'Malley stayed here and he was peeling potatoes at the open fire at the hob. He had potatoes. There were potatoes left over, as there usually would be in the countryside. He was peeling them and Mickey's mother was apologising that she wished she had something better and he said, "Ah if we always have half as good, we'd be very lucky." He trained Volunteers in the nearby field here. Just adjacent to us.[46]

In early 1919 O'Malley (later a well-known author) spent time training IRA Volunteers across Clare. During that time he also stayed for a period at Patrick Howard's house in Tarmon, outside Kilrush. Patrick's son, Michael, remembered O'Malley at his home as a child:

> He did because he was goin' around training the IRA and he was here for nearly a week … Yes. Down the haggard, they'd be there in the daytime. They'd be drillin' and firing shots and trainin'. I'd see them down there … The only thing I remember. I witnessed that. There's a lake down there and 'tis, I suppose, a mile away and there was a dog above on a yoke sitting. A dog! So one of the boys said, "I bet you wouldn't shoot him." So he didn't kill the dog but they looked after and the bullet was stuck in the timber under him … he had a great shot shur.[47]

Amongst the IRA officers with whom O'Malley worked closely in early 1919 was Ignatius O'Neill, one of the most significant figures in the Mid Clare Brigade. Having served with the Irish Guards in the First World War, O'Neill had military experience, which was put into effective use when he returned and joined the 4th Battalion of the brigade, of which he became commandant. O'Neill was injured on a number of occasions during the revolutionary period and on one occasion recovered at McCormacks' in Tullaha:

> Ignatius O'Neill was here ... he was wounded and they saw the Tans comin' over the road from here and they said the lorries were coming. He said, "I can't move. I'm too sick," he said. "Put a revolver in each of my hands," he said, "and I'll kill as many as I can" and he said to Pete, "You don't mind if the house goes up?" "I don't give a damn," says Pete, because they burned O'Loughlins', they burned Torpeys' and they burned Markhams'. This house was left.[48]

A similar story was told to me about Moloneys' safe house in Illaunbaun, where O'Neill was first moved following his wounding at the Rineen ambush on 22 September 1920. The Moloney home was one of the most reliable safe houses in the county. Ellie Moloney spoke on occasion to P.J. Donnellan about the period when her home was used as shelter by some of the most wanted IRA men in the country.[49] Micheál O'Connell also recalled a story he inherited in his native townland of Moy regarding Moloneys' safe house:

> Oh, you heard about every man that was wounded and where they were brought and the devil knows what. I knew where every man was carried. Ignatius O'Neill now got wounded in Rineen and he was

carried on the side of a creel [large wicker basket for carrying turf or other items] whatever you like to call it. 'Twas Moloneys' house there in the back, all the way from Freigh. That was a long way I'll tell you. Micklo Curtin! He was livin' there over the road, not so far. He got wounded in Rineen too. And they carried him over to Lynchs' in the mountain. And aul Hillery [Dr Michael Hillery] came out there by night, several nights and tended him. And Ignatius O'Neill was above there at Moloneys' on the top of the hill. And the army, the British Army I suppose you'd call 'em, they arrived over at the bridge there, White's Bridge, searching around for the boys [IRA]. And someone came in to Moloneys' and told O'Neill. And he only said to 'em, "Bring me in my gun and clear the house." That was the order! I'll never forget that. "Bring in my rifle to me now let ye go out of the house" ... Oh, he was goin' to die fightin'! ... The road was too bad. That's all that saved a few of 'em and no one went in.[50]

According to P.J. Donnellan, at another point when it was felt the arrival of the British forces was imminent, forty-two-year-old Ellie Moloney managed to carry O'Neill out of the house and got him to the safety of the mountains above their home.

At the Moloney home during that time was P.J.'s aunt, Mary Donnellan, who was a sixteen-year-old girl when the Rineen ambush occurred. While the wounded Ignatius O'Neill was being sheltered in Moloneys', it was probably Mary Donnellan who was dispatched to meet the local doctor, Michael Hillery (father of Ireland's sixth president, Patrick) at a place known as White's Bridge, to convey him to the Moloney home and the wounded IRA man.[51]

Like the Moloneys in Illaunbaun, there is no doubting that the McCormacks' home and the area of Tullaha in Kilfenora were important ground for the IRA. This was illustrated by their use by the Mid Clare Brigade before the Monreal ambush in December 1920. IRA leader Joe Barrett later wrote that:

> Long before the dawn of that winter day had broken over the hills, there had been a clatter of arms and equipment and an urgency of movement under the roofs of Tullaghea [*sic*] in the Kilfenora district in the homes of the O'Donoghues, the O'Loughlins and McCormacks.[52]

Ultimately, the Black and Tans did come, and they burned many houses in the townland of Tullaha. Fortunately, the McCormacks' home was spared and so they were in a position to continue to offer shelter to those in need – this time their neighbours. 'The O'Loughlins here. When they were burned. The whole family came up here and stayed in this house. Can you imagine? Mother and father and children.' Reflecting back on the period, Teasie McCormack remembers speaking to her mother-in-law, Norah, about it. Norah had been in America and had returned to Kilfenora in 1909. Soon after, her home became a safe house of the republican struggle, drawing significant hardships and privations on herself and her family. However, Teasie insisted that Norah always emphasised how positive the whole experience ultimately was:

> Well, she said, times were tough. Often she didn't go to bed [as] there wouldn't be a place for her to sleep. She wouldn't eat a morsel of meat in case one of the Volunteers needed it. And still she said it was the happiest six years of her life and nobody thought of themselves. They never dwelt on their own problems.[53]

I have visited multiple safe houses, now derelict, which testify to a careful selection by the IRA. In the mountains above Tulla, in Ballyoughtra, Knockjames, republican Liam Mellows stayed for an extended period with two comrades, Frank Hynes and Alfie Monaghan, in an old derelict cottage described as an 'old cowl' or 'bothán'. The building belonged to a man called Michael Moloney, described as 'a great old republican' by Tom McNamara from Crusheen.[54] In his home in Crusheen in 2012, Tom recalled the tradition he had heard surrounding the Mellows case:

> They had him down in the wood for a day or two and it was my mother's brother, Pattie Fogarty, who got him from there to Knockjames. When they were taking him away, they had him in a sidecar and the sidecar covered in fleeces of wool. The same as you were going to sell wool. And to the best of my memory, I think it was a sister or aunt of Tommy Daly that got nun's clothes for him.[55] They used to describe him as a small, light, fair-haired man. He was very safe there, they wouldn't tell. They got him to America then and he collected a lot of funds for 'em [republican movement] there.[56]

McNamara's respect for Mellows came through in the interview, lamenting that 'the poor man then when he came back he was executed', which related to Mellows' later execution by the Free State on 8 December 1922. In 2010 the late Pat O'Halloran from Kiltannon in Tulla claimed that prior to his move into the house in Knockjames, Mellows had spent a number of days hidden in the Twomeen caves in Tulla.[57] Con Hogan, whose father, Tom, was a captain in the East Clare IRA, also inherited the story of Mellows' stay in the area. He recalled how a fiddle played by Mellows at the hideout in Tulla was kept in his home for many decades.[58]

'My father would have to stay up outside all night'
Many safe houses had direct connections with the republican movement. When asked if locals supported the IRA in her native

Killimer in west Clare, Mae Crowe pointed to the obvious reality that, 'Ah, they would of course because shur they were all their sons. They were all their own sons and their brothers.'[59] For P.J. Clancy in Knockroe, the role of his own house in the period was a touchstone within his family memory:

> Oh, God they were very involved. 'Twas always a safe house, do you know. A safe house was that you could safely come and stay and to be watched as well you know and guarded ... 'twas raided regularly. They often see him [Micho Clancy] going out the back door but they could never get him. The cow cabins would be outside do you see and he put up those big flags against the cabin do you see and made the heap of dung agin it do you see and he'd run in there. 'Twas real safe now.[60]

Like P.J. Clancy in north Clare, in the east of the county Mick Ryan spoke about his father's time 'on the run' and the frequent disturbance of slumber: 'I know that Mrs [Nora] Ryan that was here [his wife Noreen's grandmother], she often got out of her bed and let in the Brennans and let 'em sleep there for the night.'[61] Seán Kiely from Claremount in east Clare recalled his father, Jack Kiely, telling him stories of keeping watch at Gortatreasa in the mountains over Broadford, while IRA men slept in the thatched home of his parents:

> My father would have to stay up outside all night while they'd [IRA] be there. Oh shur if he was caught, the Lord Save us! He'd have to do duty then. Out on the height ... The house was down in a kind of a hollow or a valley and he'd a clear view from the height. No one could come in on them you see. There was only one way in. They'd have the old-time lanterns that time and he'd see them [British forces]. He'd have to stay out on duty while they'd be there.[62]

The constant awareness that raids could come at any time was borne out in the Kiely family tradition. Seán's story illuminates what is now an entirely abandoned townland. His family home has now given way to afforestation and is no more to be seen. Back in 1921, light still shone in the townland of Gortatreasa:

> There was one night in particular he told me that they [Black and Tans] called to the house. There didn't happen to be anyone there that particular night only himself and his mother. That time the stick would be along the back of the door that was the way they had a lock on the door into the wall. The Tans knocked on the door and said, "Open the door!" The father said, "Wait till I put on my trousers." "You'll have lots of time to put on your trousers, open the door!" they roared in. They put their shoulder to the door anyway and drove it in![63]

Once, the sleeping Volunteers were roused suddenly from their beds and scattered to the surrounding countryside when they were informed by thirty-three-year-old Jack Kiely that lights were seen down the road from the house:

> The Tans had some smell of it got that they were up around the area. One night my father saw this light coming up at Guerins' [their neighbours], down the road. But 'twas Guerins taking pigs to Limerick! But he had told whoever was in the house to clear. I know that's what the father told me. This was a good bit before my time. He was telling me that when there would be any of the men that was 'on the run', he'd have to stay out that night and keep an eye out to make sure there wasn't an attack made.[64]

Michael Howard from Tarmon in west Clare was proud that his home was 'a great IRA house' regularly used by the republican movement. His early childhood experience was dominated by landmark memories of IRA Volunteers meeting in his house. At six years of age, Michael would watch intently as men gathered in his home 'before and after ambushes'. On occasion Michael would help clean the guns with the fighters. In 2011, at the age of ninety-six, a year before he passed away, Howard proudly remembered:

> 1915 I was born, do you know, and it was in 1920 then and 1921 I was a few years old. I used to be hearing they used to have speeches and all that and about ambushes. I'd be listening and I used to even clean the guns with them after ambushes. There was a Paddy Mescall, he was very good to work and he'd take up maybe a Mauser gun or maybe a Lee Enfield to see which one of them was heavier than the other. We'd a shop here and he'd go up to the scale and put the rifles on it to see their weight.

Howard claimed that Volunteers arrived at his home after an ambush in Burrane in Killimer. This ambush took place in August 1920, when the West Clare Brigade's 1st Battalion surprised a horse-drawn truckload of Black and Tans. The horses were commandeered, the truck burned and the Black and Tans subsequently released.[65] Following this successful and bloodless action, some of those involved made their way three miles north to Howards':

> They came up here for their dinner and my mother [Susan Howard] was sick at the time and Paddy Mescall never told her. Paddy was told to tell her to have the dinner ready for them … Lucky enough she had a pot of potatoes down for the pigs and they were good potatoes. So Paddy went up and he pulled a fletch of bacon off of the

rafter and they had their dinner ... Willie [Shanahan] was in that ambush.

As a child, Michael had seen what were young IRA Volunteers at his home, sometimes injured. One memory presents a wounded IRA man sitting calmly in Michael's home with a bloodied bandage on his head. Michael suggested this may have been Willie Shanahan. Nine decades later, however, he could not be sure, but the image remained clear:

> I'm not sure now to be honest with you was he here one night or was it his brother, Marty. I remember he had a bandage around his head where he got wounded. Whether 'twas either Marty or Willie Shanahan now I won't say. Ah 'twas this room here. There was no partition there and 'twas all a big kitchen and a big open hearth there.

For Michael, a declared supporter of the IRA, the men in his memory were giants:

> Oh they were good cool men and they'd face anything. They were. They used to keep the rifles outside in the hay. There would often be forty rifles there. Stuck in the reek of hay, they'd have them stuck in the far end. No one would know they were there.[66]

Shelter – from a Landlord's House to a Grave

On occasion the most unlikely of houses proved the safest. Jimmy Gleeson from Coore told how his father, Matt, and other republicans were once securely billeted in the upstairs of Colonel Frederick St Leger Tottenham's 'big house' in Mount Callan, while British soldiers were being entertained downstairs.[67] A friendly relationship between republicans and Tottenham was unlikely, however, if the testimony of Patrick 'Pako' Kerin was anything to go by. In his statement to the BMH, Kerin, a captain in the 4th Battalion of the Mid Clare IRA, outlined how on one occasion during an IRA raid for arms, Tottenham put up a fierce resistance, which had to be violently suppressed by the raiders.[68] However, for Jimmy Gleeson, it was revealing that he was 'one of the few landlords who was never burned out'.[69]

In the late 1930s one pupil in Bodyke National School in east Clare noted another form of rebel seclusion, close to the local Catholic church and where previous outlaws had also been sheltered:

> Our parish church was built in a place where the priest was hidden. It was very secure and in the time of the Black and Tans, 1920–21, the "boys on the run had a dugout". There is a big stretch of bog land near it and it was easy to escape.[70]

When the extravagant surrounds of an estate house or the familiar turf-warmed cottage were unavailable, the IRA in Clare often used natural features in the landscape for accommodation. Man-made dugouts were used in various places across the county, in secluded fields and usually in locations with a surrounding support base. For example, dugouts were discovered during research in Kilmihil, Labasheeda, Bodyke, Kilkishen, Kildysart, Cranny and Clonlara. John Corry, interviewed in Fermoy, Co. Cork, in 2012, recalled his father's description of a makeshift home during the war. Martin Corry from Clondrinagh in west Clare was a captain in the West Clare IRA Brigade and later a Free State officer:

> They stayed out in the bog. Covered it with sallies and rushes and put a type of a roof on it with four poles. Obviously the sides were

covered in. They slept there in my father's farm in Clondrinagh. He lived out there for a good while because the Tans knew about him. How they were fed was Uncle Steven, who was the youngest, used to bring the food out to them.[71]

Like John Corry's, Mick Ryan's father had been an active IRA man and like Martin Corry, Jackie 'Bishop' Ryan spent considerable periods sleeping out in the open countryside, when shelter was not available indoors. In Sallybank, in southeast Clare, an IRA dugout was located adjacent to a wooded area to achieve maximum concealment. In December 2013 Mick reflected on the perils of sleeping in such makeshift environments:

> Ah shur there was lots of stories. The Larkin side of it. They couldn't sleep at home either. They had a dugout made over in Leitrim bog, where they used to sleep for the night. They were in the dugout one night and this fella passed beside 'em and they knew him. But he escaped being shot because they interceded for him. He shouldn't have been there ... I suppose they kind of knew the ones; they used to keep away from them people [informers]. [72]

In a literal 'field interview' in 2011, ninety-two-year-old John O'Connell moved quickly ahead of me, as he knowingly made his way across his farm in Labasheeda. He had spoken many times about the IRA dugout that had been made on his land, to shelter IRA men 'on the run'. The dugout, which was located deep inland, was burrowed three metres into the field and hollowed out enough to create space to thatch the makeshift shelter. Timber reinforced the interior and a bed was brought as furniture. The dugout was excavated into the slant of a hill, which meant that from the top road (the only access point), it could not be seen in the landscape:

'Twas dug into the field. There was a good fall in the field. That was a big advantage ... and then 'twas near a ditch, 'twas near a fence. You couldn't see it from the road above, the Sliabh Liag road. No hope at all you'd see it from the road above. There was a hill above you in the fall of the ground down.[73]

Natural underground spaces were also used across the county. The combination of weather, time and landscape has produced many extensive cave systems in Clare. In the 100 square miles of the Burren's limestone landscape many caves exist, some of which were used for shelter by the IRA. The caves of Kilcorney as well as a souterrain system (underground chamber) in Ballyvaughan enfolded men 'on the run' within the embrace of their own natural heritage. Likewise, the Twomeen (Kiltannon) caves in Tulla, which span a 500-metre-long section of the Kiltannon River, from which the Hell River flows into the parish of Clooney/Quin, sheltered within them men who were wanted by the crown.[74]

Multiple interviewees attest that the War of Independence was a time of extreme danger, abnormality and volatility. The stories from that period of eighty-six-year-old Jimmy Gleeson, whose father, Matt, was a member of the 4th Battalion of the West Clare IRA, underlined this:

> Well, you see, they knew that this was an IRA house so they constantly raided here. Being a public house, they were constantly lookin' for them. But they [IRA] had their hideouts and, believe it or not the vaults in the graveyard were one of the areas where they slept. They used to stack up the coffins in the vaults ... The graveyards in Killernan. Most of the outside ring of the graveyard are vaults. And some of the vaults, the doors are on the inside of the grave but some of them are on the outside ... So what they used to do was they'd get into the

vault, stack the coffins on one side and sleep on the other side of the vault. They were nice little houses, like. Slated, perfectly dry and they maintained that they were more afraid of the living than the dead!⁷⁵

At the same time as Matt Gleeson and his comrades lay to rest among the faithful departed in Killernan, burial tombs in Kilsarcon graveyard in north Kerry were opened by tired and hunted Volunteers who equally 'had no fear of the dead'.⁷⁶ Jeremiah Moriarty from Kilsarcon, Currow, Co. Kerry was a member of the Currow Company, 1st Battalion, Kerry No. 2 Brigade. During the War of Independence, Moriarty spent much of his time with Humphrey Murphy, who was initially the leader of the Currow Company and was later appointed O/C of Kerry No. 2 Brigade.⁷⁷ Moriarty's son, the late Jerry Moriarty, explained in an interview in 2015 that his father, who is now buried in Kilsarcon graveyard, regularly slept in a tomb there with Murphy to evade the British forces throughout the War of Independence.

While it is evident that the IRA had a strong support network across Co. Clare, on other occasions doors were undoubtedly opened more in fear than support. For example, a west Clare interviewee recalled how his father, a member of the 2nd Battalion, Mid Clare IRA Brigade, had to produce a revolver to elicit food from a family while he was 'on the run' late one night in Ballynacally:

> He was right weak with the hunger. This old couple anyway. I forget the house, but 'tis demolished now anyway. They were in bed. 'Twas all homemade bread that time and they had a cake of bread made for the morning. 'Twas a grand moonlit night and he had the revolver. He knocked at the window. He said, "Give me out a can of milk and a pick of bread, I'm starving with the hunger." "Go away," they said.

> "We have nothing," they said. The father shoved up the aul window and he pointed in the revolver and he said, "Give it out to me quick." And ah, the old woman and man jumped out of the bed and into the kitchen and gave him out a half can of, or a jug of milk and a half a loaf of bread. He went away and he sat down outside on a moonlit night with a half can of milk and a cake of bread and he left the can up on the window and he shouted, "Thank you". Shur they were inside shakin'![78]

As well as the danger and disruption consistent with providing a safe house, John Minogue from Scariff, who was born in 1924, recalled how his father often spoke of the pressure that this sometimes put on families in a more everyday sense:

> He spoke a good share about them. He was tellin' me one time that he was here and he went over to where he had a cock of hay. He went over anyway to some field and he was pullin' out the hay and he pulled out three revolvers out of it. Them would be the old type. So he told some of the crowd around like that they were there. There was a man there, Ferrick Griffin they used to call him. Those that were 'on the run'. Ferrick killed two pigs and they ate the two pigs there, those that were 'on the run'. There was a dugout there overhead Daltons, Croaghrum. They used to stay there in the night-time.[79]

For a typical rural family, a large fattened pig could be a source of food for up to six months, yet, in the space of a day, Ferrick Griffin saw two of his prized pigs disappear into the mouths of hungry republicans.

For their support to the republican struggle, the Griffin family have the claim of being the only safe house to be memorialised in Clare and possibly in Ireland. In St Cronin's graveyard in

Tuamgraney, the headstone of Michael Griffin from Derrymore in Scariff records its erection 'by his friends for harbouring IRA men "on the run" during the Black and Tan period'.[80]

Gelignite for Turf: Behind the Doors of a Safe House

P.J. Magner from Ross in Kilbaha was steeped in lore and tradition. During a long series of interviews I undertook with him, he contributed much to the historical record. At his home near the famed Bridges of Ross, he spent his later years regaling all who would listen with stories of the past. When no one was there to ask a question, he revealed to me that the time was spent '*ag smaoineamh* (thinking) all day'. His home was a safe house during the War of Independence:

> There was two Sinn Féiners captured in my house by the Black and Tans. Two Sinn Féiners. One of 'em was, ah, they were well hidden. When the knock came to the door or the window my father delayed a long time. They had their routine. And they'd be gone away but for one of the Sinn Féiners had his jacket left on the chair. They [Black and Tans] were going away and they spotted the jacket and they had to search in earnest then! They found 'em … one of 'em was [Patrick] Mescall from Cooraclare direction and the other one was McGrath, Dinny McGrath from Dromelihy … [laughs] They were under my grandmother in the bed! They had gone in underneath, down in the bottom of the bed. They'd never find 'em only for the jacket. The bloody bugger if he brought the jacket with him they wouldn't be captured at all![81]

P.J. spoke about how close his family home came to being burned down and also how his father, forty-one-year-old farmer Patrick Magner, was beaten by the Black and Tans:

But there was a sergeant of the police with them, they'd burn it the same night. They were goin' to throw petrol on it. 'Twas a sow thatched house. There was a sergeant of police and he was goin' out especially with the Tans to calm 'em down ... he prevented them from burning it ... the Tans struck my father. They fisted him and marked his face and that.

Dinny McGrath, who was arrested at Magners', later spoke to Doonbeg poet Pádraig Haugh about his feelings towards the Black and Tans. McGrath was an attendee at the emotionally charged funeral of Willie Shanahan and Michael McNamara in Doonbeg in December 1920, after the men had been murdered by crown forces, as Haugh described:

'Twas Christmas eve then that Willie Shanahan and Mac were buried in Doonbeg and yer man came to the funeral and he told me that he had a grenade in his hand and if the Tans appeared they were goin' to get it![82]

With IRA Volunteers 'on the run', came weapons. The men who sought shelter throughout the countryside were men engaged in a violent war against the British forces. Often a safe house would be used as a location to either prepare for an ambush or deal with the aftermath of an IRA action. Sometimes, the steady glow of an open-hearth fire would illuminate the careful assembly of bomb materials. Over a number of years I recorded the memories of Fr Martin Bugler, a native of Scariff, who has spent over six decades as a Roman Catholic priest in New Zealand. In 2014 he wrote to elaborate on some of the oral tradition he had received before he emigrated in the 1950s, and one story in particular about the night gelignite became a solid fuel:

> On my father's side, grandmother – a widow of about nine years – with three sons and two daughters, living in Moynoe ... The oldest son, Andrew, was significantly involved in the fight for freedom ... Some of 'the boys' [IRA] were in the kitchen drying a stick of gelignite in front of the fire. Grandma, mistaking it for a sod of turf moved it into the fire and in due time came quite an explosion! Differing degrees of damage, depending on who was telling the story and who was listening![83]

For many safe or 'known' houses, the sudden sound of approaching engines or a loud bang on the door signalled a raid by Black and Tans. In most cases the prudent action was to stand back and hope that the house would not be burned to the ground. However, on occasion interventions were required and in many cases this was left to the women, those left behind. Ninety-six-year-old Johnny Doyle from Broadford recalled one such incident involving his then thirty-eight-year-old mother, Bridgid. He explains first how it was his father's involvement that drew attention to them:

> My father was joined with the IRA. Thade McGrath and Tom McGrath was one of the IRA leaders as well. My father was deep enough mixed up with 'em. That's why they put him in jail. He used to carry two revolvers a weight of his time. There was an awful lot of guns in this house one time ... There was a big cupboard there and there was a lot of stuff thrown in it. There was a big case for gunpowder ... My father and my mother used to load cartridges and load bullets and that's what they wanted the gunpowder for. They [crown forces] dumped it down on the ground and they didn't know what was in it. But Katy and Maggie, the two girls were in bed this morning and a soldier made a sweep to go up the stairs and my mother caught him by the shoulder and she said, "You're not to go up there.

There are two girls up there in bed and you are not going up there until they come down." And the officer was there and he ordered the soldier to stand back. But my mother was a tough little woman![84]

'Listening around the old turf fire' – A safe townland

Over the mountains from Broadford, almost the entire townland of Caherhurley in Bodyke provided safe houses to the republican movement. The solidarity shown in the past was a source of pride for Jimmy Walsh, whose father, Michael, better known as Sonny, was his reference point for local history. The childhood of Sonny Walsh, who later became a well-known poet and storyteller, was dominated by the fight for independence. According to Jimmy, a former Bodyke and Clare hurler, the firm presence of the Black and Tans in local memory was reinforced by ever-circulating stories in his youth:

> Since I was able to walk I was actually listening around the old turf fire under the thatch roof about what the British did to us and the Black and Tans. They were always described as the corner boys of London and the outcasts of prisons and what have you. I heard that since I was able to walk, and it never left our mind how us Irish people were treated by the British in those days. It was frightening … When you think of the Tans driving through a little townland like Caherhurley and in reprisal for knowing that maybe there was IRA activity in the place, they shot the geese and goslings swimming in the pond. It showed the ruthlessness that those Black and Tans were capable of.[85]

Falling within the 4th Battalion area of the East Clare IRA Brigade, the topography of Caherhurley offered a relatively safe haven for republicans 'on the run'. The townland is situated at the foot of the Sliabh Bearnagh mountains, overlooking the villages of Bodyke and Tuamgraney, as well as Scariff to the north. Over the mountain pass to the southwest lay Kilbane, where an active IRA network existed. To the southeast of the townland, IRA Volunteers were able to move towards Killaloe and Limerick. A curious Jimmy Walsh listened carefully to how his elders spoke about the period, affirming 'they would speak quietly but very passionately about what happened around here'.

In the early 1920s over five miles of the landscape could be seen towards the west from the gable of Walsh's home, in a time before the encroachment of forestry. On one occasion, while casting his gaze across the open landscape, Sonny Walsh noticed the irregular movement of a convoy of vehicles, not common in the locality, but known. The Black and Tans were turning into the townland of Caherhurley at a place known locally as 'Corney's Cross'. Pivoting quickly, Sonny ran 'in his bare feet and short pants' towards the O'Brien homestead, where he informed sleeping IRA Volunteers of the impending arrival of British forces.[86] On that occasion, thanks to Sonny Walsh, the young IRA Volunteers were able to make their escape. The O'Brien house, as well as other safe houses in the townland, all faced north, with the Sliabh Bearnagh mountain range at their back. As the crown forces neared, the republicans retreated from the back of the house and moved southwards into a mountain landscape where no vehicle could travel. The young IRA men made their way over the crest of a hill called Knocknellican and moved quickly across an area of bog named 'The Lane', before disappearing into the embrace of their own landscape, just as the Black and Tans broke in the door of O'Brien's.

On another occasion, when a combined force of Auxiliaries, Black and Tans and RIC entered Caherhurley, they passed through a place called Ballydonaghane, where a young IRA Volunteer called Tommy Bolton was working with his uncle. He was taken and roughly thrown into the back of a military lorry, before the convoy moved on towards the home of Sonny Walsh, where once again IRA Volunteers were resting. Recorded in 1989, Bolton vividly remembered:

> They took us off the road and they took us in around into Caherhurley. Joe Noonan of Tuamgraney. He was staying inside in the old house and Sonny Walsh's. Jimmy Walsh is now in the old thatched house. There was more of the boys up the hill. They took Joe. Joe used to often trace it with me. He was a great friend of the Walshes. He used to stay there. But he, he only came out to the kitchen and he only had one leggin' on. He had only one red leggin' on. We used to wear red leggings that time, the Volunteers. When he saw your man at the door, he put his hand in his hip pocket. He hadn't it [revolver]. 'Twas left inside in the table at the bed. He told me if I had it, he said, he was down at the door if all Caherhurley went up.[87]

With the British forces occupied with Joe Noonan, the revolver left behind was quietly lifted by young Sonny Walsh, who managed to make his way out the back of the house and hide the weapon under a whitethorn bush, shown many years later to his son, Jimmy. When, as a young man, Jimmy Walsh spoke to an older Joe Noonan, the story of the latter's arrest was a repeated topic of conversation. In April 2018 Jimmy recalled those conversations:

> Joe told me that story often. I remember well he looked into my eyes and spoke about the day that an Auxie arrested him at my grandfather's house. The Auxiliaries had separated and Joe told me that when he was arrested by one, another man was at Timmy Malone's

house where he was hoping to capture Malone, who was in the IRA as well. Both of the Auxies had hand grenades on them. At one point, while Joe was walking beside the Auxie, he asked could he tie the lace on his boot. He told me this straight, that when he was bending down tying his lace over the road from the house, he thought to attack this Auxiliary, but then my old grandmother [Margaret Walsh] came to his mind. She had been thirteen years bedridden and he knew that if he attacked him, the house would be burned around her.[88]

A previous story (see pp. 80–1) had suggested that Joe Noonan was released by the crown forces after his singing endeared him to his captors. However, Jimmy revealed that Noonan's liberation was not solely based on his vocal ability. Noonan informed Jimmy that while in conversation with his arresting Auxiliary, it was established that the officer knew Joe's brother, John, a teacher in Donegal. This personal connection was later given as the reason the officer insisted to Joe that if his colleagues at any stage attempted to throw him from the lorry, 'to hold on to the calf of my leg and don't let go because if you do, they'll claim you were trying to escape and shoot you dead'.[89]

The activity of the crown forces in Caherhurley at this point would seem to have been part of a broader sweep across an area that had frustrated them for months. A letter I received from Australia by a native of the neighbouring townland of Corragnoe picked up the story:

> The Tans went from Caherhurley to Corragnoe where they took Johnny Ryan and his brother Patsy. They [Ryans] always kept their money in a sock. So Patsy said to one of the Tans, "I have just got a call from nature, is it all right with you?" So he allowed him and as he was passing the cow house door, he fired the sock with the money

into the cow house. Now they proceeded to walk from Corragnoe down across the field and hills down to Ballymalone and down apast Hill's house in Ballymalone. As they were walking along Patsy moved slowly and quietly beside Johnny. He said, "Johnny, if I'm not coming back, the sock is in the cow house." They proceeded on to Tuamgraney and they stood 'em with their backs to St Cronan's church in Tuamgraney, where their interrogation began.[90]

The correspondent, Joe Fitzgerald, lived his young life in Corragnoe before emigrating with his entire family to Australia. His mother's family home had formed part of that day's events. During the War of Independence, the home was owned by his uncle, Michael Ryan:

Mike Ryan had got word that the Tans were arriving, so he locked the door and took his shotgun with him to where he hid in a valley where he hid the shotgun which he covered over in moss. That shotgun remained there for an awful lot of years ... What's more interesting is that the Tans bayoneted the door of Mike Ryan's house which he had locked and left, and those marks remained on the door of Fitzgerald's house when my father, Martin, inherited it from Mike Ryan right into the 1940s.[91]

Martin Fitzgerald first noticed the marks on the door of the old house when he inherited his uncle's home in the 1940s. In July 2018 I met with his son, the above-mentioned Joe, when he returned from Australia to spend a number of months in his native home. Joe told me of how his father had replaced the door in the 1940s, but had taken one lath from the original (with bayonet marks) and integrated it into the new entrance. He encouraged his son: 'don't let anyone destroy that'. The marks were a memory trigger for a time when Martin Fitzgerald's people endured tremendous oppression, and he was insistent that they be retained as a reminder. The evidence of the stabbing blades also took Martin back to his own childhood, when he witnessed the Black and Tans in action in his townland of Currakyle:

> I often remember my father [Martin Fitzgerald] recalling the day he was a young boy in the home place above in Currakyle, looking out the rear window of the house. He saw his father [Patrick] on the road below the house, coming along with a load of hay to go foddering the cattle. He saw this group of British forces coming on horseback. They were going over to Turkenna Lodge where they used to be based.[92] They put my grandfather up against the bank and started to prod the hay with bayonets to see if he was carrying anything for the IRA. They let him go all right. They didn't hurt him but it was something that my father never forgot.[93]

Over time, while Joe was living in Australia, the door's historic lath was inadvertently destroyed when the doorway was once again replaced. The homestead still stands, however, and in the townland of Corragnoe and surrounding area, the memory endures.

Micheál Brennan, the O/C of the East Clare IRA Brigade, spent at least three weeks in the area in October 1920, after he had been injured in an action in O'Brien's Bridge. During that period he was moved between at least five houses, until his wound had healed sufficiently to enable him to return to active service. There was some frustration afterwards in the area when it was felt that Brennan had failed to sufficiently acknowledge the support he received there. He did reverently refer to such supporters as the movement's 'solid base' on whom the IRA 'depended for everything and without them could not have existed'.[94] However,

Tommy Bolton, who operated under Brennan as a scout, angrily recalled the IRA leader in a 1989 recording:

> Ah he'd be comin' and goin'. He was the head officer in charge of the whole thing. I delivered him some dispatches in my time. And do you know. He's gone and he was no good! He was no good. He never thought a bit about the people that minded him and slept out all night minding him. He never came back to see 'em. He never came back. He stopped a lot of time above with my son-in-law's father and the present Mrs Brady. And I remember her father to tell me, he used to card play with him and that he got up a basket of apples from where Bill Bleach is now. Tom Scanlon that time. You know that was a backward place. He was inside there too. I'll never forget Dinny Moloney: 'He ate 'em like a sow and he never gave the girl an apple and she got out of her bed and gave him her bed.' No I won't deny it of 'em at all. He never came back to see us. There was only the one man as far as I remember and he was [P.J.] Rutledge.[95] And he said, "Only for the country lad and the private Volunteer, we'd make no hand of that job."[96]

4

'BORN WILD'

STORIES OF THE EXTRAORDINARY

FREEDOM FIGHTERS

> They were a tough race of people. I have done a fair bit of travelling in my time and I would say they were a unique race of people. They were tough. They could go for a long time ... without food and stuff and they didn't expect too much. I would say one thing for 'em ... I would like to have 'em behind me if I was in a tight corner! They weren't afraid of anything and ah, on top of that too they probably, they weren't maybe the nicest people in the world to their wives and families. They were kind of born wild, if you like. But they were hard men. Real hard men! ... they didn't go back from anybody.[1]

The son of one West Clare IRA Volunteer reflected for a moment, before offering the above characterisation of his father, Matt Gleeson, and his comrades. Jimmy Gleeson had grown up in Coore, hearing tales of IRA actions against British oppressors. At the age of eighty-five and having served in the American military himself, he had developed a more rounded picture of the men he heard about while growing up in west Clare. He knew that as with any association of mortal men, dishonesty and malice could penetrate. Nevertheless, the central characteristics that he heard praised as a child remained firmly impressed on his mind when he was asked to offer a reflection on the men who fought against the Black and Tans.

It is certain that memory is selective and sometimes chooses where to emphasise and where to understate. Nonetheless, there is no doubting the very sincere admiration held by many for the IRA Volunteers who took up arms during the War of Independence. When asked about local incidents in his native area of Caher, Flagmount and Kilanena, Ned Keane was keen to illuminate the heroic actions of two of the most famous fighters from his area:

> They were goin' up Curra one day. Up Currakyle and there did about a hundred riding horses came in from Woodford. They [British forces] were moving from Woodford to Feakle. And they fired on them but there did a couple of horses go back to Woodford with no riders and there was only the two of 'em [IRA] in it! They [British] made out that ah, they said that they met a whole regiment of Irish lads and they only met two![2]

The ambush referred to by Ned Keane occurred in June 1921 in Currakyle, near Flagmount in east Clare and 'they' were Seán Moroney and Pat Houlihan, two senior IRA officers in the East Clare Brigade. During an IRA action in the Sliabh Aughty mountains the men were confronted by a large force of British military. Houlihan and Moroney, who were armed with service rifles, ordered the others in the small group to run. Moroney records that he and Houlihan then lay down and engaged the force of mounted soldiers. Firing continued for over thirty minutes until the two IRA men were able to slip away into a ravine. A plane circled the area later, as Moroney and Houlihan hid within the landscape. Moroney detailed that the 'military lost three killed, some wounded, and several horses killed and some wounded. Our losses were two bicycles.' They established later that the force was 300 strong and was part of a larger contingent who were making a determined and coordinated effort to capture the East Clare IRA's ASU.[3]

In east Clare, amongst the older generation, the name Pat Houlihan was for decades synonymous with the time of the Black and Tans. Houlihan was born into a Fenian family at Doorus, Caher, close to Lough Graney. He was given charge of the East Clare IRA's 6th Battalion with the rank of commandant and fought in several actions. He was regarded as a 'hard gunman'. Although in 1927 he became a Fianna Fáil TD, he was forever identified with his time fighting against the crown forces. Ned Keane's father, James, was a friend and cousin of Houlihan, and spoke to his son about a day when Houlihan proved his skill with a gun:

> When Pat was goin' to Ballyturin he crossed into a field of ours to talk to my father and my father made out he [Pat] wouldn't have a great shot. But he went back and he went around the road and he was about three or four hundred yards from him and he said, "You can put up [a] straw hat on a fork and see whether I have a shot or not." And he did and he cut the hat to bits off the top of the fork! A rifle bullet.[4]

In 2013 Bernie Burchell wrote from Cheshire in England to contribute her family tradition to the research. Bernie had grown up hearing stories about the involvement of her uncles from Clare, Jim and Tom 'Brody' Lillis, in the 'trouble times':

> Uncle Tom (Brody Lillis) spent the trouble times in Dublin. My mother told us they were not sure where he was and hoping he was safe. He said, "One has to practice walking like a tramp, wear old

boots and an old sack on my back." As he also had a few old coats in the sack, and shoes, no one expected him to have guns … One time when my grandmother was ill, Uncle Jim [Lillis] came to visit her dressed as a woman, complete with a veiled hat which was worn by ladies at the time. He was 'dressed' by McInerneys who lived outside Kilrush and taken to Tarmon in a pony and trap. They were stopped on the way by the Tans who heard Jim Lillis was in the area. Mr McInerney said it was his aunt who was visiting.[5]

'They were goin' to suffer, remember'

Over the following decades, stories of bravery, particularly of fallen Volunteers, were nurtured and reinforced by commemorative activity, which ebbed and flowed with the broader patterns of political life. In all parts of Clare, certain stories and memories seem to tower over others.

In the east of the county, the admiration in local social memory for the Scariff Martyrs, the four young men murdered by crown forces on the Bridge of Killaloe in November 1920, is striking. Tom Lynch, born in 1929, recalled in relation to the four men that, 'They'd talk with reverence and they'd nearly pray for them.'[6] According to Michael O'Gorman, in Scariff, the town where three of the men worked and lived, 'There was great reverence, like, if they could have canonised them they'd have done it.'[7]

In west Clare the story of 'Mac and Shanahan', two west Clare IRA Volunteers similarly murdered by British forces in December 1920, was a comparable touchstone for the period. Cooraclare native John Queally affirmed that the story of Michael McNamara and William Shanahan was 'always in the human consciousness of the people of the locality'.[8] For Dympna Bonfield from Kilbaha in west Clare, who was born in the late 1930s, the involvement of her mother, as well as her aunts and uncles in the republican movement, meant that the War of Independence and stories of the Black and Tans, as well as 'Mac and Shanahan', were part of the 'cultural background' to her upbringing:

> I remember my mother talking about that. You can't remember much of the detail of it but that it was a whole kind of a cultural background to it all. Old IRA and the Black and Tans. An uncle of mine then had been in prison and he was supposed to have been taken in the lorry with Mac and Shanahan who were both shot and he was in the lorry with them and he was beaten with rifle butts and he spent a lot of time in prison.[9]

Willie Shanahan and Michael McNamara were both actively involved in the IRA in west Clare and had participated in numerous actions. They were arrested in a remote house near Doonbeg on 17 December 1920. The men were severely beaten and accused of being involved in the death of a British magistrate, Captain Alan Lendrum, the previous September. Although Shanahan is reported to have driven Lendrum's car to be disposed of, he was not involved in the incident. The men were taken first to Kilrush Barracks, where they were tortured and beaten. While being transferred to Ennis on 22 December, McNamara was taken from the lorry and murdered. It has been strongly suggested that he was dragged for some distance, which left his body mangled.[10]

Shanahan, who watched his friend being so brutally murdered, was then taken to Ennis where he was tortured for at least six hours, before being murdered and later thrown in the grounds of the County Infirmary with his hands and feet bound, part of his head blown off by an explosive bullet and his body severely mutilated. It is not surprising that such a harrowing story endured in local memory, as did respect for the two men:

> Oh there would be great respect for the Shanahan crowd and Mac there was. There was in Doonbeg, there was great respect ... Everyone felt it bad now for Mac and Shanahan because they were both innocent men. Maybe they took part in ambushes but they injured nobody at the same time or done nothing wrong. But regardless of who the Tans captured that time, they were goin' to suffer, remember. They were going to show no mercy to anybody. They told Mac and Shanahan they'd be let go if they told names of who was there and all. They wouldn't be let go! Don't you know what you were goin' to get from the Tans when they captured 'em, do you see? But they gave no names, they stood on their feet and told nothing and ... gave their lives and that was all.[11]

Similar to the passage just quoted from Willie Whelan above, Joe 'Jack' Sexton in Mullagh recorded:

> Ah they were, they were. There was two fine boys back near Doonbeg. They were wanted ... They were. They never slept at home. Different houses every night. This night, they parted with their friend, they thought and they went to this house and weren't they spied on. They were tied to a lorry and pulled to Ennis.[12]

In the War of Independence, the ordinary lived alongside the extraordinary. During my research, I was given access to a private diary kept by Seán Griffin from Ballyea, a member of the 2nd Battalion, Mid Clare IRA Brigade. The diary documents Griffin's experiences throughout the War of Independence and his later incarceration during the Civil War, in which he took the anti-Treaty side. On Tuesday 21 May 1920 Griffin recorded that he and his comrades 'Engaged [in an] ambush on British Marines at Ballynacally.'[13] The following day, on Wednesday 22 May, he wrote in his diary that he 'Got Friesian cow in calf' and 'bought four bags of nuts for wainlins [*sic*]'.[14] Griffin's entries illustrate powerfully that many of the IRA Volunteers who engaged in ambushes against trained and professional soldiers were themselves ordinary farmers and workers. They had to try to continue to live ordinary lives and perform their expected duties in the home, farm or workplace in the midst of confronting an empire. Griffin's record is reminiscent of what Corkery described in west Cork: 'the few against the many, the inexpert against the professional, the clumsy makeshift against the perfected weapon'.[15]

'THE SPIRITS OF THE BLACK AND TANS':
THE SUPERNATURAL

> A fairy car used go on the old green road. It is said that those people in the fairy cars were the spirits of the Black and Tans who did bad deeds to the Irish in the year 1921. Long ago the people believed.[16]

Co. Clare has long been recognised for its deep folklore and traditional heritage. It is unsurprising therefore that stories of the War of Independence intersect with aspects of folk belief, including the supernatural. In 1928 the *Irish Independent* reported that 'women and children and most of the men in part of the district of Mullagh in west Clare would not leave their homes after dark because of stories of the appearance of a ghost'. The paper recorded that the ghost was seen moving about between 9 p.m. and midnight. It was said 'to be a man of military appearance, wearing a trench coat and [he] carries what appears to be a rifle'. It was also reported that one local man attempted to converse with the ghost, only to receive a military salute before the ghostly visitor disappeared.[17] A decade later, Pat Garrahy, a seventy-two-year-old native of Moy in north Clare, who was interviewed as part of the Schools' Folklore Scheme in the late 1930s, testified that, along with a number of others, he too had seen the figure of a soldier in uniform:

> During the period of the late Anglo-Irish struggle [War of Independence] a soldier who was stationed at Ennistymon was shot dead in an ambush near the gate of M. Ross Roses's [Major Ross Rose] house on the hill outside Lahinch. Several people, including the above [Garrahy], have seen the figure of a soldier in uniform standing as it were on sentry at the gate since that ambush. Sometimes it is seen marching up and down the avenue leading to that house entrance.[18]

Interviews in the east of the county attest to a belief that a Black and Tan ghost was also present in Glenwood, where an ambush occurred in January 1921. One interviewee, who grew up in the area, spoke in 2014 about the tradition and how a local member of An Garda Síochána charged that on one occasion he had been attacked by the spirit:

> Oh, the ghost! [laughs] There was a Guard called Bill Kearney there one time. He was a small man from west Cork. Very clever but a devil to summons you! The local lads had him told all about the Tans of course and Glenwood and all that. He was comin' one night from Sixmilebridge. I don't know in the hell what he was doing there but he was coming cycling past Glenwood and he arrived in an awful panic saying that there were hands clawing at his legs as he was passing the ambush site in Glenwood during the night. Oh, he was frightened out of his wits! I don't know if anyone paid any heed to him but he wasn't a drinking man at all, so he definitely believed it himself. That was known around the area.[19]

When, after his traumatic episode at Glenwood, the shaken Garda Kearney reported to the police barracks in Broadford the following day, he may not have been aware that another spirit was said to have lingered in that building also! A tradition has been documented that the ghost of Willie O'Brien, shot by a Free State soldier during a dispute at the former RIC barracks in the village, was periodically seen, and that his step would be heard on the stairs in the barracks. The late Seán Crowe outlined the tradition in an interview in 2011:

> He [O'Brien] was a very strong man and strong-minded. He was struggling with an officer in the Free State army and he got shot coming down the stairs of the barracks [in Broadford]. It is said that his ghost is in the old barrack the whole time. I heard a story that during the [Second World] war years the LDF [Local Defence Force] were staying in the barrack overnight. They'd be armed and they'd stay there overnight in their turn. The Guards [An Garda Síochána] would be gone to bed. The Guards would be there also but there would be no stir but when they'd lie down to sleep this step would come in the stairs. But never when they were up! 'Twas general knowledge that it was the ghost of O'Brien. 'Twas generally accepted that it was true.[20]

In west Clare, a number of interviewees relayed the strong belief that the lights of Captain Alan Lendrum's motor car could be seen on the roads of west Clare in the decades after his killing by the IRA on 22 September 1920.[21] Lendrum was an ex-British Army officer from Tyrone, who had recently been appointed acting resident magistrate at Kilkee when he was confronted by members of the IRA at Caherfeenick. The IRA claimed that the intention was to take papers from Lendrum but, in the confusion of the incident, the magistrate was shot dead.[22] The mother of Senan Fitzmartin from Doonbeg told of seeing the light of Lendrum's motor car rising every night at the Caherfeenick gates and going across the land.[23] Other interviewees testified that children who refused to go to bed at night would be ushered into their rooms with the warning that 'Lendrum's lights were coming'.[24] According to Joe 'Jack' Sexton in Mullagh, 'the auld people used to say that so many times. 'Twould pass, the noise of the car.'[25] For ninety-three-year-old Willie Whelan, the story was firmly believed in his native Doonbeg, but only, he insisted, amongst 'an older crowd':

> Ah it used be back in our country. Ah it used be back around the sandhills where he was buried. We used be told it anyway. Ah we used be told that. Anyone of my age group now didn't see it. They were an older crowd![26]

John Kelly grew up in Cree and from an early age was introduced to the story of Captain Lendrum. However, as a much older man in 2012, he spoke about other elderly people who were aware of the ghostly presence:

> That's right, I was talking to an old lady recently. She's in her nineties now and she said, when they were young, the old people, they'd look to the west and they'd see the lights in Kilkee and they'd say "Come on let ye, quick into bed, there's Lendrum's lights." The lady said they used to be frightened and they believed it was Lendrum's car, which it wasn't at all at all. It was the lights in Kilkee! But she always remembered, "Come on, into bed, there's Lendrum's car!"[27]

The American anthropologist Conrad Arensberg noted that it

was only after his colleague Solon T. Kimball had an apparent experience with the supernatural that the arms of the Clare community opened to him in a welcoming embrace. This incident occurred when Kimball – who was conducting research there in the early 1930s – visited a local public house in Ennis and commented to those inside that he 'saw a shadow moving at the door'.[28] It was believed locally that the spirit of a member of the Black and Tans shot near the pub lingered there.[29] The seeming appearance of the ghost to Kimball was enough to ingratiate him with the locals. According to Arensberg, after this glimpse of the supernatural Kimball was 'in'.[30] The spirit was believed to have been that of a Sergeant Rue of the Royal Scots, who was killed in the Market Square in Ennis on 16 April 1921 when a bomb was thrown into Shaughnessy's public house, where crown forces regularly were entertained by the proprietor, Kate Shaughnessy.[31]

'OH, I SEE, THE HOLY FAMILY, PLEASE PASS ON': HUMOUR IN MEMORY

Humour is a critical element of the human condition. Writing in Brixton prison in England in 1920, Sinn Féin Lord Mayor of Cork Terence MacSwiney affirmed that 'a revolution will surely fail when its leaders have no sense of humour'.[32] It is not surprising, therefore, that many amusing stories have been passed on relating to the revolutionary period. It is, however, extraordinary that within such turmoil and violence, humour and entertainment were able to break through on occasion.

The recorded histories show that men engaged in the most serious levels of violence were capable of comedy. Having attacked the British forces stationed in Kilrush in April 1921, almost sixty members of the East Clare IRA, who had travelled across the county for the action, began their slow journey home. The leader of the flying column, Micheál Brennan, kept a military and detached command of his unit, aware that danger was everywhere as they made their way on foot towards the village of Cree. There they would billet in local republican safe houses. Despite the solemnity and discipline which characterised the march, two of Brennan's more senior men decided to introduce some humour to the situation:

> On the way, two column men (Joe Clancy and Martin McNamara) cantered up to me riding donkeys they had collected on the road and inquired if a mounted advance guard was all right with me. It was; so they took post in advance to the cheers of their very tired and probably envious comrades.[33]

A donkey was also at the centre of a tale told in an interview conducted for RTÉ radio and first broadcast in November 1985, with Ennistymon native Paddy O'Dwyer. In one story relayed to the presenter, Kevin O'Connor, O'Dwyer explained that at the time of the War of Independence he had 'a wild ass' that was very difficult to control. O'Dwyer skilfully described how on one occasion, when passing the Black and Tans, he was told to halt but while he was willing to comply, his donkey refused to heed the command. Having finally come to a stop, Paddy was taken back to the barracks in Ennistymon by the crown forces. While in captivity, Paddy witnessed the 'Tans getting up on the ass's back' whereupon the hoofed animal once again stubbornly refused to cooperate. Paddy proudly related how the ass declined to move for the British forces, whom he noted were playing 'God Save the King' on a mouth organ. According to Paddy, John Daly, a local solicitor, ventured out from his office close by to establish the reason for the commotion. Having assessed the situation, and apparently recognising the well-known animal, Daly informed the assembled crown forces that, 'Ye might as well be idle boys. The Devil of one of ye will put one leg out before the other' (will not make the donkey move). After the Black and Tans reputedly informed Daly that they had a rather brutal method of 'getting the bastard going', the solicitor exclaimed: 'Don't ye know very well that that fella is a Sinn Féiner? He won't go! Ye'll have to stop playing that "God Save the King". Let ye rattle up "The Soldier's Song" and he'll go!'[34]

'Here was the East Clare Brigade!'

The IRA's East Clare Brigade engaged in many actions against the British forces during the Irish War of Independence. Glenwood, Cratloe and Meelick count among significant ambushes executed by the brigade. Deep into the War of Independence the crown forces in the area were intimately aware of the danger it posed. As a precaution, as the war developed, the British travelled in larger groups to defend against attack by republicans. Only on occasion did they travel in smaller numbers. On one such occasion, when three Black and Tans stopped at a shop in east Clare, the sound of the local brigade being called to assemble was sufficient to warrant immediate retreat. Teresa Flynn, who was born in December 1930, remembered Joe Minogue from the east Clare village of Mountshannon humorously recalling the day the East Clare Brigade was called upon, despite the fact that the man calling was the only member of that brigade present! Teresa described the location of the incident as told by Joe:

> The same gate, 'tis still there, a big double iron gate and I pass and I pray for 'em all, the darlings. There was a very staunch IRA man in that yard when the Tans pulled up and there was a guy who had gone

in for a packet of Woodbines and there was only the two of them [Tans] in the yard. Charlie Turner called on the East Clare Brigade to assemble [by shouting for them to come together] and the lad that had gone for the packet of Woodbines leaped the six-bar gate and ran up the field, terrified out of his mind! [laughs] And he [Joe] said, "Here was the East Clare Brigade!" He wasn't a member, but shur the Tans took off in a frenzy because they thought, "Oh well, we're going to be attacked here." East Clare Brigade. [laughs] But Joe Minogue, Joe was so funny. He said, "the East Clare Brigade". If the East Clare Brigade were depending on him, he'd have scaled the gate and gone running too![35]

'They jumped in the air!'

Often traumatic episodes were softened by humorous elements over time. Tuesday 16 November 1920 was a dark day for the people of East Clare. On that morning, four young men were captured by members of G Division of the Auxiliaries stationed in Killaloe. The men were taken back to Killaloe, tortured and brutally murdered on the bridge linking Ballina in north Tipperary to Killaloe in east Clare. The event remains a potent milestone in the social memory of east Clare. In time, when some of those associated with the incident were able to look back on that dark moment, the light of humour was able to break through on occasion. Tommy Holland from Whitegate grew up hearing about the Scariff Martyrs, of McMahon, Rodgers, Gildea and Egan, and of their violent deaths. It was often a struggle to obtain the information that a curious young Tommy sought. However, one story rooted in that time was forthcoming. After the Auxiliaries had captured the four young men at Williamstown House in Whitegate, they made their way to the nearby townland of Nutgrove and to Tommy Holland's family home:

> They raided the house … onto the house there was a dairy and onto the dairy there was a boiling house, where people used to boil a lot of stuff for pigs and Indian meal and corn and there was always a fire down. It was November and the door was closed but the boiling house was full of steam. And they always laughed at the idea when the Tans busted in the door, a big fog of steam came out and they could see they jumped in the air! They thought they were blown up! They thought it was a bomb. They got great enjoyment out of telling about the fright the Tans got, or the Auxiliaries, whichever one of 'em it was![36]

On a separate occasion, the Black and Tans were raiding houses in the area of Annagh on the outskirts of Feakle parish, close to the village of Bodyke, when they arrived at the home of Francis and Margaret O'Grady. Like the men who raided the Holland homestead in November 1920, these men were wary of what they might find. Peggy Hogan, who was born on 23 June 1925, remembered a story told to her by her father, Rodger O'Grady, who was at his home when the Black and Tans came:

> They were also in our house that day and they went up to a room off of the kitchen and we had a separator for separating milk and he got all excited and he said, "I think I have a find. I think I have a find!" So they came in anyway and they stood over it and one of the Tans knew it was a separator for separating milk. They thought 'twas for makin' some kind of bombs! [laughs][37]

The Black and Tan Bullock

For IRA Volunteers seeking shelter when being hunted by crown forces, the more remote and desolate location they found, the safer they felt. In Clonkerry East, in the parish of Labasheeda,

IRA Volunteer Jamie Corbett and some of his comrades of the 1st Battalion, West Clare IRA Brigade, had assembled late one night in a remote, derelict outhouse. While severely lacking in comfort and warmth, it offered security and safety, or at least that is what they thought. A sudden thud at the door made them think for one frightening moment that the Black and Tans had arrived at their secret hideout:

> Before they had the dugout they were staying in an aul workman's house over there. They used to be inside of it. I heard Jamie saying one night that they were there and 'twas mighty cold and they went step dancing. They went step dancing. At least they had some kind of steps anyway. And didn't a wallop come to the door! Anyone would think 'twas a blow from a rifle, the end of a rifle. An aul bullock's horn [laughs]. He gave a bit of a dander to 'em all right but one of 'em stole around to see what was happening, went out the other door. But 'twas the aul beast that was there [laughs].[38]

'Halt, who goes there?'

In 2008 Mellie Enright, who was born in 1914, recalled a story about two old ladies walking past a military sentry box in her native Kilmihil in west Clare. The sentry box had been installed due to the increasing republican activity in the area during the war. It was a Friday and the women had earlier collected their pension of five shillings.[39] They made their way home, lost in the comfort of their own conversation:

> We had the RIC there. Nobody could come in from that side. They'd be stopped. There was a sentry box outside the thing and [a soldier] inside of that then to say, "Halt, who goes by? Stop to be recognised." And where the old creamery was, if you were going over the Ennis

road, there was a sentry box above behind the wall. There was a high wall so he had a full view of who was over there. It was "Halt" day or night, it didn't matter if they didn't recognise you. "Who goes by?" Well if you were the lord lieutenant, it didn't matter, you had to halt. He didn't know you were the lord lieutenant and if you were okay, he'd say, "Okay, pass on." We had no other experience of that except that there were two old ladies going over one night [laughs] and they were after getting their pension on a Friday. A pension that time was five shillings and of course it was an awful lot of money to the one that had no money … They were rich with five bob a week! They could buy their little groceries or an odd little *tá sé* [alcoholic drink] and they might buy a bottle of stout on the Friday … but they were what they'd call now, "middling merry" … They were going over anyway this night and one of them was going over a bit of the way with this one … They were passing the barracks now going over and they forgot that the sentry was there, forgot all about a sentry or anything! The next thing the lad above knew who was there because he was used to them and he says, "Halt, who goes by?" "Oh, Jesus, Mary and Joseph!" says one of them … and yer man as quick as anything says, "Oh, I see, the Holy Family, please pass on." 'Twas the only time I heard of one of the British lads saying a prayer! [laughs][40]

In east Clare a sentry also startled two local men who were returning from a long day's work at the bog in Ballymacdonnell in Bodyke. Palkie McNamara from Scariff, who was ninety-six when interviewed in 2011, relayed the story:

> I remember a funny incident. There was a sentry on duty there from six in the evening to six in the morning. If you were passing, they'd say, "Halt, who goes there?" There was a man named Hanrahan, working in a bog in Ballymacdonnell. He was coming home late at

night and one of the young Hogans was with him. The sentry said, "Halt, who goes there?" Hanrahan didn't say anything but the young Jim Hogan piped up, "John and I comin' from the bog, sir!"⁴¹

Young Hogan's overly familiar declaration to a bemused British soldier was either the result of nerves or the brashness of youth.

Excitement can produce peculiar results on occasion. In O'Callaghan's Mills one local supporter of the national cause was called upon to perform the important duty of introducing the former Irish Parliamentary Party, Independent and then Sinn Féin politician Laurence Ginnell to a baffled crowd outside Mass. It is likely that Ginnell, a strong supporter of land agitation, was in the area due to the prevalence of cattle drives there. Such was the excitement of performing this duty that, having stepped forward to the platform, the would-be master of ceremonies introduced the waiting crowd to 'Larry Ginnell, the man who fought and died for Ireland!'⁴²

Among those assembled to hear the above unfortunate introduction was my grandfather, a well-known character in the area in which Ginnell had come to speak. Bartholomew 'Batty' McNamara from Claremount had been active in the increasing land agitation and 'cattle drives' in the area. On 9 February 1918 he was listed in the *Clare Champion* as appearing in court with ten other defendants in relation to cattle driving in the Broadford and O'Callaghan's Mills district.⁴³ In the same month he was arrested with several others for refusing to allow timber at Derrymore Mills to be taken and used as trench reinforcement for the First World War, which was ongoing at the time.⁴⁴ The late Paddy Gleeson, at the age of 104, recalled 'Batty Mac' in 2008 and testified to the way in which humour was a central medium for the transmission of lore and memory:

He could walk in there to the two of us and he'd have the two of us laughing in five minutes. That's the way to look at Batty Mac. I never saw a frown on his face. That was another character of his. You can be bloody well sure me or anybody else ever saw a wicked puss on him in any shape or form. Good-humoured in every way of the world. He was full of humour ... He had such humour that he was noted by everyone shur as Batty Mac and when you were talkin' of Batty Mac you were talking about a funny character!

Paddy explained how when Batty was taken to jail in 1918, following his arrest with twenty-two others, his humour managed to break down some of the tension within the jail:

He was taken on with the rest of 'em into jail ... They got a month in jail anyway and sometimes he was so funny that the warders for a finish got the president or the governor of the prison to listen to him and have a chat with him. He was there one side [of the prison cell] and they questioning him and the humour going on. The questions they'd ask him and the answers he'd give 'em back. 'Twas a concert more than anything![45]

There are many stories associated with Batty Mac, most of which seem to have humorous connotations. On one occasion he avoided arrest by the British forces at Kelly's public house in O'Callaghan's Mills. After Auxiliaries arrived and began questioning locals, Batty, who was in the kitchen of the pub, placed the carcass of a goose over his head and successfully passed himself off as somewhat insane. Having been lined up outside with other locals, he spontaneously began to sing songs to 'entertain' the arresting Auxiliaries, which according to the late Seán Crowe managed to lighten the mood of the tense occasion. A suitably impressed

Auxiliary took off his cap and passed it around to the nervous locals to solicit a donation for the entertainer. Laughing, Seán Crowe recalled in 2011 that Batty then singled out a man called Michael Campbell, who himself owned a public house, telling the amused Auxiliary, 'That fella is a wealthy man, make sure he pays more!'[46]

A final story sees Batty Mac facing a judge in Cork, where he had been taken after he and a friend had occupied a recently abandoned landlord house in the Claremount area. For the occasion, Batty is reputed to have worn a bright yellow waistcoat, recently sent to him by his sisters, who had years earlier emigrated to America. After the judge questioned which of the defendants was 'the farmer's son' and which 'the labouring boy', Batty rose to declare, 'I'm the right honourable labouring boy your honour!' Commenting on his impressive attire, the judge is reputed to have said he would have considered him to be instead a farmer's son. The judge finally decided to release the two men with a stern warning not to reoffend. Batty, having demanded a right of reply, boldly informed the judge, 'Here we are, two poor men of the land, who are brought to court for taking shelter from the rain! You're now asking us to make our way from Cork to Clare without a bob! Shur we'll have to do the same thing again on our way home!'[47]

Batty McNamara was buried in Broadford graveyard on 9 November 1969 at the age of eighty-seven, the Irish tricolour having rested on his coffin as a mark of respect from his neighbours and former comrades.[48]

The Fox Hunter's Reel

In any period of turmoil, the light of entertainment breaks through. Co. Clare has long been a seat of storytellers and musicians, often competing, at other times complementing each other, and never far apart. While 'on the run' in east Clare, two Mayo republicans immersed themselves in the traditional music of the countryside and bequeathed to the people a tune, which hangs on the musical breeze to this day:

> They were from West Mayo, Belmullet side. Ah, Concannon and Joyce. They were noted, ah they were the leading lights in a big ambush and there was a big price on their head. After the ambush they had to get out of the place, which they did and they worked their way, they had to take a circuitous route and they had to go into Longford and work their way down through the midlands. They finally wound up in Derrynahalla, Doireguillan. They joined up with the republicans there. Tom Clune and others. They were great musicians and they used to play up at Dinans', Mrs Dinan and Peter Dinan, at Maghera Cross. They brought tunes. I know one tune that they brought there and it wasn't known. 'Twas used very frequently after at country dances. They brought the tune with 'em and 'twasn't known. It wasn't known in southeast Clare anyway and they left it behind 'em and 'twas very much used afterwards in later years. The Fox Hunter's Reel! The people that got it made it known that it came from these two men.[49]

'Jazus boy I was there'

In west Clare, in the late 1950s, at Gleeson's pub in Coore, a local man was regaling the assembled customers with stories of his days of fighting the British forces. Jimmy Gleeson, the pub owner, whose own father, Matt, had been a member of the West Clare IRA Brigade's 4th Battalion, watched knowingly as the stories unfolded. At such social scenes it was rare for the teller, particularly an older man, to be interrupted. Following a two-year anthropological study conducted in Clare in the 1930s, American researchers Arensberg and Kimball found that when an older man spoke at a social gathering, like the one in Coore: 'At such times the important news of the countryside disseminates itself. Political judgements are formed. It is the bold man who enters an opinion.'[50] However, Jimmy Gleeson recalls that on this occasion the pertinacity of youth managed to break through the prevailing norms and a 'bold man' entered an opinion:

> Oh ya, he maintained that he was in the Rineen ambush. I don't have a list of the people who were in it. He was bragging about it in the pub and there was a young fella there fairly well into his cups [under the influence of alcohol]. He was talking about the way the ambush went, do you know. He had the chest stickin' out! The young fella said to him, "Where were you in 1014 when Brian Boru needed you?" Pako answered straight away, "Jazus boy I was there!"[51]

Pako Kerin from Knocklistrane in Miltown Malbay was not at the Battle of Clontarf in 1014. He was, however, a key participant at the ambush of Rineen in 1920 and, ironically, along with his comrades at Rineen, was later caricatured in song as one of 'the dauntless sons of Brian Boru'.[52] During the War of Independence, Kerin was O/C of the Glendine Company, 4th Battalion, Mid Clare IRA Brigade, one of the most active in the county.

Gleeson's pub in Coore, Miltown Malbay, was opened in the mid-1800s. For more than a century and a half the pub was a fulcrum for lore, music, tradition and story, until it closed in 2003.[53] The declaration of its last owner, Jimmy Gleeson, that 'we had the greatest bunch of historians comin' into that place there outside', no doubt captures the essence of the innumerable assemblies in Gleeson's pub.[54] There is also little doubt that truth and fiction lived a happy coexistence in such a place of social relief.

The late Joe 'Jack' Sexton from Mountscott in Mullagh passed away in 2012 at the age of ninety-two. Two years previously, he told me how his uncle, Tadgh MacMahon, would speak about the Rineen ambush while working on the family farm. He also remembered later being in Gleeson's pub hearing Tadgh claim to have fought at Rineen. Unlike the boasts of Pako Kerin, however, the assertions of Tadgh MacMahon were without foundation, according to his nephew:

> I remember he had one story that he used tell. Well the day he was making up hay, making a reek of hay over there in the meadow and my father was with him. But the Rineen ambush, he used trace it. He had himself in the finish convinced he was there. He had told it so often. We were one night over in Gleeson's in the pub for a couple of drinks and there was three lads there from Kilrush and the pub knew it well, do you know, that 'twas damn lies he was tellin'! He traced it, do you know, how he was inside the wall at Rineen and he peltin' these hand grenades and how he lodged it inside the lorry and how all of 'em was killed. Oh, he had it brought to perfection! And how did he get there? He was at a brother's house in Moy and they were makin' the grenades and the lads asked, "Can he be trusted?", and they said he could. So he made them with 'em. And the man wasn't there no more than I was! No![55]

5

'A CORNER OF THE GRAVE'

STORIES OF SILENCE

'A LOT DIDN'T BELIEVE IT EVER HAPPENED':
BURIED MEMORIES

On Monday 14 May 2018 the body of a British soldier was exhumed in the north Clare townland of Moy. The remains were taken to Grangegorman Military Cemetery in Dublin, where he was buried. The body of nineteen-year-old Private George Duff Chalmers had lain in the hills over Moy for ninety-seven years. Chalmers was a member of the 2nd Battalion of the British Army's Royal Scots, based in Clare during the War of Independence. He died on 11 June 1921 at Drumbaun after he was captured and executed by members of the IRA. The reburial of the soldier was greeted positively by the local community. While they could not forget the violence of the force in which Chalmers was a member, the story was now a human one and a soldier's body was now back within reach of his family.

Regrettably, however, the agencies involved in the exhumation were pointed in their lack of any consultation with local people or landowners.[1] That locals only became aware of the exhumation when vehicles arrived on site was a source of frustration for many. The approach taken by the agencies failed to acknowledge the role played by local people in preserving and marking the site, and showed a regrettable lack of understanding and respect. Critically, it demonstrated the failure of officialdom to recognise the value of local memory and tradition.

The surrounding media attention focused largely on the age of the soldier, the tragedy of his death and the loneliness of his remains. There was little reference to the violence and murders perpetrated by his regiment, or the broader repression of local people in which he was likely a participant. The media also failed to note that the men who executed Chalmers were also young men in their early twenties. Strikingly, there was little reference in any of the considerable media coverage to the role played by memory in the retrieval of his body. It was not the detailed British archives or the subsequent Irish government records that held his story for almost 100 years. Nor was it referred to within the considerable historiography that has claimed to chronicle the revolutionary struggle. Instead, the story of the remains of the young soldier who rested in the local landscape had been preserved within the enduring fold of oral tradition and memory.[2]

'The boys spotted him and took for the road after him': Private George Duff Chalmers

On 10 June 1921 a party of British soldiers from the Royal Scots travelled to the remote townland of Moughna in north Clare to deliver a jury summons to sixty-one-year-old Tom Tuttle. Reportedly, on the way back from delivering the summons, Private Duff Chalmers left the unit in the Lavoreen area. The soldier was soon arrested by local IRA Volunteers, who had been tracking the movements of the convoy.[3]

There has been some dispute as to Chalmers' motivation for leaving his convoy and about the exact circumstances of his capture, court martial and subsequent execution. While the suggestion that he was making his way to see a young girl he was courting in the area has found a foothold in local memory, it is not the only theory. It has also been suggested that Chalmers was presenting himself as 'kind of simple' in order to obtain information on local republicans. While this may not have been the case, it certainly was the impression of the IRA who encountered him. It is also possible that neither of these stories was the truth and that a more simple reason for his departure or ejection from his convoy could be the explanation.

What is beyond dispute is that a British soldier who had been in Ireland for a considerable period, and who had been injured over six months previously in an ambush (Monreal) by the IRA, was acutely aware that walking in a known republican area while wearing a British Army uniform was dangerous. That the incident occurred deep into the war, in a period when the dynamics of violence and danger were well established, makes the reason for his presence there even more peculiar. The last sighting of the soldier before his capture was in the garden of the Tuttle home, where he was seen smoking a cigarette before departing on his final journey.[4]

Both Seamus Hennessy and Steve Gallagher, active IRA men in the Mid Clare Brigade, were involved in the capture and later court martial of Chalmers. At the court martial, held in a remote quarry above Moy, Chalmers was sentenced to death on suspicion of being a spy and was executed at the same site.[5] The tendency for British intelligence to dispatch apparent deserters in order to gain information from local people had been noted by the IRA and, with the increasing danger posed by spies, such extreme decisions were often taken. An IRA report noted that 'A Private of the Royal Scots who dropped off one of four lorries passing through

C. Coy area, was captured by two riflemen after a chase. The Bn. staff being satisfied that his object in leaving the lorry was to seek information, had him executed on the same date.'[6] When asked about the incident, P.J. Clancy stated that he had heard about it later in life than he might have expected:

> 'Twas late enough when I heard about that, you know. There'd be a few different tellins about it. Someone said 'twas to go to meet someone he was and more had it that he was let out to pretend he was kind of simple in order to get information from people ... 'Twas said that they sent him out as a kind of a foolish fella that didn't know much ... It didn't make sense for one man to go out on his own with what they were doing.[7]

A certain folklore has evolved from the incident, including reference to the spot where Chalmers was executed, with P.J. suggesting 'that spot now, ever after, it held green'. This peculiarity was confirmed by P.J. Donnellan, whose forestry land was close to the site. Like them, Dinny Costelloe had also gleaned something remarkable about the place of execution. When I asked Dinny if he had heard about Chalmer's execution, or had been aware of the burial site, he explained: 'I did, and the place took fire and the place where he was buried never took fire. Isn't that remarkable?'[8] Dinny also claimed that a pig had been killed and the blood spread around the human blood to conceal the incident. Here, it is possible that Dinny was confusing the story of Chalmers with that of Private George Robertson (a British serviceman executed by the IRA in Connolly eight months before Chalmers), where the suggestion that a pig was killed to conceal the evidence of his death was recorded in local tradition. (The Robertson case is discussed on pages 210–13.)

In 2009 I sat in the front room of Micheál O'Connell's home in the townland of Moy. Micheál, who was born in 1918, was typical of his generation. He, too, had grown up in the shadow of the most turbulent and violent period of modern Irish history. Having spent his entire life in the townland of Moy, he knew it and the surrounding landscape intimately.[9] When asked about the suggestion that a British serviceman was buried locally, he responded:

> I'll tell you the whole lot of it! They were stayin' below at the Ennistymon hospital, the British soldiers and of course they had a share of duty to do in regard [to] summons to people, to keep law and order. This soldier was sent out one day with a summons, up to Tuttles', for to attend such a court … And he came out with his summons and delivered it to Tuttle. He was goin' with some lady down near Lahinch at the time. Instead of goin' back the road he came out, he came down Clooneyogan over here. And of course, the boys [IRA] spotted him and took for the road after him. They caught him halfway down near Lahinch. They court-martialled him and brought him up and shot him and buried him.[10]

Micheál explained that in the locality, many people refused to believe that the event took place or that a soldier still rested in the bog above Moy:

> A lot didn't believe it ever happened. Patsy Connors used to be comin' here to me often, tellin' stories and all. Patsy used to say "Is it true?" "'Tis true Patsy," says I. By God, didn't he open a corner of the grave and he got the uniform. He did. Ah, he closed it fast!

As the years rolled on there was a further deepening of the story, as Micheál continued:

But then there was another old man, livin' back the mountain there, Pat Lynch was his name. He'd often go to Miltown and come home late at night and the Devil knows what. But the point about it was, he was in the middle of the crowd that brought him out from Moloney's quarry, they held the court martial in it. He was with 'em bringing him up the mountain opening the grave and burying him. The grave is there to be seen at the present day. But I'd say fifteen years ago, or twenty, some of the Miltown boys used to come out cutting turf there in Ballaun.[11] But they came out this day there was three or four of 'em in it and they said, "Shur tis a cod about the soldier bein' buried there." Someone said, "The grave is above there." Faith, they opened the grave but they closed it just as quick!

Sitting back on his chair in Moy, holding his walking stick between his two time-worn hands, as night was moving in and as the interview was coming towards its natural end, Micheál concluded, 'they were funny times and quare times and dangerous times and no respect for life either'.

The story of Chalmers is undoubtedly a profound example of the value of local memory. Without the endurance of the oral tradition associated with the event, the body of Chalmers would never have been located. Exactly why Chalmers left the convoy, and where the young soldier was going, will likely never be known for certain. What is certain is that the only pathway towards his body and his story's recovery was through the local oral tradition. In order to make sense out of the story, an understanding of the local geography and landscape, as well as its history, was critical.

Chalmers was buried just fifty feet from the boundary of P.J. Donnellan's forestry, close to an area called 'the dry lake'. P.J. had, over time, sought to preserve the site and worked with others to mark the grave. Although he grew up with a strong republican background, he was capable of understanding the human story in its political and historic context. While deeply aware of the damage done by the forces to which Chalmers was aligned, his human empathy ensured that the site was cared for with sensitivity over time. Regrettably, this was not acknowledged in the final part of the story in 2018.

'He managed to carve his initials': The story of Private George Robertson

Lance Corporal Alexander McPherson, who featured centrally in the murder of Charles Lynch on 21 October 1920 (see pp. 68–72), was captured just weeks later with Private George Robertson near the village of Connolly by local IRA Volunteers led by Mick Meere. While being held captive at the home of forty-four-year-old Mick Eustace, Furroor, in the parish of Kilmaley, McPherson managed to trick his guard and escape, leaving Robertson behind. When one of the Eustace family later married Nora Corry from Clounlaheen, the story of Robertson and McPherson was introduced to Catherine Talty's community. In 2013, at the age of ninety-seven, Catherine explained, referring to the solders as 'Tans':

> The IRA, they captured these two Tans. I don't know exactly where and they brought them all the way down to, I think, Lisroe. Two different houses. One was Eustace and I don't know what the other one was. There was one big, strong, able-bodied man looking after the fella who shot Charlie Lynch after. He went to load a gun and he had some problem and your Black and Tan [McPherson] said, "Oh, I'll do that for you" and shur you know the result, shur he took off, of course. Anyway, the one that was imprisoned in Eustaces', I think he was only there a night when the IRA took him [referring to

the execution of Private George Robertson] and that was it ... And of course the Tans traced back shur because they knew, McPherson knew where they had been imprisoned. Your man had been tied to a chair but he managed to carve his, ah, his initials or his name on the chair and they found it. And all they did to the family was they burned the house.[12]

McPherson had escaped by persuading IRA Volunteer Hugh Hehir to part with his gun on the pretence of instructing him on how to load it properly. After his escape, the IRA, who had been maintaining guard over the two soldiers, realised that to hold Robertson, whom McPherson had made no attempt to liberate, was too dangerous. They executed Robertson soon after and reputedly buried him in a bog in the parish of Connolly, which was owned by Colonel Frederick St Leger Tottenham, a local unionist landlord.

McPherson later returned to the scene with his fellow crown forces and identified the Eustaces' home through marks that he had carved into the furniture with a tobacco knife. At one farm in which he was held captive, he had carved his initials into the rafters of an outdoor toilet. All the houses identified by McPherson were searched and burned, in addition to thirty tons of hay, in reprisal.[13]

There have been alternative accounts of Robertson's death, which indicate he was more brutally and clumsily killed than the straightforward execution that may have been typical in such circumstances. Fr Pat Gaynor, a republican priest, wrote many decades later that he had heard Robertson was not killed in his initial attempted execution. Instead, Gaynor claimed it was botched and that instead of being executed by gunfire, he was eventually bludgeoned on the side of a road with a stone. However, this account has been robustly disputed by others, including Pádraig Óg Ó Ruairc, who has carefully analysed the Robertson case.[14]

I myself recorded a second version of the story from storyteller Francie Kenneally from Leeds in Miltown Malbay. From the 1970s to the 1990s Francie travelled across Ireland and England, speaking at storytelling festivals like the Irish Centre in Hammersmith and the Sidmouth International Folk Festival, and he was featured on *The Pure Drop* for RTÉ. Francie insisted that the story of Robertson was only known locally and at that point had failed to reach the official narrative on the period:

> But there is another story and 'twasn't in the recording but I heard it now. They took two aul Tans prisoner in Connolly ... I don't know did they keep 'em handcuffed or not but they had no right jail for 'em. 'Twas farmhouses. But it seems, they were like themselves. They brought 'em one night to a dance, to a country dance and didn't one of 'em mark a chair with a penknife unknown to 'em. That was all right anyway. They went out long-jumpin' one day. These two Tans, they were two great athletes. They were two fine boys! They took off their coats and they were jumpin' and didn't they make a run for it! They followed 'em and they caught one of 'em and they killed him with a spade. This is the story now. The other fella went down to Dunógan Castle and he went up on the top of a hill where Dunógan Castle was. 'Twas an old castle now and he saw Miltown. He came up across and there was a Sinn Féiner diggin' spuds now and the strange thing was he had the rifle in the garden. He shot a crow or two that morning ... The Tan passed him out. He didn't know who he was. He was digging spuds with his father. He passed out the garden and this Sinn Féiner noticed his clothes were a bit torn. I suppose thorny wire on the run from Connolly. He saw Miltown and he came up. He landed at the barrack, where the Bank [of Ireland] is now ... he went

in and he told his story to the Tans. They equipped him anyway with new clothes and gave him a feed and all that. He told them about the mark in the chair. They went on to Connolly and found the chair and burned the house ... 'twas told locally anyway.[15]

Francie's version is different in many ways from that of Catherine Talty and of the more generally accepted view of the incident. However, that McPherson and Robertson were initially brought to house dances and believed to have been deserters was confirmed by Ennis IRA member Paddy 'Con' McMahon.[16] What is certain about this story is that it occupied a part of the broader historical consciousness and oral tradition of the area, as affirmed by the various tellings, and as such is of tremendous importance.

6

CARRYING WOUNDS

STORIES OF PAIN

'I REMEMBER KISSING MY FATHER GOODBYE':
ANTHONY 'MURRAY' MCGUANE
In November 1941, in the west Clare townland of Coore, a young girl ran behind a heavy curtain and cried. Although she did not fully understand her own tears, they were induced by knowing something was wrong, as evidenced by the countenance of others, the quietness, the sad looks, her older sister's pained expression. She had just kissed her father. He was cold and still. A gentle hand reached behind the curtain and encouraged young Catherine McGuane to come out from her place of emotional shelter. She had to now follow the coffin of her father, Anthony McGuane – a former member of west Clare IRA – on his final journey to Coore church.

In 2014 this daughter of Anthony McGuane wrote to me from Australia and described these events. I had encountered her father's name in a number of interviews in that area, but had never seen him mentioned in any book or record of the period. His goddaughter, Mary Dollard, who was born in 1922 in the nearby townland of Maherantaisce, grew up hearing stories about the man known affectionately as 'Murray'. I recorded Mary at her home in Limerick on a number of occasions between 2012 and 2014. Mary's early life was typical of most rural children of her generation. As she lay in the cradle, a violent war was being fought around her. In Dublin a man called Collins had orchestrated a guerrilla conflict against the British Empire which reached into the very fields of her own townland. By the time she was baptised into the Christian faith, the man who stood as godfather for her – a man who had already spent a number of years fighting in the struggle for independence as a remote disciple of Collins – now stood against Collins in an increasingly bitter Civil War. Anthony 'Murray' McGuane was the first connection she had to that turbulent history. She remembered him 'as jolly and funny, a decent man' and fondly recalled a ring that 'Murray' made for her mother Mary 'from a florin'.[1] Thus, when she heard about the revolutionary period many years later, it was through the eyes of such personal understanding.

Sitting at her home in Kennedy Park in Limerick, where she had lived with her late husband, Pat Dollard, Mary declared in the first of a series of interviews: 'Oh, our house was a safe house. Oh my father was always telling us. IRA men up in the garret [attic room] … The guns all hidden and they'd polish 'em.' In 2012 Mary recalled the story of a raid on their family home told to her by her father, Tom. The raid was carried out by the Black and Tans and the story centred around her godfather, Anthony 'Murray' McGuane, the republican reference point for her family. Mary's story about 'Murray' intersected powerfully with more intimate connections to the Coore republican, presented later in this section:

> I remember hearing about the night that they raided our house. Anthony was caught there. He was in his early twenties. He was brought out and there was a trench above. If you were thrown into that you could say goodbye … They left the jeep [Crossley tender] up the road because it would warn people. They came in and they caught him and took him out. My father was telling us that everyone

in the house was shivering. They put out the paraffin lamps because if you were seen looking out, you were in trouble! They didn't know which direction they were gone. They left it about a half an hour and they were waiting for the shots. They waited for a half hour and there was no sound. Eventually someone ventured out with a lamp. They started calling [whispers], "Anthony, Anthony, Anthony." They went up the roads but there was no sign of lights or anything. They walked up further and called him. He was down in the trench. Of course it was pitch dark. At this stage the car was gone miles out the road.[2]

At this point, like a practiced storyteller, Mary had submerged deep into her story and narrated her father's instructions to his family as they tried to rescue 'Murray' McGuane:

"Get ladders quickly, get ladders." They had to bring him up in the darkness. He was drenched wet and he was shivering. He was definitely suffering from hypothermia. They brought him into our house and of course the blazing fire and they warmed him. Somebody, his sisters, I suppose, got clothes belonging to my father. There was no running water in those days. They had a big aluminium bath. They carried him down and they put him in the bath. Ah, but the fellas were tougher then. He [Anthony] was 'on the run' and he was in jail and he did weeks and months there. He came back out and came to the fire. He was fine then, but the shock never left him.

After Anthony McGuane had been warmed up and was sitting on the hob, next to the blazing open fire in Maherantaisce, Mary's father ventured a question about his experience. According to Mary, Anthony replied, 'Nothing ... They just trained their guns on me. Made sure the flash lamps showed the guns.' Chillingly, according to the story recounted to Mary, Anthony told those listening attentively that he was asked by the Black and Tans if he 'had any message for his mother before they shot him'.

In 2013 the late Mary Dollard recalled sadly that, less than two decades after this incident, Anthony died as a young man, leaving his wife, Bridget, and a young family behind:

> He died at the age of forty-five. He died from a simple cold. My father often would be telling us. "If you don't do your homework, you'll be put in jail and you'll be like Anthony on bread and water." I was in the cradle ... I didn't think I'd ever hear anything about the War of Independence or the Troubles after I left Maherantaisce.[3]

Anthony McGuane joined B Company of the 4th Battalion, West Clare IRA Brigade in 1917 and was later appointed company section commander. In September 1919 he enrolled as a member of the ASU and was involved in all actions of that group, including raids for arms and explosives, road cutting, collecting rates and guarding RIC prisoners. He was also a participant in an ambush at Dunógan in September 1920, and the armed defence of Mullagh later that month, when Black and Tans threatened to burn it as a reprisal for the Rineen ambush and the killing of Captain Alan Lendrum. His sister, Mary, was a captain in the Coore Company of Cumann na mBan. She later emigrated to America, where she continued to support the republican movement.

Having taken the republican side in the Civil War, McGuane was arrested in May 1923 by Free State forces, badly beaten and interned for eleven months. During this time he was on hunger strike for fifteen days. He was released in March 1924 with others and returned to Coore.[4]

In the next townland of Clounlaheen, Catherine Talty was then almost eight years old. She witnessed the return of Anthony

McGuane and other local republicans, recalling: 'There were bonfires. They were heroes.'⁵ She remembered Anthony later as 'a constant visitor' to their home in Clounlaheen in the 1930s and characterised his personality as 'very lively, very jolly and lovely'.⁶ In Catherine's home there are multiple reminders of the past, carefully preserved by a proud bearer of tradition. Among her considerable collection is a piece of lace mantle decoration made by Anthony while in prison. She also recalled Anthony patiently teaching her the skills he learned in jail, and remembered fondly making a tea cosy with him during one of his many visits. Catherine sadly recalled Anthony's death from pneumonia in the early 1940s:

> He died of pneumonia ... He left a young family. Oh, God, I suppose Anthony the youngest one was only a few years. But that family. Those girls. My God, those girls worked like any man!⁷

Although Catherine stated emphatically that 'there was nothing weak about Anthony McGuane when he came back from prison', it is highly probable that the effects of volunteerism and imprisonment may have compromised his health, which manifested later in his inability to combat pneumonia and his death at a young age.

The Moroney family in Dunógan and the Murphy family in Maherantaisce, the families of both Catherine Talty and Mary Dollard, mourned deeply the loss of Anthony McGuane. In fact, on 22 November 1941 his entire community mourned the loss of a man they had loved and respected. Perhaps his role in the struggle for freedom seemed less important then – two decades having passed since the deadliest year of the war – but it was not forgotten. His story was preserved within family tradition and Anthony McGuane's grandson, Seán Cox, a US district judge in Michigan, America, grew up hearing stories about his grandfather. He communicated some of the family's knowledge about Anthony:

> We do know that he was imprisoned during the rebellion [War of Independence] and again during the Civil War ... That he was a leader in Co. Clare ... That he captured British soldiers and held them for ransom ... That the hostages, at times, were held on the farm ... that guns and ammunition were hidden on the farm and underneath the floor of the cottage.[8]

Anthony's sister, Mary, emigrated to Detroit in the late 1920s and remained very active in the republican movement there. Mary was a key source of information about the revolutionary period for the Cox family. I asked her grand-nephew Seán to describe how Mary spoke about the period:

> Pride [of involvement in the republican struggle] and contempt for the Black and Tans. Loved talking about Molly McMahon [republican leader in west Clare] and the march to Kilrush to see de Valera. Mary was hit on the face by a Black and Tan during the arrest of her brother outside a house in Coore.[9]

After my contact with her son, Margaret McGuane Cox wrote to me from America in April 2018. She is the oldest surviving child of Anthony McGuane and his wife Bridget. Margaret was just eight years old when her father became very ill in early November 1941. He had contracted pneumonia and with no penicillin available, the only treatment was sulphur. In her letter, Margaret remembered worryingly observing as her father became increasingly delirious with fever. She recalled that he was unable to sleep for days and had to be constantly attended to. At the end of the second week, Dr Michael Hillery came, and to Margaret's intense relief, reported that the fever had lifted.[10] Painfully, however, she then explained how her father went to sleep early on the morning of 22 November and never woke again. The following day in the loft of their home, she held her youngest sister, Tess, close and watched as, below, the adults in the house seemed busy but distracted. More neighbours than was normal were visiting. She then watched as the priest arrived and heard the devastating words from her Aunt Mary's mouth, that her dear father was dead. Margaret tried to remain composed in spite of the devastation that had shaken her world to the core. She later saw her father laid out in a brown habit, the customary dress for the deceased at the time. Seventy-nine years later, she remembered kissing her father's lifeless body, the cold of his brow a painful sensation that confirmed he was gone.[11]

In November 1941, when her home seemed unsettled, six-year-old Catherine 'Kitty' McGuane looked to her older sister, Margaret, for guidance. She could sense from Margaret that something was profoundly wrong, but back then could not understand it. In 2014 Catherine, then a nun living in Western Australia, also answered a letter I wrote enquiring about her father's IRA past as well as general memories. She kindly responded:

> My father passed away on 22 November 1941 RIP. I was six years and three months. The only recollection I have of my father was the Halloween before he died. He bought apples for us children, as was the custom for the occasion. My brother, who was two years younger than me, had a bigger apple than me, which I tried to take from him. My father had to come to the rescue![12]

The untold human story of the War of Independence was movingly conveyed by Sr Catherine's only other memory of her father:

> The second memory of my father was the night he died. I was asleep and my aunt took me to a neighbour's house. I remember it was dark and I was aware something unusual was happening but at the time I didn't know that my father was dying. In those days the corpse was in the home until it was taken to the church. I remember kissing my father goodbye in the coffin before he was taken to the church. I went behind a window curtain and cried until I was found and for the next thirty years funerals were very painful for me.[13]

The story of Anthony McGuane is like that of innumerable other local republicans across the country, whose stories did not endure and spread like those of national figures such as Michael Collins or Éamon de Valera. Within their own townlands and families, however, their names and their stories have persisted across the generations.[14]

'He was dead before the last of us was born': Mick Killoury

In August 2012 I interviewed John Kelly from the parish of Cree in west Clare. While preparing for the interview, I discovered that the father of John's wife, Phil, was Michael 'Mick' Killoury, a captain in C Company of the 2nd Battalion, West Clare IRA Brigade, and later a commandant in the anti-Treaty IRA.[15]

Killoury (sometimes spelt Killourhy) was born in the townland of Cloonakilla, Kilmihil at the turn of the twentieth century into a large farming family. He was one of thirteen children born to Michael and Mary Killoury. Like many young men in his community, he joined the IRA in 1917 and later rose through the ranks.

One of the most significant incidents in which he was involved was an ambush on 18 April 1920 in his native Kilmihil. There, he was part of a small IRA unit that attacked the RIC outside the local Catholic church. The ambush led to the death of one RIC sergeant, Patrick Carroll, and also Mick's IRA comrade Seán Breen, with whom he had acted as part of a two-man covering party. (The story is explored in more detail in the following chapter.) Following this incident, Killoury spent a considerable period of time 'on the run', including a long period in a man-made dugout in Clonreddan, four miles from the parish of Kilmihil, where he was concealed with at least six other IRA Volunteers. According to IRA Commandant Bill Haugh, on 29 May 1921 Killoury was surprised by a large contingent of British forces in Kilmihil, whereupon 'he pluckily opened fire on them'. Haugh also noted that Killoury 'wrenched' his ankle during this exchange.[16]

In 2012, when I arrived at the house deep in the parish of Cree, Killoury's daughter Phil gave me a warm welcome. Her countenance indicated that she was happy for the focus to remain on her husband, John, and the considerable knowledge and tradition that he possessed. John was a dream interviewee: engaging, interested in the process, informative and willing to share his knowledge.

However, whether through instinct or scholarly pursuit, I was also determined to draw Phil into the narrative. I had presented her with an obituary of her father, outlining some of his military activities, so a declaration of interest had been made. Around the midpoint of the interview, and conscious that Phil was not offering memory, I tried to gently pull her in and ventured a question. With equal care, Phil spoke about the man who died when she was just a young girl. In fact, as she explained, her father, who passed away on 15 November 1945, was dead before his last child was born. Phil explained that it was only when she was older that she began to hear about her father's central involvement in the IRA and realised his commitment to the republican movement and the struggle for independence. On occasion she met old men while working as a nurse in the County Home, who, upon realising her identity, would declare, 'Nurse! I slept with your father', in reference to their days 'on the run' together around west Clare. In this way, over many years, Phil began to gradually discover the story of IRA Captain Mick Killoury. However, despite being presented in adulthood with a gradual disclosure of her father's revolutionary past, her own childhood memories revealed perhaps a deeper insight. In 2012 she tenderly but acutely recalled her father:

> Daddy was always sick when we were children. He was most of the time in a Dublin hospital when we were young. He had a wound in his back. I remember the wound in his back when he was at home from the time. I remember the smell of my father! He was on morphine. I remember the smell of morphine. He was on morphine every day, while he was at home. He was dead before the last of us was born.[17]

Phil's sensory recollection of her father's pain, resulting from a wound received during the War of Independence, is a testimony only retrievable through memory. Long after his war had ended, Mick Killoury wore the wounds of his involvement. Pain was a constant companion and a daily *aide-memoire* of his days in the IRA until he died as a young man in 1945.

His obituary reflected on his patriotism and commitment and listed actions in which Killoury had bravely participated. Speaking at his graveside, his former comrade Michael McMahon affirmed that Killoury had 'died for Ireland as surely as if he had died on the field of battle' and reminded those assembled that his death was 'directly as a result of the privations and hardships he endured in those days of trial and trouble'. He praised Killoury for his 'steadfastness and cool courage in the face of danger and his unswerving loyalty to the cause which he espoused'. In addressing Killoury's family and children, McMahon poignantly conceded that 'they alone can measure the depth of their grief'.[18] Sixty-seven years after her father was buried, Phil, in her simple recollection, bore perhaps a deeper and more eloquent testimony to her father's revolutionary commitment than official records ever could.

'You'd hear him screaming sometimes in the night': Joe Clancy

It is officially recorded that Joe Clancy from Kilkishen in east Clare joined the British Army and served in France and that later he became training officer in the East Clare IRA Brigade.[19] One of eight children, Joe was born on 19 June 1899 to John and Bridget Clancy in Teeronea, Kilkishen. In 1914, at the outbreak of the First World War, Joe was a fifteen-year-old carpenter's apprentice. A year later he ran away to join the 2nd Battalion of the Munster Fusiliers at New (later Sarsfield) Barracks in Limerick. Within weeks, he was serving in trenches of the First World War, as was his friend, Martin 'Neighbour' McNamara, also from Kilkishen. After his discharge in July 1918, Clancy returned home with a Distinguished Conduct Medal (DCM), as well as two German automatic pistols, a short Webley and a quantity of ammunition. Joe kept the medal but immediately handed over the guns and ammunition to the IRA, which he joined shortly thereafter.

Clancy went on to fight in many of the major Clare ambushes, including Cratloe, Glenwood and Kilrush.[20] He and his friend,

Martin 'Neighbour' McNamara, have etched themselves into the republican folklore of that period, with many exploits and near misses which have endured in the local memory around Kilkishen and east Clare. On one occasion, for example, McNamara was shot in the knee by Black and Tans while escaping from a public house in Kilkishen. The following day he was conveyed to a safe house in a cart drawn by an ass, and later brought to a hospital in Limerick hidden in a load of hay. Within a short time, he was back on active service.

On 11 March 1956 Joe Clancy made a statement to the BMH outlining salient details of his IRA activity.[21] Five years later, in August 1961, he died. In March 1963 a large memorial was erected over his grave in Killaloe Cemetery.[22] However, none of this official record tells us about the personal impact this period had on Clancy. Local people say that later in life Clancy was a well-known 'character' and was the subject of many humorous stories and escapades. One interviewee recalled how Joe would regularly take great pleasure from his boast of having pensions from both the IRA and the British Army! His nephew remembered him in 2010:

> God be with him; he was a hard man. Then Joe joined the Irish Army and he became a captain. He always said he went through four wars. He said, "I was in France, the IRA, the Irish Army and the worst of 'em all, my feckin' mother-in-law." [laughs][23]

One Killaloe-based interviewee recalled seeing Clancy in the 1950s, breaking through the roof slates of the building which then operated as the barracks of the Irish police service, An Garda Síochána. Clancy had earlier been taken in by police on the charge of being drunk and disorderly. The former soldier and guerrilla fighter made his way to the top of the three-storey building and appeared through a hole in the roof to hurl verbal abuse at the amused policemen and assembled crowd below. Back in 1920 Clancy was a different type of character but was also seen on the roof of an RIC building. In his BMH statement he recalled standing on the roof of Scariff RIC Barracks in September 1920, while throwing hand grenades down on the RIC men inside. On that occasion he was trapped on the roof and had to be rescued by some of his fellow Volunteers, who managed to get a ladder up to him amidst continued defensive rifle fire from the RIC inside. Although no one was killed in the incident, this attack resulted in the withdrawal of the RIC and British forces from the barracks in the days that followed, a result that was seen as a victory for the local IRA.

During an interview with the late Jack Quigley from Killaloe in 2012, I asked about Joe Clancy. It transpired that not only did the interviewee remember him vividly, but for a period as a child his bedroom was adjacent to Clancy's, who lived in the next house in Newtown in Killaloe. Jack spoke with feeling about his one-time neighbour and offered a short story about a former British Auxiliary seeking Joe out in the years after the War of Independence:

> He was in the troubled times, you know, but he was also in the British Army. He got the military medal for bravery. He was a sergeant. And years after, he showed me the letter, it would be the 1930s, I suppose. But he had a letter from this former Black and Tan, an officer. He was an officer. He was an Auxiliary, not a Black and Tan. He had taken this medal [DCM awarded to Clancy for his service in the First World War] during some raid in a house around Kilkishen. Joe was from Kilkishen. And he sent him the medal, "One soldier to

another," he said. "I can't bear to keep it." He went to the trouble of finding out where he was, this English man.²⁴

Quigley was insistent that the fighting days of Joe Clancy had a severe impact on his nerves. There, in his room, the young Jack Quigley regularly heard the private internalised pain and torment of Clancy not expressed in any official record:

> Oh God yes, oh God, I do. And he lived beside me in the next room to me one time, out there in Newtown. And I often heard him, oh God almighty, you'd hear him screamin' sometimes in the night!²⁵

Jack Quigley's aural recollections of a tormented Joe Clancy go perhaps closer to the story of the one-time British soldier and IRA Volunteer than official records have been capable of doing. Only in memory did this revelation rest.

7

'DORMANT SYMPATHIES'

STORIES OF DEATH

The Shooting of Seán Bréen

> We went up and stood outside the window. Children were not shy of looking in a window or a door because we went into each other's houses. We could see him [Breen] lying inside on the sofa. He was there, inert of course, but the people were there.[1]

Ninety-two years later, the image of a dying Seán Breen remained firmly imprinted on the memory of Mellie Enright when I recorded her in December 2008. Much living had taken place in the meantime. Life continued, the seasons came and went, but for Mellie and for many people in Kilmihil, the day Seán Breen was killed remained a permanent mark on their memory.

On 18 April 1920 Seán (also known as John) Breen, a twenty-two-year-old quartermaster in the 2nd Battalion of the West Clare IRA Brigade, together with four of his comrades – John O'Dea, Peter McMahon, Martin Melican and Mick Killoury – had ambushed a group of RIC men outside Kilmihil church in west Clare. It was the first armed attack on crown forces in the battalion area. Before the ambush, the area had been comparatively quiet, although a certain distance between the civilians and police had been in evidence, as explained by one Kilmihil native in

1997: 'I remember strangely enough that even though we went everywhere as children, in and out everywhere, we always had a kind of a reluctance to go anywhere near the barracks'.[2] By early 1920 that relationship had, of course, soured significantly. The Black and Tans had been introduced and, increasingly, RIC members were deemed complicit in the brutal actions of their new colleagues.

On the morning of the ambush, the tall, athletic Breen left his home in Kiltumper early. The day was fine as he made the three-mile journey to the village of Kilmihil. From the RIC barracks in the village, Sergeant Patrick Carroll emerged. Carroll, from Co. Meath, was forty-one and unmarried, and had been stationed in Kerry and Armagh before transferring to Clare in October 1919. He had arrived in Kilmihil only five weeks before. He, along with Constables Patrick Martyn and Daniel Collins, had been appointed to guard his colleagues in the RIC, including Head Constable Bernard Hoare, on their way to and from Mass. By 1920 in Kilmihil it had become customary for those attending Mass from the RIC to be given an armed escort to and from the church. The IRA unit had planned to approach the police from behind and attack this armed escort, which invariably brought up the rear of the group. Breen's apparent role in the ambush was to cover the retreat of the leading attackers. He was joined in that task by Mick Killoury, another native of Kilmihil.

When the last of the RIC men had left the church and walked approximately fifty yards from the house of prayer, the shooting started. According to Eoin Shanahan, it was Martin Melican who shot Sergeant Carroll, who died immediately. Constable Collins was shot by O'Dea but survived the attack. Peter McMahon attempted to shoot at Constable Martyn but his revolver, allegedly stolen from a returned Canadian soldier, malfunctioned.

As planned, the three leading attackers retreated following the initial shooting. With McMahon's gun unfired, Constable Martyn was left alive, which ultimately proved fatal for Breen, as he and Killoury were left dealing with the return fire of the RIC. In this chaotic reality, it would seem Breen's height was a distinct disadvantage. In the ensuing shootout, Breen was fatally wounded by Constable Martyn.[3] It is strongly suggested by John Flanagan in his BMH statement that Breen failed to fire at Martyn when the latter ran into the crowd of civilians for cover, afraid he would injure an innocent bystander.[4] As he hesitated, Martyn shot him.

In the panic and mayhem that followed the ambush, sixteen civilians were badly wounded, many from bombs thrown by the police. At the inquest into the incident, which took place in the local schoolhouse on Friday 14 May, it was established that the RIC had walked inside the church gates carrying concealed bombs, which indicates a certain awareness of danger and a readiness to risk the lives of civilians.

The death of Seán Breen is one of those peculiar historical phenomena that present a dilemma for the bearer of this memory, given the location and context of the IRA attack. Breen was a committed local republican. In the energised period of mid-1917 he had joined his local company of Irish Volunteers. Over the following years he remained an active and committed participant in IRA activities. In early 1918 he was arrested and imprisoned in Dundalk, where he met republicans from all across the country. Upon his release he immediately returned to active service. In parallel to his IRA activity, as the oldest and only son in his family, he worked the family farm with his father, Michael, and was well known in the local community. In a documentary broadcast in 1997, Kilmihil native Tom Hogan remembered Breen as a young man:

When I was a youngster I remember John Breen. The spring evenings, he'd be passing our house. He'd be passing through our yard … he was a fine, tall, strapping young fella. Looked very big entirely to my mind at that age. His father was Michael Breen, Kiltumper and his mother was Catherine Breen … his mother was a very nice lady, a very lovely lady. His father worked hard. He had to work very hard after John died … John Breen spent the week before he was killed cuttin' turf, himself and John McNamara. 'Twas very sad how he died because it was a very badly planned operation. He shouldn't have been in it at all. He was at least six inches over the ordinary people around him. Anyway, it wasn't a proper place for that with people coming out from Mass.[5]

The feeling that the IRA action was both badly planned and ill-conceived is firmly voiced in local memory. The fact that Breen and his comrades were in the IRA was understood. So, too, was the inevitability of violence. However, to deliberately force an intersection of religious devotion and violence was deemed unnecessary, and has somewhat tempered the social memory of the incident.

Oral tradition surrounding the death of Breen circulated well beyond the boundaries of the west Clare parish of Kilmihil. Nine miles southeast of the village, in the parish of Coolmeen, Michael 'Marshall' McMahon spoke of the incident, referring to another participant in the ambush. McMahon asserted the belief that twenty-five-year-old Mick Killoury, who, like Breen, was a native of Kilmihil, was saved by the intervention of a British soldier: 'He was lying in a trench and didn't one of the British soldiers look out and say, "stay there you're safe, stay where you are".'[6] According to the historian Eoin Shanahan, while making his getaway Killoury had concealed himself under a culvert near the townland of

Lacken, after discarding his boots to give the impression he had run ahead barefoot. This may have presented an opportunity for a kind or disinterested soldier to turn a blind eye.⁷ When referring to the death of Breen, McMahon described how the older people in his parish of Coolmeen saw the incident:

> You see Carroll, Sergeant Carroll was shot and what happened [to] Breen was, he ran across to pick up Carroll's rifle. He broke cover and he ran across to pick up the rifle, do you see. Shur he was a sittin' duck. Era shur, there wouldn't have been any great experience … He was a big tall man but he was only twenty-two but he was an officer in the IRA all right … He died below at Dinsey Breen's, because Dinsey Breen would be his uncle … Oh shur it had a fierce impact on his father and mother.⁸

In Cranny, three miles closer to Kilmihil, Morgie O'Connell often heard the tale of Seán Breen in his youth. In a recording in 2014 O'Connell explained:

> Shur they tried to kill three of 'em [RIC] in Kilmihil again … the time of John Breen. He was one of the lads that tried to kill 'em. They made out that the guns didn't go off at all with two of 'em when they tried to fire at the police … shur one of 'em [RIC] turned around and shur Breen was a very tall fella and the police had guns as well. They wanted to have 'em that time! He shot Breen shur in the forehead. That was the end of Breen. There was great confusion in Kilmihil. The Tans were in Kilmihil that time too! They got an account. They were over here on the Ennis road, around Lacken or the school there. They went up then around the street in Kilmihil with their guns and they firing shots, shur they terrified everyone … There was an aul woman shouting at the priest to "Bring out Jesus to stop the shootin'." But

they fired up in the air; they didn't shoot anyone because there was none of their men shot at.[9]

Closer in age and in geography than McMahon and O'Connell was Timmy Ryan, who died at the age of 102 in June 2012. In 2008 I recorded Timmy at his home in Corgrigg, just three miles from the village of Kilmihil. In the same house, on 18 April 1920, a nine-year-old Timmy listened intently as he heard his father's animated tones following his return from Mass. Forty-nine-year-old John Ryan delivered the news that two men had been killed in an ambush at Kilmihil. He also explained that a bomb had exploded beside him, but to his own amazement he was unharmed. Although the Ryan family were aware of the violent nature of the time they lived in, such an intimate exposure at such an apparently safe setting left those who were present in deep shock. Timmy Ryan listened and listened. So too did his brother, John, before fetching his coat and, despite his parents' objections, heading on his way to the second Mass of the morning. At sixteen, he was old enough to make his own mind up but perhaps not old enough to appreciate the true meaning of danger:

> I was here. I remember it well. They were coming from Mass talking about it. I know my father was at Mass. That was first Mass and they didn't want him [John] to go to second Mass, do you see, and still and all, he went. My father was talking about the bomb that landed and burst beside him and broke Johnno Carey's window and he didn't get a scratch even though it hopped near him. I was only a young lad … The police threw it to scatter the crowd.[10]

Fifty-one-year-old shopkeeper John Carey was wounded in the left leg when a bomb was thrown close to where he and John

Ryan stood, watching aghast as the violence unfolded. Twelve-year-old John McMahon, just three years Timmy's senior, was also wounded badly when fragments of a bomb thrown by the RIC entered his hip. Both Carey and McMahon were caught up in the hysterical panic that reverberated throughout the crowd in the immediate aftermath of the ambush. Old and young ran for shelter where they could find it, imagining each sound of a bullet or bomb was getting closer and closer:

> That time there used to be seagrass and all coming to Kilmihil. 'Twas around the month of April. There was an aul lady going around looking for Mikey, her son, afraid that he'd be shot. And the lord, didn't they find Mikey lying under a heap of plants. A heap of cabbage plants, he was so frightened.[11]

Within a short time, the local military arrived on the scene and soon the Black and Tans were on the streets of Kilmihil. Locals still in the village were eager to depart:

> Then the police landed and soldiers. They came up. Tom Fitz's father. He drove up through the street with a pony and trap and the soldier was out. Tom says, "Oh, I'll have to go past you." "Well, an order is an order," says the soldier, "if you don't go back you'll be shot." That finished Tom!

Timmy remembered the way in which the incident was discussed in Kilmihil in the months and years that followed. In 2008 he described his understanding of the incident:

> It wasn't nice, do you see. There'd be three Peelers going to Mass. They wouldn't be armed or anything. When Mass would be over,

three more would be armed and they'd come down to bring 'em back. Breen always said that he'd never shoot an unarmed man, do you see, and I suppose he stuck to his word. The three police came down and the sergeant was shot dead and another lad got badly wounded … Breen then was supposed to be there in the sideways in case they missed their target … But of course, the trained man, do you see, he was quicker than him. God, he picked Breen out of the crowd! He was a decent man in one way. He saw [Mick] Killoury jumping in over the ditch, there was a bit of a wall there but with the crowd he couldn't get him. He didn't fire. He raised the revolver but the crowd [was in the way] … Breen went to shoot this policeman but he was quicker. I suppose Breen was fairly up on it but he didn't [shoot]. A lot said it wasn't [a] nice thing, coming from Mass. More shur was delighted. That's the way things go on.[12]

Reflecting back on the incident that occurred almost nine decades before he put the story to record, Timmy spoke of the human impact of the episode:

He was an only son. I knew his sister. Well it was tough on an aul [Michael] Breen, do you know. This lad was always a kind of a mad IRA man. He was arrested some time before that. He got some time in jail. It seems he was a determined kind of a lad.

'A platoon ran past the house'

On the morning of the ambush, within the village of Kilmihil, six-year-old Mellie Enright was excited to see various people from outlying areas enter her home as they did most Sundays before Mass. Each Sunday, Mass-goers arrived for their weekly service on ponies and cars, the principal mode of conveyance for communicants. On wet days the cushions and rugs which offered some comfort for those travelling were left inside the door of the Enrights' for the duration of Mass. Typically, after Mass was over and 'while their husbands were having a few words on the street, the women would come in and wait for them to come down to tackle up'. On that Sunday morning, for a curious and alert Mellie, nothing seemed out of the ordinary. Awaiting the arrival of those women, she continued to play, far away in the world of her own imagination:

> Well now, we were in that position and I was playing around the kitchen floor and the door opened in with the first crowd that came in from Mass. They were all very, I thought, frightened-looking. I knew they were different from any other Sunday, when they used to come in slow and laughing and talking. "Oh we'll be all burned out. We'll be all burned out. We'll be all burned in Kilmihil today. Kilmihil will be burned out today." Of course I was looking up at them and I was amazed. I had heard shooting now but I hadn't known what it meant. I'd say ten minutes before that. Across the road there was an old creamery and 'twas there, there was a detachment of the British. The resident ones. We were used to seeing them going back and forth … they were always at least in twos … We took it for granted that they were there and we were not to mix with them or that we weren't to be rude to them … But these women came in and I couldn't understand why would Kilmihil be burned and my mother said, "What's on?" I had heard this rifle shooting or whatever it was. We had heard it but we didn't know what it meant and immediately after that a whole lot of the lads over [Highland Light Infantry], a platoon, ran past the house and they had the rifles at the ready in their hands and we hadn't seen that. I was talking to myself of course [laughs]. "Mellie, why are they bringing the guns?" They were all running, full tilt! We could hear the noise but didn't know what

it meant. They [the women] said, "There's a man killed. There's a man killed. There may be two of them killed. We'll be burned out of Kilmihil today." They were just hoping that they'd get home going in that direction before anyone would meet them. They'd be killed too if they were on the road. They'd take them as being part of the ambush of whatever.[13]

Mellie's memory moves to the very moment of the ambush. She heard the shots, saw the reaction of the local people and witnessed with her own eyes the hurried movements of soldiers called to engage in an incident of violence. Even at six, Mellie knew that something significant had occurred:

We were all ears then to know. The man was shot and he died and who was he and who died? It dribbled down to the fact that there was an RIC man shot and there was a local man shot. The RIC went to Mass in twos. They travelled in twos for protection and they always had their revolvers in their pockets. As well as that then of course, they knew there was a group of IRA in the parish and of course, their families and themselves were under suspicion. They were always being watched going up and goin' down. Their family were only doing the ordinary thing. But if you had [a] son or a cousin or a nephew or a niece [in the republican movement] you'd be watched. They were all going down to Mass and just as Fr Hayes, the Lord have mercy on him … he would be with the people but he couldn't say that. He'd have to be quiet. He heard the shooting. He went right out of the sacristy and the shooting was a little bit down from where he was … He said, "In the honour of God, whatever has happened," he said, "will ye do no more!" He went down, I suppose, to see could he give absolution to whoever was down. Both of them were Catholics. They were after coming out of Mass.

Whatever, whether 'twas bad management. 'Twas a wrong time, you know, to do it. There was a chap coming down that was taller in the group going down along. He was one of the boys [IRA] all right but he was a good height. That was John Breen now and I heard that he didn't do the shooting at all. That 'twas someone else did it, but someone from the back here shot the RIC man and he went down. The one that was beside him then, you see, turned around, immediately, and seeing the head over the others, he fired. He assumed that this was the man that fired the shot. He fired at him and he went down ...

Fr Hayes' request for them to cease operations worked, anyway. But I suppose they had some way of sending word to Ennis and within ten or fifteen minutes and I was still below at home, these lorries came in from Ennis ... flying off the road, filled with British military, out from the Ennis crowd. That was the fear then, that they'd go on the rampage. They had burnt different villages for similar offences. They'd set fire to a house and let it burn away and go into the pub and demand drink. Oh, they got it and when they got all the drink they wanted then they'd smash bottle and glasses, mirrors and all and leave the place in a shambles. But that didn't happen here that day.[14]

Across Kilmihil, people returned hurriedly to their homes and closed their doors. In the village, after a tense number of hours, the practical need to care for the wounded began to bring back some sense of calm. The wounding of Seán Breen was such that death was inevitable. He was removed to the home of his uncle, who ran a shop and public house in the village, and from there to the surgery of Dr Daly for a post-mortem the following day. On the evening of the ambush, Breen was treated with as much tenderness and care as possible, by locals who were eventually given access. Breen's father,

Michael, had earlier been turned away from his dying son by British forces. Aware that his injuries were fatal, Dr Daly administered palliative treatment. Fr Hayes prayed for a man who was already gone. His mother prayed harder, as she watched helplessly while her son 'moaned heavily … his powerful countenance … no longer discernible, his heart's blood flowing'.¹⁵ Their eyes were fixed on the dying young man and they did not notice the two young girls who gazed curiously in the window behind them:

> I was only six years and another girl and I, Dossy Clancy. We were there the two of us now on the evening when all this quietened down. The body of John Breen was brought down to the main street where Dr Daly was living … 'twas brought down to his dispensary. His house had the dispensary at the time … and he was left inside in his own front room on the couch. We wanted to know like children now, "What was it like to be shot?" We went up and stood outside the window. Children were not shy of looking in a window or a door because we went into each other's houses. We could see him [Breen] lying inside on the sofa. He was there, inert of course, but the people were there. He was unconscious; he died that evening. But of course, he had the priest and the doctor.¹⁶

When, days later, Breen was buried in his native Kilmihil, all businesses and houses were fully shuttered and the tricolour was displayed from each window. All farming was stopped in deference to the fallen republican. As mournful crowds moved slowly and quietly past the scene where panic and violence reigned just days earlier, a blizzard blew in the village of Kilmihil.¹⁷ Through the showers of falling sleet, mourners were able to see the arrival of an armoured car and the careful placement of Lewis machine guns in clear view of the public. One gun was trained on the coffin as they passed the RIC barracks and continued to Kilmihil graveyard.[18] Mellie recalled:

> I also remember the day of the funeral but of course we wouldn't be let out to the funeral. The place was thick with people. They came from all over ... I remember seeing them, going up and down. They used to say that place was black with people.[19]

Eleven days after the ambush, Catherine Breen wrote to her sister in Australia, expressing the sense of immeasurable pain she felt that day:

> Sorry that my letter is not one of joy. Perhaps the saddest in the history of our family. But we have one thing to look to with pride and joy that my darling child has been ever devoted to his religion and his country. It had been my wish to be with him in his last agony, and to offer his poor soul to God. He could not speak, but he moaned heavily. His powerful countenance was no longer discernible – his heart's blood flowing. He was a true soldier of Ireland. He gave all to Ireland. How many a lonely glen and valley did he call on his duty, he never missed and how he'd try not to let us know when he'd return. "Mother, I can use my silken paws sometimes like the cats." He was the most affectionate child that ever lived. If he wished he could have saved himself, but I hope his innocent death has saved the multitude.[20]

During my research, a collection of letters privately held for over nine decades in Buffalo, New York, was discovered. Having been given access to the collection, I was surprised to find a previously unpublished letter, handwritten by Catherine Breen on 11 October 1923. The Black and Tans were gone, her son had been dead for over three years and now Ireland was in the grip of an increasingly bitter Civil War. The letter, published for the first time in full below, bears powerful testimony to the enduring pain felt by Catherine, as well as her resilient belief in the cause of Irish freedom:

Our Lady's Hill,
Kiltumper,
11.10.23

My dear Mrs O'Gorman,

It's almost time I should write and thank you for your gift, which I appreciate very much. I expect both yourself and your boy got back to your family safe and sound. So dear old Ireland is in the balance again, with England and the orange at the heavy end. It's an anxious time now waiting for the turn of events. I wonder if the dead could speak what would they think of the whole situation. I am sending you a few papers together with Dr Mannix's farewell speech.[21] I know you have all the news in the Irish world, while we only get a sketch in the Free State papers. However, I don't feel like writing now, for alas 'How many dormant sympathies of sad recollections does Christmas time awaken'. I am enclosing the original photo of Seáns [sic], taken when on his way home from Dundalk jail in May 1918. He was almost twenty years then. The one I send you was also taken on the same day but it was copied out of a group and his shoulders and body did not come out so well. If you are taking any copy, I think this would be the best. If you ever find it convenient you may return it to me. It's the only one of the original copies I have. I expect all the home folks in Buffalo are well, especially the boys, our republican soldiers. How cruel they have been treated after their fight for freedom. Sometime when I'll be in better mood, I will write you a long letter and tell you about poor Seán, my poor dead boy. Michael wishes to be remembered to you and Martin. All the family join with me in wishing you a very Happy and prosperous New Year.

Lovingly your friend,

Mrs. C. Breen, Kilmihil[22]

In her letter, Catherine quoted the American writer and philosopher Elber Hubbard, when she pondered, 'How many dormant sympathies of sad recollections does Christmas time awaken?' The sadness and emotion emanates from the faded pages, bearing testimony to the pain she would carry to her grave decades later, in September 1947.

'Francie' – The Murder of Francis Murphy

While certain categories of memory and stories are easily triggered, other areas of remembrance are more deeply hidden and difficult to disclose. Legacies of the revolutionary period take many forms. Many of the most profound stories linger in silence. On 26 April 1965, in Ennistymon Hospital, Una Garvey from Glann, Ennistymon was about to enter a third day in a coma.[23] Her son, who was painfully aware that his mother was dying, sat beside her bed and lifted his head as his mother somehow began to move. Una Garvey gradually elevated herself on one elbow, enough to be able to reach her hand to where her rosary beads had been hanging since she entered the hospital three weeks earlier. She fumbled the beads in her weakened hands before gently kissing the crucifix and with her remaining strength she uttered just three words. Her son listened to his mother as he had never listened before. She whispered, 'Francie, Francie, Francie.' They were the last words that Una Garvey ever said. In 2011 her son remembered sadly that the following day his mother 'fell asleep forever'.

Forty-six years before she died, Una had held her dying fifteen-year-old brother in her arms, as he bled to death in their cottage in Glann, Ennistymon. Francis Murphy had been shot in the chest through the window, allegedly by British forces, as he sat reading by the fire on the night of 14 August 1919.[24] It was to her young brother, Francie, that she called at the end. A bullet's echo can thus last a long time when it ends the life of a family member. The case of Una Garvey illustrates how memory can be a very real part of a person's consciousness, even when it is not disclosed publicly. Flan Garvey, the nephew of Francis Murphy, was interviewed in 2011:

> An uncle of mine was fifteen when one night he was sitting beside the fireside in Glann in the homeplace. He was the only one up, the rest of them were gone to bed. He was reading with the old oil lamp, I suppose, or candle or whatever it was beside the fireplace and then suddenly there were shots fired and he was shot dead through the window from the front of the house. Those bullet marks were in the windows for years up until the 1950s. And my mother, the Lord have mercy on her, ran down out of her bed; she ran down and found him on the floor of course and he was bleeding. She was whispering the Act of Contrition into his ear when her father roared at her, "Una get back to bed, get back to bed they're still out there." But that was it; he was killed.[25]

Murphy's killing was characterised by the local Catholic priest at the time, Rev. Mullins, as a 'most foul, brutal and savage murder which took place in the parish', and he asserted 'it was murder which cried to the Heavens for vengeance'.[26] The incident was an ever-present, if largely unacknowledged, feature of the family's upbringing, a presence aided visibly by the bullet marks which remained embedded in the family home.²⁷ Flan Garvey spoke of a certain awareness of his uncle's story, but also of the fact that the details were never fully disclosed:

> I was born in 1943, so I presume my memory would go back to maybe age four or five. One thing that was always in our house was the rosary, the rosary was sacrosanct. I remember about my uncle Francie and the rosary, my mother never talked about this incident except twice a year … Both on the night of her brother's birthday and the night of the anniversary of his death, she would say, "We'll say the last decade of the rosary *as Gaeilge* for Uncle Francie" and that was it!²⁸

James Lynch, coroner for north Clare, opened an inquest into the incident on 15 August 1919. At the inquest Francie's father, John, a prominent member of the Gaelic League, former rural district councillor and member of Ennistymon Board of Guardians, informed those assembled that he had retired to bed at approximately 10.20 p.m., leaving his fifteen-year-old son reading by the fireside. Around two hours later he was woken from his sleep by the sound of loud gunshots and mortar falling in his room. Having rushed to the kitchen, he saw his son lying in a pool of blood. At the inquest Pete Connole, a night watchman for the West Clare Railway, gave evidence which supported the theory that the murder was carried out by British military forces. The motivation was said to have been revenge for the recent shooting of Sergeant O'Riordan and Constable Murphy by the local IRA, at a place called '81 Cross' on 4 August, shortly before the incident in Glann.

Another suggestion, that Francie Murphy's death was instead the result of a local land issue and that John Murphy had assisted a boycotted neighbour, has also lingered within social memory. There is abundant evidence that land conflicts were often violent and did result in brutal murders. However, the active and aggressive role of the military in pursuing those responsible for the deaths of Murphy and O'Riordan, including the arrest and interrogation of several innocent local people, as well as the reportedly hostile raiding of numerous local houses, reinforces the possibility of their involvement in Francie's death. Significantly, the inspector general of the RIC noted, in his private communications for August, that the bullet used was 'of a military pattern'.[29]

That the British were anxious to deflect attention from this case is shown by a minute sent to the commander-in-chief of the British forces in Ireland in the weeks after the murder. Sent by William Evelyn Wylie, the solicitor who prosecuted 160 rebels after the Easter Rising, it discouraged a public enquiry. Wylie pointed to 'matters which have happened in the District which would furnish material for cross examination'. Members of the military had broken windows of homes who had lights on after 7 p.m., held up a hotel in Lisdoonvarna with a revolver, threatened to shoot a Catholic priest in the street and intimidated locals with bayonets. Concerned for the British position, Wylie underlined how this would make 'an unpleasant impression' if made public and suggested that the military court of inquiry, held in secret, should be sufficient to exonerate the crown forces.[30]

Michael Knightly, who worked within the intelligence section of the 1st Battalion, Dublin IRA Brigade, was visiting Ennistymon on a separate issue the day after Murphy's murder. Knightly investigated the incident and reported to Arthur Griffith his firm belief that British crown forces were responsible. Griffith took the allegation seriously and engaged Patrick Lynch as the solicitor for the Murphy family.[31]

The jury that sat at the inquest into Francie's death concluded that the murder was carried out by the British military, who had been seen in the area on the night in question, as revenge for the shooting of the two policemen. The behaviour of crown forces over the following two years would certainly remove any doubt as to their capacity to exact revenge. The jury passed the following verdict: 'Francis Murphy, of Glann, Ennistymon was unlawfully and wilfully murdered ... by a bullet unlawfully and wilfully fired by members of the military ... which caused immediate death'.[32]

Although no monument is erected to the memory of Francie Murphy, the story remains a key moment in the period for the people of Ennistymon and the surrounding area. For Nora Canavan, who was eleven years of age when Francie was murdered, the event was a profoundly sad one for her community. In 2012 she remembered sadly: 'They fired in through the window and killed him ... a young lad. That was bad. Oh shur everyone was very upset. Oh, very, very upset.'[33] In Nora's neighbouring townland of Knockroe, P.J. Clancy, who over his life became increasingly interested in the revolutionary period, had also been aware of the incident:

> Oh God yes. Shur, I heard different stories ... I remember the bullet hole in the window. That stopped on and on. High up in the high pane you know. I was often wondering, why did someone fire so high up inside? ... I found out after that the lower panes were riddled but they left the top one. There had been several in the lower panes but they replaced the lower panes, you see.[34]

According to P.J., one local tradition suggested that Murphy 'was inclined to dress up a lot in Boy Scout [Fianna] uniform and they [British forces] had a set taken on him, you know, and that he was reading late that night'. Whatever the exact circumstance of Francie Murphy's death, on 14 August 1919 the lives of the Murphy family in Glann, Ennistymon were shattered by bullets fired from outside their home. A fifteen-year-old boy, who was reading by his own turf fire, had his life brutally ended.

When, ninety-two years later, his nephew was asked to recount the impact that this episode had, he explained how on occasion he would hear about his uncle's death from neighbours. At fairs, when it was discovered he was the nephew of Francie Murphy, this would also be discussed with deep sympathy. Within his own family, however, the story was rarely mentioned. Yet Flan revealed that when his uncle, Andrew (Francis Murphy's twin brother), returned from Australia a number of years previously, he decided to bring up the story of Francie. When Andrew began to cry inconsolably at the mention of his name, Flan became finally aware that such pain was perhaps best left within the fold of silence, and so he did not ask again. There the story rested, within the silence of a family, until a moment of profound disclosure brought it forth without a question to trigger it. It was towards the end of the interview in 2011 that Francie's nephew offered the profoundly personal memory which had enforced an appreciation in him of the way in which silence can linger for many years, over a memory:

> An awful strange thing happened, Tomás, in time. In 1965, when my mother lay dying in Ennistymon hospital. She was in a coma and the coma lasted for three days. And I was present for this because I have good faith, but if I wasn't present for this I would not believe it, no matter who would tell me. I was beside her bed in the middle of the three days, the second day, we'll say. She was lying on the bed, out of it for all intents and purposes. And whatever strength she got, she raised herself up from the pillow, far enough to be able to get

her hand to where her rosary beads were. She kissed the crucifix and said the following. And this is all she said at the end of her life ... "Francie, Francie, Francie". And it struck me. Well did she see him? What happened at that split second? But they were the last three words she ever spoke in her life.[35]

'Uncle Tom was shot and burnt': Tom Connole

Maureen Connole, who died in August 2011, was keenly aware of her role as 'the last of the Connoles in north Clare'. A year earlier, Maureen – then over ninety years of age – wrote to Clare MacDonagh in Melbourne, Australia, outlining some of the details surrounding her family's connection to the War of Independence. MacDonagh had submitted a questionnaire to Maureen, who was, as always, willing to communicate her family story. In the handwritten response, Maureen wrote about how a journey to America as a young woman revealed some of her own family connection to the period:

> On my first visit to USA on arrival at the customs in Boston, the head officer said, "Are you any relation of Joe Connole?" I said, "Yes, my father." He hugged me and cried. He said, "He saved my life when we arrived off the ships in Belfast [while being taken to Ballykinlar Internment Camp] when the riff-raff attacked us with bricks and bottles. He was fearless." The ship's captain threatened to fire on them [internees]. He [head customs officer] told me, "You are not staying in any hotel. You are my guest." This is how loyal they were.

In the correspondence, Maureen also reflected on the impact Joe Connole's involvement with the republican movement had on their family:

My mother had a terrifying time while my father was interned. It was not from British military but the auxiliary force, the 'Black and Tans'. They harassed her every night. They would search my cot and Nancy's [Maureen's sister] bed with rifles and bayonets. They painted the name over the door and poisoned her dogs and gave live bullets to the children.[36]

Maureen concluded her response to the curious Australian by stating: 'I feel very proud of the Connole name. No native ever calls me anything but M. Connole. I'm past ninety years so it seems I am the only person here who suffered from the troubles.'

In her response to Clare MacDonagh, Maureen made no mention of her uncle, Tom Connole. That was a deeper memory and one filled with as much pain as pride. Maureen spoke to me about him, but always with sadness and only after an explicit question. In Ennistymon, on the night of 22 September 1920, at approximately 9 p.m., the local town hall in Ennistymon was burned down, commencing a night of incomparable terror, a night that ended in the brutal murder of Tom.

The people of the town had predicted the night would be filled with dread. The Rineen ambush executed by the Mid Clare IRA Brigade earlier that day had left six police dead and enraged the military and police in the area. In a private tape recording conducted in 1978, Barney O'Higgins, a participant in the ambush, described the tranquillity of the morning of the IRA action. With other members of the 4th Battalion, O'Higgins had arrived in the townland of Leeds in the parish of Miltown Malbay at approximately 5 a.m. on 22 September:

> From Leeds hill you could see half of West Clare county. A lovely morning, no sign of life, no sound, cattle lying on the warm grass. The

only disturbance was the barking of dogs at the houses we passed by as much as to say, "Where are ye going at this early hour?"[37]

A short time later the men were in position, where they lay in wait for many hours before their target arrived from Ennistymon. Reflecting on the Black and Tans and RIC who regularly travelled that road, O'Higgins later commented: 'When they set out for Miltown that lovely morning, they did not think there was a force to stand up against them.'[38] In various strategic positions around Dromin hill, up to sixty IRA Volunteers waited and watched intensely for the Crossley tender to return from Miltown Malbay to its base in Ennistymon. An initial mix-up at the site meant that the tender was allowed to pass unmolested on its way to Miltown. It was determined to ensure its journey home would be less serene.[39] The waiting Volunteers then watched as a couple married that morning in Carrigaholt drove in a Ford car on their way to their honeymoon in the Spa town of Lisdoonvarna.[40] The smiling couple passed by, unaware they were moving through an ambush site and that serious violence would occur there only moments later. As the sound of the Ford faded, the crackle of a Crossley tender engine was heard. The ambush, which only lasted a matter of minutes, left all six occupants of the tender dead. One constable escaped but was tracked down and shot dead by two Volunteers below the ambush site.[41]

That night, as reprisals began in Ennistymon, Maureen Connole's uncle, Tom, a thirty-one-year-old secretary of the Irish Transport and General Workers' Union, was confronted at his home.[42] Connole, together with his twenty-four-year-old wife, Helena, and their two infant children were removed from their home, which was then set on fire.[43] The men who confronted Connole that night were approximately twenty-five members of the British military stationed in Ennistymon. While the Black and Tans played their part in the night's terror, the death of Connole was at the hands of the regular army, under the command of an officer. Despite the pleas of his wife, Connole was shot and thrown into his own burning home. His charred remains were found the following morning. The allegation that Connole was still alive when he was thrown into the fire remains firmly rooted in local belief.[44] James Queally from Cregg, Lahinch, who was born in 1863, recorded the belief when he was asked to contribute to the Schools' Folklore Scheme, eighteen years after the incident. In 1938 he noted that after the Rineen ambush, British soldiers 'found an insurance card in a boy's pocket' and that on that card was 'Connole, Ennistymon, Co. Clare'. He explained that the soldiers later made their way to Tom's home and affirmed that 'They caught Connole and they threw him into the middle of a blazing fire and burned him.'[45] While Connole's brother, Joseph, was a member of the IRA and was on a reserve list for the Rineen ambush, Tom does not seem to have been an active member.[46]

Helena Connole informed a court hearing four months after the incident that she had begged on her knees for her husband's life, but was dragged away by her feet by soldiers.[47] She then testified that she heard shots and saw her house go up in flames. On 11 October Connole's brother, Joe, wrote a letter, which was printed in *The Freeman's Journal*, underlining the agonising experience of his sister-in-law:

> She asked to be allowed to return to the cottage for a shawl to cover her half-naked child, who had just got out of bed, but this was also roughly refused and she was driven at a bayonet's point along a *botharín* to a neighbour's house … Immediately she saw her cottage on fire and heard two shots. These shots sent Tom Connole

to eternity ... that night the wife of Tom Connole prayed and wept and hoped that her husband was still alive.[48]

The following morning, 23 September, as smoke ascended from the town of Ennistymon, Helena Connole emerged nervous and frightened from an old farmhouse to begin searching in a vain hope for her young husband. At the same time, a young man was returning cautiously from farm work and observed the destruction in his native town. In 1985 Paddy O'Dwyer remembered his vision of Tom Connole's home:

> The following morning, I was comin' over milking the cows and I saw the smoke coming out the window, no roof. The house was roofless. There was two lads there and they were diggin' him out, taking him out and he was underneath the mortar and the slate, the whole thing collapsed in on top of him and there was nothing of the mortal remains only bones, all the flesh was burned away.[49]

On the hills above Ennistymon that morning was Tom Connole's brother, Joe, who, with other republicans, had worryingly observed the town of Ennistymon emit an ominous red glow towards the sky. Joe's daughter described the return of her father the following morning and the gradual realisation of what had taken place beneath that glow:

> He returned in the morning. He saw, they all saw from the country, the sky was red. They knew there was terrible work done. And he knew himself that the Rineen ambush was to take place because as I told you, five of them were left on reserve, he was one of them ... And the first people who were coming out to him, they were sympathising with him. They were coming out the church way, this way down. And

he thought, God did something happen his mother? She lived alone in the old family home in Church Street where she had a small shop as well. And he thought it was her and he called into her on the way down and she was fine. She [Joe Connole's mother] knew nothing until he came in home to Parliament Street and he heard it.⁵⁰

Joe was soon at the home of his brother where, with others, he found the charred remains. Three local men – Michael Dundon, Joe Flaherty and Denis Molloy – later gave evidence of finding the body of Connole. Flaherty testified that Connole 'was unrecognisable and a person could only see the bones. All the flesh was burned off but part of the chest remained.' A white bone pocketknife, a scissors and a half crown were used to identify the victim.⁵¹

For Maureen Connole, the story of her uncle, Tom, was an absent presence. She explained that her father 'never really wanted to talk about it ... unless my mother might tell us and he might confirm whatever she said':

> The thing that I always heard. That evening my father returned. He was 'on the run'. And there was this woman from Ennistymon and she was the cook and waitress and everything above in the [British] army barracks. The barracks was at the end of our street. He was just going in home. He was coming back. He'd do that now and again and stay a night and be gone again. And as she came towards him, she risked her life of course and her job to talk to him. But she spoke as she approached him and she said, "Joe, you're coming back the wrong day, go away, there will be trouble." And he waited at the door. She was going for messages. And on her way back now I don't know exactly what she told him: "I overheard it discussed at the dinner today. They said the Connoles are in for it tonight." It was the night my uncle was killed. And he went and he came back in the morning.⁵²

Patrick Connole was just four months old when he was hurriedly swept up by one hand of his mother, the other dragging his two-year-old brother, Jack. The sudden movement from the warmth of their home to the bleak cold of the September air may have been discernible to little Patrick. The shouting of soldiers, the crying of his mother and his brother, and the two loud bangs were all just disturbing noise to the infant. Over his life the sounds of that night formed a perpetual echo. Ninety-eight years later his daughter, Helena Marconetto, wrote to me from England:

> All I know is that it ruined my dad's whole life. He was a baby and his dad was snatched away from him. He never called his stepfather Dad. He always talked about his dad and always loved Ireland. His life would have been a lot happier if this incident had never happened. When he died at a young age, his older brother Jack came to the funeral. He couldn't wait to get back to Ireland, due to what the English had done in Ireland.

The incident became known to Helena when she was a child and was discussed often in the family home:

> My grandmother, from what I have been told, was left on the street with a baby (my dad) and a two-year-old. That night, my grandfather had stayed in their cottage because of his wife and children. Other men had fled the town as they were aware of the reprisals ... I was told by my grandmother that Tom had lent his coat to someone. Inside the pocket he had left something that had his name and address on. The Black and Tans found the coat and on that basis had killed an innocent man. My grandmother begged them not to kill him, she was running with him as they dragged him out of the cottage. While she was with her husband, another Black and Tan

told her that her cottage was burning down. Her children were asleep in the cottage so she had to run back to save her children. While she was trying to save her children, Tom was shot.[53] They then threw his body into the burning cottage and my grandmother was left without her husband and home.[54]

There is a slight difference in Helena's version to that of Joe Connole. While Helena had heard in her family tradition that her grandmother had run back to save the children, it seems she was instead a short distance up the road with her two sons, outside a neighbour's house, when her husband was shot. It also appears from Joe's account that she may not have been aware that her husband was dead until the following morning.

The reprisals in the three towns of Ennistymon, Lahinch and Miltown Malbay involved the burning of at least twenty-six houses and the deaths of six people, including Tom Connole. Not surprisingly, when recalling the case of Connole, the brutal nature of his death was stressed. Paddy O'Dwyer remarked how Connole was saying his rosary when an officer knocked on the door and demanded he come out:

> So it seems they took him out, they shot him on the road and they dragged him down ... there's a cross there in memory of him. Three of the soldiers sent the wife up the Pound Road and she had this child in her arms and they kept her covered with the rifles above ... He was dying at the time, in a dying condition. One of the officers said, "Take him up now," he says, the houses was in flames at the time, "and throw him into the flames." The other three and the officer dragged him up and the heat was so bad that the officer caught him in his arms and he only went half way and flung him in through the doorway into the flames. And the house was burning mad ... the

whole thing collapsed in on top of him and there was nothing of the mortal remains only bones, all the flesh was burned away.⁵⁵

P.J. Clancy visited with Maureen Connole and spoke to her about Tom. Clancy's parents were also involved in the republican movement:

> I went to Maureen Connole above and I was going till she died after that … She didn't talk that much entirely but she told me that his remains was able to fit inside in a little biscuit box, he was so badly burned there was only a handful of bones. It was supposed that they threw him into the blazing house and he not dead. She had the three bullets that they fired, I saw 'em because his brother [Joe Connole] went up the following morning and he found them outside across the road.⁵⁶

Later that year, at highly tense meetings between Archbishop of Perth Dr Patrick Clune and British Prime Minister David Lloyd George on 1 December 1920, the case of Connole was brought up. Rev. Monsignor J.T. McMahon, who was secretary to Clune in 1920, detailed how the young man whose wife was 'rocking the cradle' was shot point blank for having muttered some opposition to his house being burned. McMahon informed Lloyd George that 'as the young man screamed with the pain of the bullet, they lifted him and threw him into his blazing house'.⁵⁷

The first monument that related to Rineen was erected on 2 November 1947. The granite memorial, in the form of a Celtic cross, was installed on Circular Road, Ennistymon, and commemorated the death of Tom Connole.⁵⁸ A journalist in the *Clare Champion* reported that the erection of the monument to Connole, which occurred twenty-seven years after his death, occasioned a strong memory trigger to the broader reprisals that followed the Rineen ambush.[59] Interestingly, the monument in Ennistymon is dedicated to 'Volunteer Tom Connole', although it appears that while Connole's brother, Joe, was in the IRA, Tom was not.[60] While delivering the oration, William Murphy, a Fine Gael councillor, explicitly outlined the intention of the memorial, which 'would serve as a very noble cause as the years roll by'.[61]

CONCLUSION

In the century that has passed since the Black and Tans left Ireland, much has been said about that difficult time. Much more has lingered in silence. Very early in my research, the common response to my enquiries about the period from family members of potential interviewees was that 'they didn't want to talk about it'. When approached respectfully and sincerely, however, I have found that most people were not only open, but happy to contribute their memories. It is true that, in some cases, memories will remain hidden and will in time fade into our past, stories untold. However, a reticence to disclose does not necessarily translate into an irretrievable narrative. A determination to forget is not the same as an inability to remember. The sixteenth-century French philosopher Michel de Montaigne was correct when he shrewdly noted that '*Nothing fixes a thing so intensely in the memory as the wish to forget it.*'[1]

This book has shown that, in most cases, stories are just answers awaiting the question. For almost two decades I have asked the questions and have become enriched by the answers. In these stories are found both the landmarks and nuances of our history. Neat chronologies and linear sequences of events do not properly encapsulate the story of our people. For too long historians have retreated to the safety of statistics and information, reluctant to move towards the milieu of life. True history, I contend, is found in the reality of life and in a lived experience. The documentation of the memory of our past infuses our present understanding with a much deeper comprehension of who we were and who we are.

Over time, some have sought to probe deeper and revise the

narrative of that time. With the passing of decades, there has been much reflection and re-evaluation. Irrespective of that ever-increasing tendency, for the generation who were there and those who were the first to inherit the emotion-filled stories, theirs was an almost unshakable position. When asked during a radio interview in 2004 to characterise the Black and Tans, 100-year-old Paddy Gleeson sensed he was being encouraged to offer a rounded answer, more suited to the politically correct culture in which it was asked. The interviewer suggested that perhaps the Black and Tans were 'not as bad as they were made out to be' and the IRA 'not as good'. Having paused briefly, Paddy was rounded but emphatic:

> I can't give a character for 'em but I suppose there was decent men through 'em but *they* done all the burning and all the beating and *they* used to come to Mass on Sundays and take people away and *they* done in the four boys from Scariff.[2]

It is important to note that, while this book has not been able to engage in any significant way with memory from the perspective of the British side of the conflict, I have interviewed several people who had family connections to the RIC, Black and Tans and regular British Army in Ireland during this period, as well as the grandson of one man executed by the IRA on the allegation that he was a spy. While, inevitably, this was more challenging to encounter and elicit, the use of oral history to explore such dimensions of our past can shine a revealing light on the experience of those, who, in the context of social memory, found themselves on the losing side.

Republican violence was as real as was the violence of the Black and Tans. From 1918 to 1923 republicans in Clare killed at least thirty-five members of the combined British forces stationed in the county. In addition, at least three alleged informers were executed by the IRA. Micheál Brennan accepted in his memoir that the IRA had 'brought terror' to the people of east Clare. However, the undoubted suffering of the local population brought about in part by the IRA seems to have been eclipsed in popular imagination and memory by the indignation and bitterness directed towards the Black and Tans – those figures who were symbolically representative of British rule in Ireland. In stories from the period, an understanding prevailed: IRA violence was a targeted means towards the goal of Irish freedom, while Black and Tan violence was perceived as indiscriminate and aimed at suppressing that drive towards liberty.

Paddy Gleeson and his generation had witnessed what others have sought to interpret. For too long they remained silent, their knowledge often only recognised when they passed from this world, an airless lament. The generation who can tell us about the Black and Tans are now gone. Their story, some of which is preserved in this book, is our inheritance in all of its complexity and nuance.

On 1 February 1922, in the north Clare town of Ennistymon, large numbers of Black and Tans began to board the many lorries that waited to take them and their military colleagues towards Ennis. From there, they would take the outbound train for Dublin and then would disperse back to their homes. Their work in Ireland was almost done. Before they departed, local schoolchildren who had assembled to witness the much-anticipated withdrawal were heard shouting 'Up Rineen' and 'Up the IRA'.[3] From the midst of the group of assembled British forces, a pin was pulled from a hand grenade and the bomb thrown angrily into the gathering. As the crowd frantically peeled back from the bouncing missile, the internal workings of the weapon passed through its lethal four-second process. The explosive charge lit, blowing apart the grenade and leaving several people badly wounded.[4] Those final four seconds of the Black and Tan's presence in Ennistymon left their mark, a postscript to a story already full of violence.

Less than an hour later, three miles south of the town, a fourteen-year-old girl called Nora Canavan (then Nora Mullins) sat overlooking the road outside her home in Monreal. From her vantage point, Nora could see a series of lorries gradually moving east. This was not an unusual scene and, in the past, had invariably been met with caution and fear. However, on this occasion there was a greater sense of ease, for she knew that the British forces were passing her road for the last time. She watched intently as the last military lorry faded from view. For a long moment she stared at an absence. Nora then took a deep, slow intake of breath and exhaled a deflating sigh. Tension lifted and her shoulders relaxed as she released the fear that had firmly gripped her for over two years. She would never forget the Black and Tans. Ninety years later, her relief at that vision of departure was evident in her tone, her breathing and countenance as she recalled, 'There was terrible joy. Oh, my goodness tonight! And the last of them, they all had to pass off down to Ennis. I said that the country was overjoyed.'[5]

APPENDIX

EXPLORING MEMORY

This book is partially based on an in-depth examination of the oral history, tradition and social memory associated with the War of Independence in Co. Clare, which formed the basis for my doctorate at the University of Limerick, completed in 2015. That doctorate was an evolution of my long-held contention about the value and need for oral history and memory in the mosaic of historical sources.

At the age of ten, having found a revolver that dated from the War of Independence concealed within decades of growth in my townland of Ballymalone, I became enchanted with the period. It was not long before I realised that, in order to understand how such a weapon could come to be concealed in my own landscape, I would have to seek out older people to be my avenue towards enlightenment. It was many years later, however, that the notion about how the past is best understood crystallised in my mind. The War of Independence, fought between a young volunteer force and a centuries-old empire, had been played out in my townland. The gun was the tangible evidence, physical remains concealed by time, nature and neglect. In physical form, some of these remnants of the war were hidden within the walls, secluded under the thatch or buried in the corner of a backward field, while others were disposed of to divest a family of its past. Others still made their way to museums in order to preserve family pride and history, and more were integrated into garden ornaments or became household keepsakes, proud evocations of a family's contribution to Irish freedom. Some lay where they were left and remain undiscovered. These artefacts, however, are only the physical remains of a story deeply embedded in the consciousness of the Irish people.

The War of Independence happened at a local level. Its impact was felt most powerfully, was understood most intimately and endured most profoundly at that local level. It follows that, in order to more deeply understand the period, the local experience should be a central focus. In this book I have argued that memory is the optimal pathway towards the recovery of that experience and that, in order to better understand the past, it is necessary to engage meaningfully with memory deep in the consciousness of local people. As historians, if our endeavour is to bring about a clearer understanding of what actually happened during a particular period or event, then we must engage with all opportunities to place ourselves close to the reality of that time. In order to address the deficit in understanding between those who remember and those who seek to interpret, the historian must, therefore, take an informed look through the lens of memory.[1]

'The time of the Tans', or the Irish War of Independence, was the temporal landmark that many people born in the early part of the twentieth century used to situate their lives within the chronology of modern Irish history. To be born during the period usually meant some association with an incident where the war came to their childhood doors. To be born in the years that followed meant that its shadow hung over most conversations and dominated discussions of the past. After almost twenty years of intensive collection work, it is evident that this chronological positioning prevailed in most parts of not just Clare, but the whole of Ireland. A 2010 socio-economic study into the post-independence generation in Co. Clare noted that the War of

Independence was clearly a key reference point for their life, much as Guy Beiner identified the 1798 Rebellion as 'an evocative category in Irish national historical consciousness' for the Irish of the nineteenth century.[1]

From a politico-military perspective, Clare offered a suitable site of research, with IRA activity largely developed along parochial and county lines. In January 1917 Clare was formed into one brigade, having previously been part of the Limerick area. This territorialisation was later consolidated and narrowed further when three brigade areas were established in east, west and mid Clare.[2]

In addition to its suitability from the above perspectives, throughout the twentieth century Clare remained a distinctly rural county. Consequently, the majority of villages and parishes maintained a similar composition to the county of the 1920s.[3] As a result, memory and oral tradition associated with the revolutionary period were more easily preserved, particularly in the rural communities. Therefore, this study evolved in the confidence that Clare offered a suitable location for engineering the confluence of history, folklore and memory in order to arrive at a more comprehensive, inclusive and complete narrative on the revolutionary period.

Recent advances in technology have also had a significant impact on the ability of oral historians and collectors to document and interpret information at greater speed and efficiency.[4] Greater technological capacity, as well as the emergence of oral history as a credible academic discipline, has led to its application across a range of subject areas and, in particular, to a greater attention to the notion of a 'history from below'.[5] Its global application has been an enlightening force in many parts of the world and has assisted in preserving the identity of persecuted peoples. In some cases, only memory can connect exiles to their native land.

Numerous international examples illuminate the value of memory to nations, particularly those who have suffered occupation. For example, an oral history project into the memory of 'Al-Nakbah', or the Nakba, in 1948 found that the widespread destruction of Palestinian homes, architecture and historic sites, which paralleled the creation and development of the state of Israel, meant that memory became increasingly important. Palestinians use the term Nakba, which means catastrophe or disaster, to symbolise the historic moment they believe their country was occupied in order to forcibly create the state of Israel. In this case, with many Palestinians expelled from their country, the only connection to their former homes was memory at individual and collective levels.[6] For many Israelis, the same period is interpreted differently, as the Israeli War of Independence or War of Liberation.

Thus, memory is a global phenomenon that can illuminate the history of a remote townland in east Clare and help bring understanding to conflicts in various parts of the world. I submit that oral history as a discipline and a resource must now be elevated to its rightful place in historical circles. Through its use, we can discover the fragments that assist us in painting a picture containing all the richness and complexity that makes up our past.

ENDNOTES

A Note on Transcription
1. The term derives from an old process of separating the fibres of flax by beating them. A 'scutch' was a wooden implement used in this process. The term found its way into the local vernacular as a way of describing inflicting violence on someone.

Introduction
1. The two IRA Volunteers had been arrested on suspicion of involvement in the killing of a magistrate, Captain Alan Lendrum, the previous September. Both men suffered extreme torture before their eventual deaths at the hands of British forces.
2. Conor Mac Clúin (known popularly as Conor Clune), was a native of Quin who had spent the last years of his young life working with the historian, nationalist and later chief herald of Ireland, Edward Mac Lysaght, in Tuamgraney. There, he and Mac Lysaght had developed a thriving Nua-Gaeltacht. In documents I have seen with Conor's signature, he always signed himself as Conor Mac Clúin. It was only after he died that he became known popularly as Conor Clune, but it is important to defer to his own preferred spelling. Although Mac Clúin is often described as a Volunteer, he was not a member of the IRA.
3. Catherine Talty Collection, Correspondence, Molly Moroney, Chicago, USA, to Mary Moroney, Clounlaheen, Co. Clare, 17 November 1921.
4. Whelan, Bernadette, *United States Foreign Policy and Ireland: From Empire to Independence, 1913–29* (Dublin, Four Courts, 2006), pp. 260–1.

5   The Fenian Brotherhood or 'Fenians' was a name used to describe an underground movement of Irish republicans who from 1858 sought to utilise any means necessary to achieve Irish independence. They were active in both Ireland and America and led an unsuccessful rebellion in 1867.

6   Muriel MacSwiney was the widow of the Sinn Féin lord mayor of Cork, Terence MacSwiney, who died after seventy-four days on hunger strike in Brixton prison in October 1920. Muriel spent a number of months touring America and fundraising for the republican movement. The RIC men Molly mentions had resigned in protest at the behaviour of their colleagues in the Black and Tans.

7   Catherine Talty Collection, correspondence, Molly Moroney to Mary Moroney, 13 December 1921.

8   *Ibid.*

9   Seán Talty from Dunsallagh joined the IRA in the late 1920s. As a child, he listened to his mother Margaret read to neighbours about events in the Tan war across Co. Clare and remembered 'you could hear a pin drop'. In June 1940 he was interned with several other republicans from west Clare in the Curragh in Co. Kildare, where he was held for three years. Seán was featured in Uinseann MacEoin's *The IRA in the Twilight Years, 1923–1948* (Dublin, Argenta Publications, 1997), pp. 826–36. Seán and Catherine were married on St Patrick's Day, 1949.

10 Catherine Talty, Clounlaheen, Mullagh, 31 March 2011.

11 Jimmy Gleeson, Coore, Co. Clare, 16 June 2011.

12 In Co. Clare, the tradition of 'cuaird' or social visiting was a central part of life in the past. It involved the visiting of a selected house, usually in the wintertime when stories would be told and the news of the community disseminated. The practice helped ensure the preservation of oral tradition and local history, particularly in rural

parts of the county.
13 Seán Kiely, O'Callaghan's Mills, Co. Clare, 22 March 2014.
14 Hopkinson, Michael, *The Irish War of Independence* (Dublin, McGill-Queen's University Press, 2002), pp. 192–7; Ferriter, Diarmuid, *The Transformation of Ireland: 1900–2000* (London, Profile Books, 2004), p. 216.
15 Hopkinson (2002), pp. 201–2; McConville, Seán, *Irish Political Prisoners, 1848–1922: Theatres of War* (London, Routledge, 2003), p. 697.
16 Ó Ruairc, Pádraig Óg, *Blood On the Banner: The Republican Struggle in Clare* (Cork, Mercier Press, 2009), pp. 325–31.
17 Sheehan, William, *British Voices from the Irish War of Independence 1918–1921: The Words of British Servicemen Who Were There* (Cork, Collins Press, 2007), p. 100.
18 Military Service Pensions Collection, 'Organization and Membership Files', http://mspcsearch.militaryarchives.ie/brief.aspx (accessed 22 May 2014).
19 McKenna, Joseph, *Guerrilla Warfare in the Irish War of Independence, 1919–1921* (Carolina, McFarland & Co., 2011), p. 124.
20 Cuimhneamh an Chláir Archive (hereafter CACA), interview with Kathleen Nash, Roscrea, Co. Tipperary, 11 October 2009.

1 'The criminals of England'

1   Ainsworth, John, 'The Black & Tans and Auxiliaries in Ireland, 1920–1921: Their Origins, Roles and Legacy', paper presented to the Annual Conference of the Queensland History Teachers' Association in Brisbane, 12 May 2001.
2   Dwyer, T. Ryle, *Tans, Terror and Troubles: Kerry's Real Fighting Story 1913–1923* (Cork, 2001), p. 183; Ryan, Meda, *Tom Barry: IRA Freedom Fighter* (Cork, 2003), p. 15; W. J. Lowe, 'Who were the Black-and-Tans?', *History Ireland*, issue 3, vol. 12 (Autumn

2004).

3   For a treatment of the racism towards the Irish in late nineteenth-century Britain, see Anthony S. Wohl, 'Racism and Anti-Irish Prejudice in Victorian England' on The Victorian Web: www.victorianweb.org/history/race/Racism.html (accessed 23 January 2018).

4   Brigadier Frederick Clarke, quoted in Sheehan (2007), p. 38.

5   Leeson, David, *The Black and Tans: British Police and Auxiliaries in the Irish War of Independence, 1920–1921* (Oxford, Oxford University Press, 2011).

6   Shanahan, Eoin, 'The Blackened Tans', *Clare Champion*, 1 November 2013.

7   CACA, interview with Martin Walsh, Creevagh, Mullagh, 7 July 2011 and interview with Seán Kiely, Claremount, O'Callaghan's Mills, Co. Clare, 22 March 2014.

8   National Folklore Collection Schools' Folklore Scheme (hereafter referred to as NFCS) Vol. 622, p. 297, John Fitzgerald, Milford, Miltown Malbay, Co. Clare; collector: Mary Fitzgerald, Miltown Girls School, Co. Clare; teacher: Una Bean Uí Bhrián.

9   NFCS Vol. 622: p. 301; Mrs P. O'Brien, St Senan's, Miltown Malbay; collector: Máire Ní Bhrian, Miltown Girls School, Co. Clare; teacher: Una Bean Uí Bhrián.

10 NFCS Vol. 622: p. 401; John Woulfe, Miltown Malbay; collector: Joe Woulfe, Miltown Boys National School; teacher: Pádraig Ó Brían.

11 NFCS Vol. p. 622: 306, Mrs Kelly, Church St, Miltown Malbay; collector: Teresa Kelly, Miltown Girls School, Co. Clare; teacher: Una Bean Uí Bhrián.

12 Kautt, William, *The Anglo-Irish War, 1916–1921, The People's War* (America, Praeger, 1999), p. 89.

13 CACA, interview with Tom Brennan, Chicago, USA, 17 February

2010.

14 'Black and Tans', British House of Commons, 3 November 1920, Vol. 134, c383W, http://hansard.millbanksystems.com/written_answers/1920/nov/03/black-and-tans (accessed 12 June 2011).

15 Private J. P. Swindlehurst, quoted in Sheehan (2007), p. 13.

16 Major General Douglas Wimberley, quoted in Sheehan (2007), p. 187.

17 Ainsworth, 'The Black & Tans and Auxiliaries in Ireland'.

18 CACA, interview with J.P. Guinnane and Paddy Clancy, Kilkishen, Co. Clare, 3 November 2010. The interview was arranged and attended by Mike Hogan, John Lenihan and Matt O'Donovan from Kilkishen.

19 CACA, interview with Flan O'Brien, Ballymalone, Tuamgraney Co. Clare, 22 October 2008.

20 P.J. Clancy, Lahinch, Co. Clare, 28 November 2013.

21 P.J. is almost certainly referring to the Jallianwala Bagh massacre (also known as the Amritsar massacre), which took place on 13 April 1919. The British Indian Army, under Colonel Reginald Dyer, fired on a crowd of unarmed protesters, mostly Sikhs, who had gathered to protest the deportation of two Indian national leaders. British reports indicated that 379 were killed, while Indian reports suggest the figure is closer to 1,000: see Narain, Savita, *The Jallianwala Bagh Massacre* (USA, Lancer Publishers, 2013).

22 CACA, interview with Maureen Connole, Ennistymon, Co. Clare, 7 May 2008.

23 Peggy Hogan, Feakle, Co. Clare, 18 February 2013.

24 Joe 'Jack' Sexton, Mullagh, Co. Clare, 16 June 2009.

25 Michael Howard, Tarmon, Kilrush, Co. Clare, 10 January 2011.

26 Kathleen Nash, 11 October 2009.

27 Joe 'Jack' Sexton, 16 June 2009.

28 Martin Walsh, 7 July 2011. Ironically in 1949, as an emigrant

in London, Walsh met a member of the British forces who was stationed in Co. Clare during 'the Black and Tan time' and the latter helped secure the young Clare man work in his newfound home.
29 Seán O'Halloran, Noughaval, Kilfenora, Co. Clare, 25 April 2012.
30 Interview for the Shannon Social History Project (SSHP) with John Murnane on 26 April 2012 (interviewed by Olive Carey).
31 Catherine Talty, 5 July 2013.
32 CACA, interview with Mary Murrihy, Miltown Malbay, Co. Clare, 12 October 2009.
33 CACA, interview with Micheál O'Connell, Moy, Co. Clare, 12 October 2009.
34 The Rineen ambush occurred on 22 September 1920 on the road between Ennistymon and Lahinch. Six members of a Black and Tan/RIC patrol were ambushed and killed by a considerable, if poorly armed, IRA force comprised of between fifty and sixty Volunteers. The ambush party were all members of the 4th Battalion, Mid Clare IRA Brigade. The resultant reprisals later that night by the British Army and the police in the three north Clare towns of Ennistymon, Lahinch and Miltown Malbay left five civilians and one active IRA Volunteer dead.
35 Billy Malone, Miltown Malbay, Co. Clare, 25 October 2013.
36 Nora Canavan, Doolin, Co. Clare, 20 April 2012.
37 In 1928, as a widower, Feilding married Kathleen Emmet of New York, the great-grandniece of the Irish revolutionary Robert Emmet.
38 'Irish Administration', British House of Commons Debate, 21 February 1921, Vol. 138, c605: http://hansard.millbanksystems.com/commons/1921/feb/21/irish-administration (accessed 4 June 2011).
39 Margaret Hoey, Carrigoran, Newmarket-on-Fergus, Co. Clare, 14

November 2008.
40 The 'Evicted Field' is the current hurling ground of Bodyke GAA Club and is situated in Tuamgraney. The 'Cathsaoireach' is across the road from the southern end of the hurling field and was the burial ground for the poor of east Clare during the Irish Famine (1845–51).
41 Field recording with Paddy Gleeson, 12 April 2009.
42 Margaret Hoey, 12 January 2009.
43 *Ibid.*
44 CACA, interview with Mae Tuohy, Feakle, Co. Clare, 13 April 2011.
45 *Ibid.*
46 Interview with Mae Tuohy, Feakle, Co. Clare, 13 April 2011.
47 Bureau of Military History Witness Statement (hereafter BMH WS) 983, Timothy Tuohy, pp. 20–1; 'Feakle Burnings', *Clare Champion*, 5 February 1921, p. 3.
48 Michael Howard, 14 December 2010. In this case, the number of guns is likely to be somewhat exaggerated, but it is certain that the Howards' was a safe house where the IRA frequently gathered.
49 Field recording with Michael Howard, 15 June 2011.
50 *Ibid.*, 16 June 2011.
51 Mick Ryan, Clonlara, Co. Clare, 10 December 2013.
52 East Clare IRA Brigade Volunteers Michael 'Brud' McMahon, Alfie Rodgers and Martin Gildea and civilian Michael Egan became known as 'the Scariff Martyrs' after their torture and murder by British forces on the night of 16 November 1920 on the Bridge of Killaloe. The four men had earlier been captured by members of G Division of the Auxiliaries, who were stationed at the Lakeside Hotel in Ballina, Tipperary. After being captured in Williamstown House, Whitegate, they were brought by boat to the Lakeside Hotel, where they were tortured for a number of

hours. They were then released to the RIC and Black and Tans, who shot the four men dead as they were being brought across the bridge connecting Ballina to Killaloe. The subsequent military court of inquiry claimed that the four men had attempted to escape. This has been largely discredited by both historians and local tradition. A monument to their memory was integrated into the north parapet of the bridge in 1923. The four men are buried side by side in Scariff churchyard.

53 Kathleen Nash, 11 October 2009.
54 During the Civil War Dan Crawford went on hunger strike as an anti-Treaty prisoner and died from its effects in October 1924, soon after his release. He is buried in Killernan Cemetery.
55 Mary Murrihy, 12 October 2009.
56 *Ibid.*
57 The Monreal ambush took place in the townland of Monreal South, three miles from the north Clare town of Ennistymon, on 18 December 1920. The ambush, under the command of Joe Barrett, Peadar O'Loughlin and Ignatius O'Neill, was well prepared and executed. However, there has been some controversy over its success, with Barrett claiming many decades later that a significant number of the British forces attacked were killed, while others involved maintained that there were no casualties on either side.
58 Nora Canavan, 25 April 2012.
59 CACA, interview with Paddy and Kitty McGough, Inagh, Co. Clare, 14 January 2011.
60 Mac Mathúna, Seosamh, *Kilfarboy: A History of a West Clare Parish* (Clare, 1978), p. 87.
61 Paddy and his father, Michael McGough, were later contracted to build and install the commemorative monument to the Rineen ambush, which was officially unveiled in 1957 by Bishop of Killaloe Dr Rodgers.

62 P.J. Clancy, 30 May 2012.
63 *Ibid.*
64 Nora Canavan, 20 April 2012 (interviewed by Frances Madigan).
65 Matthew Birmingham, Moyasta, Co. Clare, 5 January 2012.
66 *Ibid.*, 16 April 2012.
67 *Ibid.*, 5 January 2012.
68 John O'Connell, Labasheeda, Co. Clare, 19 October 2012.
69 Jamie Corbett was born in May 1892 to John and Susan Corbett. During the War of Independence he spent a period of time in Crumlin Road jail. In the Civil War he took the pro-Treaty side and was in Kildysart Barracks when it was attacked by anti-Treaty forces. He later married Lillie Stevens from Cranny and lived in Galway until he died in 1980. Correspondence from John Corbett to me, 15 January 2018.
70 John O'Connell, 19 October 2012.
71 *Ibid.*
72 CACA, interview with Michael 'Hooky' Farrell, Tintrim, Whitegate, Co. Clare, 26 April 2011.
73 *Ibid.*
74 Martin Walsh, 7 July 2011.
75 Timmy Ryan, Kilmihil, Co. Clare, 21 December 2008.
76 Palkie McNamara, Killaloe, Co. Clare, 22 November 2011.
77 Ó Súilleabháin, Micheál, *Where Mountainy Men Have Sown: War and Peace in Rebel Cork in the Turbulent Years 1916–21* (Kerry, Anvil Books, 1965), pp. 8–9.
78 John S. Kelly, private collection, interview with Tommy Bolton, Tuamgraney, Co. Clare, 11 June 1989 (copy in my possession).
79 Personal folklore journal entry, 13 March 1996 (author's collection).
80 Mary Murrihy, 12 October 2009.
81 John O'Connell, 16 October 2012.
82 Gerome Griffin, Ballyea, Co. Clare, 12 May 2005.

83 Captain Rigby was commander of the local military unit stationed in Scariff during the War of Independence. A homemade bomb was at one stage thrown into the back premises of Mrs Moroney's, where he was staying.
84 Michael O'Gorman, 27 September 2011.
85 CACA, interview with Seamus O'Donnell, 26 September 2011 (interviewed by Geraldine Greene).
86 Edward Lynch, BMH WS 1333, p. 10.
87 'Sensational Report from Miltown', *Clare Champion*, 23 October 1920, p. 3; 'Another Miltown Malbay Tragedy', *Saturday Record*, 30 October 1920, p. 6. A British military court of inquiry presented an alternative account, which suggested that the soldiers were attacked by 'civilians' with pitchforks and that in the ensuing confusion, Lynch was shot by accident: National Archives, Kew (hereafter NAUK), War Office papers (hereafter WO) WO 35/153A; WO 35/89.
88 Charlie Lynch, Breaffa North, Co. Clare, 21 February 2014.
89 *Ibid.*
90 Despite being 'wanted' by the Clare IRA, McPherson escaped and returned to Scotland.
91 Charlie Lynch, 21 February 2014.

2 'Run for it'

1 J.P. Guinnane and Paddy Clancy, 3 November 2010.
2 SSHP, John Murnane on 26 April 2012.
3 This is most likely William A. Bentley, a former lieutenant colonel in the Clare Militia and head of the Bentley family in 1920. The Bentley family received land in Co. Clare in the mid seventeenth century and ran an estate of over 2,000 acres in Broadford until the twentieth century. Digby Bentley was the last of the family to reside in Hurlerstown House in Broadford, which he did until he

died in 1952. According to a story collected by Kathleen Gunning in 1938, an officer in the Cromwellian army returning from the siege of Limerick (1691) camped close to the site and was given 'all of the country that he could see from the townland of Mongbouee where the camp was situated' for his services to the army.

4   CACA, interview with Johnny Doyle, Broadford, 20 October 2011.
5   John Dillon's uncle, John Molony, had been killed in 1881 during a dispute between the tenants and landlord on the O'Callaghan estate, later known in local folk memory as 'The Battle of Bodyke'. The killing of Molony in 1881 encouraged his nephew to later become an active IRA fighter during the War of Independence. In the 1911 Census, his name was filled out as Seághan Uí Diullún.
6   Flan O'Brien, Ballymalone, Tuamgraney Co. Clare, 22 October 2008.
7   *Ibid.*
8   Annie Noonan, Croom, Co. Limerick, 24 June 2013.
9   Seán Kiely, 10 April 2018.
10 Bridget 'Baba' Durack, Tuamgraney, Co. Clare, 9 October 2008.
11 Annamae McNamara, Ballymalone, Tuamgraney, Co. Clare, 12 November 2017.
12 John Michael Tobin, Laccaroe, Feakle, Co. Clare, 11 March 2013.
13 Peadar Clancy from Cranny in west Clare was a senior republican in the Dublin Brigade of the IRA. On 21 November 1920 Clancy, together with his comrade Dick McKee and Conor Mac Clúin (Clune), was tortured and murdered in Dublin Castle by members of F Company of the Auxiliaries. Mac Clúin had travelled to Dublin from east Clare with the historian and genealogist Edward Mac Lysaght on Gaelic League business and was not a member of the IRA.
14 Morgan 'Morgie' O'Connell, Cranny, Co. Clare, 9 June 2012.

ENDNOTES 285

15 Maeve Hayes, Killaloe, Co. Clare, 10 November 2017.
16 'Collecting the rates' referred to the collection of statutory charges from local businesses, the income of which was used to part fund the local authority. By 1920 the republican movement had assumed this role as part of their gradual takeover of administrative power in Ireland.
17 A *súgán* was a chair made from woven straw ropes and was a feature of most rural Irish houses. More specifically, the *súgán* referred to the rope but became the term used for the chair.
18 Maeve Hayes, Killaloe, Co. Clare, 10 November 2017.
19 Jimmy Hanrahan, Ennis, Co. Clare, 12 April 2012.
20 Katie McCormack had been committed to Irish republicanism long before the Easter Rising of 1916. She sheltered republicans in her hotel in Ennistymon, including Ernest Blythe, Eamon Waldron and Liam Mellows, and continued to actively support men 'on the run' during the War of Independence. In the Irish Civil War, Katie took a firmly anti-Treaty position and undertook two hunger strikes in Kilmainham. After Katie died in 1943, the press recorded that 'the large concourse at the funeral paid fitting tribute to a life devoted to Ireland's Freedom. A loyal member of Cumann na mBan, her house and her time were always at the disposal of the boys on the run.'
21 Teasie McCormack, Kilfenora, Co. Clare, 25 April 2012.
22 Catherine Talty, 31 October 2013.
23 Michael O'Gorman, 27 September 2011.
24 *Ibid.*
25 Richard Brangan Baker was a Methodist from Blackrock in Cork, who was a bicycle merchant with businesses in many parts of Ireland including Fermoy in Cork and Ennis in Co. Clare.
26 John O'Connell, 13 September 2011.
27 *Ibid.*, 13 September 2011. Another local story sees Paddy Clancy

again surrounded in a church, this time on the occasion of a Mass for the soul of Peadar Clancy, who had been murdered in Dublin. In this story, Paddy and another IRA Volunteer, Martin Corry from Cranny, remain in the church and wait for the Black and Tans to go: see Ó Comhraí, Cormac and Ó Comhraí, Stiofán, *Peadar Clancy: Easter Rising Hero, Bloody Sunday Martyr* (Galway, Cranny Publications, 2016).
28 The Glenwood ambush on 20 January 1921 was the single biggest military operation undertaken in the East Clare IRA Brigade area. On the road between Broadford and Sixmilebridge, thirty-seven members of the East Clare IRA Brigade ambushed a contingent of eight police, killing six. Two escaped. There followed significant reprisals and burnings but, unlike after the Rineen ambush of September 1920, no civilian died as a result.
29 J.P. Guinnane and Paddy Clancy, 3 November 2010.
30 *Ibid.*
31 Joseph Clancy, BMH WS 1370, pp. 6–7.
32 After increasing attacks on Belfast Catholics by unionists from 1920, Dáil Éireann voted for a boycott of all Belfast goods. Sinn Féin proposed the boycott in response to the attacks but also to demonstrate that it could damage unionist businesses and make partition impossible. The boat referred to by Michael McMahon (*The Glenkoy*) was burned as part of the boycott.
33 Michael 'Marshall' McMahon and John Cleary, Kildysart, Co. Clare, 10 January 2011.
34 Morgan 'Morgie' O'Connell, 9 June 2012.
35 'Constable killed in Kilrush', *The Irish Times*, 23 August 1920.
36 Michael Howard, 10 January 2011.
37 Micheál O'Connell (Querrin) Collection, interview with Jack Dunleavy, Kilrush, Co. Clare, 12 June 2008.
38 Catherine Talty, 31 October 2013.

39   Gleeson Collections, West Clare IRA Papers, Patrick McMahon, 4th Battalion Volunteer. (Signed by Jeremiah Killeen, O/C 4th Battalion, West Clare Brigade.)
40   Kearns, Kevin C., *Dublin Tenement Life: An Oral History* (Dublin, Gill & Macmillan, 2006), p. 84.
41   Paddy Gleeson, 15 May 2004.
42   The townland was incorrectly spelled as 'Kielty' in press reports.
43   'Of Enormous Importance', *Clare Champion*, 29 January 1921, p. 1.
44   Hopkinson (2002), p. 80; Williams, W. J., *Report of the Irish White Cross to 31st August, 1922* (Dublin, Martin Lester Ltd, 1922), p. 48. For details of the extent and effect of reprisals by crown forces against the civilian population in Ireland see 'Chronicle of Events in Irish Daily Independent', Liaison Papers 1921–1922, Military Archives Dublin, Box 1, LE 1/1.
45   Breathneach, Seamus, *The Irish Police: From Earliest Times to the Present Day* (Dublin, Anvil Books, 1974), p. 90.
46   Ó Ruairc (2009), p. 127.
47   O'Malley, Ernie, *Raids and Rallies* (Dublin, Anvil Books, 1982), p. 116.
48   Liam Haugh, BMH WS 474, p. 19. Commonly referred to as 'Bill' Haugh.
49   CLCCA/PP/8.1, 'Letter from Lahinch detailing Rineen reprisals' September 1920.
50   NFCS Vol. 586: p. 27; contributor unnamed; collector: Sheila Baylee, Belvoir National School, Co. Clare; teacher: Bríd Ní Chadhla.
51   Micheál Brennan, BMH WS 1068, p. 74.
52   Johnny Doyle, 20 October 2011; Patrick Savage was, in 1921, a twenty-five-year-old member of the East Clare IRA Brigade.
53   J.P. Guinnane and Paddy Clancy, 3 November 2010. The two members of the Black and Tans who escaped were Constable Selve and Sergeant Egan.

54 *Ibid.*
55 Nora Canavan, 20 April 2012.
56 *Ibid.*, 25 April 2012.
57 Paddy and Kitty McGough, 14 January 2011.
58 Margaret Hoey, 12 January 2009 (video recording conducted by Matt Kelly of Matt Kelly Productions).
59 'Ambush at Clonloum', *Clare Champion*, 22 January 1921, p. 5.
60 Phil and Kitty McGrath, Dublin, 4 April 2014.
61 *Ibid.*
62 Phil McGrath Collection, Correspondence, Pat 'Thade' McGrath to his sister Kit, January 1921. Tom McGrath is buried in Glasnevin Cemetery in Dublin, adjacent to Arthur Griffith. Pat died in 1959 and is buried in Killuran graveyard in O'Callaghan's Mills, Co. Clare.
63 Mick Ryan, Sallybank, Clonlara, Co. Clare, 10 December 2013.
64 *Ibid.*
65 Tom Brennan, 17 February 2010.
66 'Military Service Pensions Applications', Cumann na mBan Clare, http://mspcsearch.militaryarchives.ie/brief.aspx (accessed 3 July 2015).
67 McGarry, Fearghal, 'Too many histories? The Bureau of Military History and Easter 1916', in *History Ireland*, issue 6, vol. 19 (Nov/Dec 2011).
68 'Nan's Struggle Commemorated', *Clare People*, 25 May 2010, p. 56.
69 The plaque can be seen at the East Clare Memorial Park in Tuamgraney.
70 Galvin Collection, letter from Mollie Lenihan to Kathleen Foley, 21 January 1937.
71 *Ibid.*, handwritten account by Kathleen Foley, 13 March 1935.
72 'De Valera Addresses Historical Ennis Meeting', *Clare Champion*, 6 November 1971, p. 6.

73 *Ibid.*
74 'More arrests', *Clare Champion*, 23 July 1917, p. 1; 'Volunteers arrested in Clare', *Clare Champion*, 8 August 1917, p. 1.
75 CACA, interview with Madeline Kileen, Ennis, Co. Clare, 30 April 2012 (interviewed by Linda Quinn).
76 J.P. Guinnane and Paddy Clancy, 3 November 2010.
77 In an oral history of Dublin's tenements, one interviewee recalled his mother having several miscarriages due to repeated shooting and raids by Black and Tans. See Kearns (2006), p. 62.
78 Tom Brennan, 17 February 2010.
79 *Ibid.*
80 Mick Ryan, 10 December 2013.
81 Pat O'Halloran, 8 November 2008; 1 October 2010.
82 Teasie McCormack, 25 April 2012.
83 'The Late Miss C. McCormack', *Clare Champion*, 3 January 1944.
84 Micheál, Austin and Patrick Brennan were active members of the East Clare IRA Brigade who adopted a pro-Treaty position in the Civil War. Micheál went on to become chief of staff in the Irish Army, while Patrick was later a TD and key figure in the establishment of the Civic Guard (later An Garda Síochána). In the Civil War in Clare, Micheál was deemed responsible, as the senior Free State officer in the area, for the execution of five Clare anti-Treaty republicans.
85 Tom Brennan, 17 February 2010.
86 Murphy, William, *Political Imprisonment and the Irish, 1912–1921* (Oxford, Oxford University Press, 2014), p. 92.
87 Phil and Kitty McGrath, 4 April 2014.
88 Teasie McCormack, 25 April 2012.
89 Interview with Jack Hogan, Newmarket-on-Fergus, Co. Clare, 18 May 2010.
90 *Ibid.*, 2 June 2011.

91 Matthews, Ann, *Dissidents: Irish Republican Women 1923–1941* (Cork, Mercier Press, 2012), p. 306; Coleman, Marie, *The Irish Revolution, 1916–1923* (New York, Routledge, 2014), p. 113.
92 Jack Hogan, 2 June 2011.
93 *Ibid.*
94 Galvin Collection, handwritten report of Cumann na mBan activities by Kathleen Foley.
95 Irish Medals, www.irishmedals.ie/British-Soldiers.php (accessed 2 March 2018).
96 Joseph Noonan, BMH WS 1287, p.12.
97 Galvin Collection, handwritten report of Cumann na mBan activities by Kathleen Foley.
98 'Nan's Struggle Commemorated', *Clare People*, 25 May 2010, p. 56.
99 Coleman (2014), p. 113.
100 Galvin Collection, handwritten report of Cumann na mBan activities by Kathleen Foley.
101 Noel Galvin speaking during an interview with Mary Galvin, Ennis, Co. Clare, 31 July 2013.
102 *Ibid.*
103 Michael Carr, handwritten interview notes: recollections of Kathleen Foley.
104 *Ibid.*
105 Galvin Collection, application of Kathleen Foley to the Minister for Defence for a Service Certificate.
106 Patricia is referring to the account given by her father, Thomas McNamara, to the BMH. See Thomas McNamara, BMH WS 1077.
107 Patricia Donnellan, Mountshannon, Co. Clare, 12 September 2012.
108 Thomas McNamara, BMH WS 1077, p. 20.
109 Patricia Donnellan, 12 September 2012.
110 Michael O'Gorman, Scariff, Co. Clare, 27 September 2011.

111 'West Clare Burnings', *Clare Champion*, 5 February 1921, p. 1.
112 *Ibid.*
113 Seán O'Sullivan, Quin, Co. Clare, 25 September 2012.
114 Tomsie O'Sullivan, Lahinch, Co. Clare, 17 October 2012 (interviewed by Frances Madigan).
115 Noreen Ryan, Sallybank, Clonlara, 13 August 2018.
116 Jimmy O'Donoghue, Kilfenora, Co. Clare, 25 October 2013.
117 Michael Howard, 14 December 2010.
118 Tommy Holland, Drumann, Whitegate, Co. Clare, 10 September 2010.
119 Ryan, Louise, 'Furies and Die-hards: Women and Irish Republicanism in the Early Twentieth Century', in *Gender and History*, Vol. 11, No. 2 (July 1999), pp. 256–75.
120 Tom Brennan, 17 February 2010.
121 Michael 'Marshall' McMahon and John Cleary, 10 January 2011.
122 P.J. Clancy, 28 November 2013.
123 *Ibid.*, 30 May 2012.
124 T.S. McDonagh, BMH WS 1540, p. 5; *Saturday Record*, 24 July 1920; *Limerick Leader*, 23 July 1920; Mac Mathúna (1978), p. 85.
125 P.J. Clancy, 30 May 2012.
126 Thomas William Conneally is buried in Killenagh graveyard (Corcomroe). According to his gravestone, he died on 11 December 1922, a year and a half after he was badly beaten by British forces. His daughter, Maria, and son-in-law, Michael, are buried in the same grave. In May 2016 their son, P.J., was laid to rest with them.
127 The Monanana ambush took place near Ennistymon in July 1921, shortly before the Truce was called. It involved a small number of men from the Mid Clare IRA Brigade who fired on a convoy of British forces. No casualties were reported and the IRA unit retreated from the ambush site. It was after this ambush that the above incident with Tom Conneally occurred.

128　P.J. Clancy, 18 May 2010.
129　Military Service Pensions Act, 1934, Application number 24863, Michael Clancy, p. 4.
130　P.J. Clancy Collection, correspondence, Steve Gallagher, Templemore, Co. Tipperary to Micho Clancy, June 1948.

3 'All their own sons'

1　Brighid Lyons Thornton, quoted in Griffith, Kenneth and O'Grady, Timothy, *Curious Journey: An Oral History of Ireland's Unfinished Revolution* (Dublin, Mercier Press, 1998), p. 160.
2　Nora Canavan, 25 April 2012; Micheál O'Connell, 12 October 2009.
3　Laffan, Michael, *The Resurrection of Ireland: The Sinn Féin Party, 1916–1921* (Cambridge, Cambridge University Press, 1999), p. 233.
4　Patrick Skeehan, Bridgetown, Co. Clare, 15 October 2010 (interviewed by Ruth Minogue).
5　Correspondence, John Moroney, Bridgetown, to me, 13 March 2018.
6　Pat O'Halloran, Tulla, Co. Clare, 8 November 2008.
7　*Ibid.*
8　*Ibid.*, 1 October 2010.
9　NAUK, Colonial Office papers (hereafter CO) 904/145 Summary of Police Reports April 1921; WO 35/154 Courts of Inquiry in lieu of Inquest, Individual Cases: MACA–MACV; *Saturday Record*, 30 April 1921, *The Cork Examiner*, 27 April 1921, *Limerick Leader*, 27 April 1921.
10　Nora Canavan, 25 April 2012.
11　Nora mistakenly states 18 September when instead the night before the ambush was Friday 17 September.
12　Nora Canavan, 25 April 2012.

13 *Ibid.*
14 'Military Order in Clare', *The Irish Times*, 20 April 1918.
15 'Scariff', *The Clare Journal*, 10 April 1920.
16 James O'Brien, 27 March 2012.
17 NFCS 622–623, Miltown Boys National School, Miltown Girls National School, Moy National School, Schools' Folklore Scheme, July 1937–December 1938. An annual commemoration had been held to three local men in Miltown who were shot dead by British forces in April 1921 at Canada Cross; see 'A Tragic Memory', *Clare Champion*, 23 April 1938, p. 5.
18 Michael 'Marshall' McMahon and John Cleary, 10 January 2011.
19 P.J. Reidy, Newmarket-on-Fergus, Co. Clare, 31 January 2012.
20 Seán Kiely, 5 October 2009.
21 John O'Connell, 16 October 2012.
22 Martin Walsh, 7 July 2011.
23 Gerome Griffin, 12 May 2005.
24 *Ibid.*
25 Paddy Gleeson, first broadcast on Clare FM, 12 May 2004.
26 CACA, interview with Micheál Falsey, Quilty, Co. Clare, 6 January 2012.
27 Martin Walsh, 7 July 2011.
28 John Minogue, Scariff, Co. Clare, 6 May 2011.
29 Paul Markham, Michael Falahee Ballyguiry and late of New York, www.markhams-of-derryguiha.com/id6.html (accessed 13 January 2018).
30 Mary Murrihy, 12 October 2009.
31 Willie Shanahan was an IRA officer in the West Clare Brigade, who, with Michael McNamara, was captured and murdered by British forces on 22 December 1920, shortly after the incident referred to above.
32 John and Phil Kelly, Cree, Co. Clare, 8 August 2012.

33 NAUK, CO 904/143, Summary of police reports, December 1920; WO 35/148, Courts of Inquiry in lieu of Inquest, Individual Cases: COM–DAV.
34 This incident was attended, it seems, by Fr Patrick Gaynor, according to Nolan. See Michael Nolan, Sinn Féin Courts in West Clare, http://kilkeehistory.com/sinn-fein-courts-west-clare/.
35 'The Blackened Tans', *Clare Champion*, 1 November 2013.
36 *Ibid.*
37 Jack Dunleavy, June 2008.
38 John (or Seán) Mullins was a captain in F Company (Clohanamore) in the 3rd Battalion of the West Clare IRA Brigade.
39 John and Phil Kelly, 8 August 2012.
40 Tom Brennan, 17 February 2010.
41 Lieutenant General A.E. Percival quoted in Sheehan (2007), p. 132.
42 Williams, Niall and Breen, Christine, *O Come Ye Back to Ireland: Our First Year in County Clare* (USA, Soho Press, 1989), p. 160.
43 Francie Kenneally, Miltown Malbay, Co. Clare, 1 February 2012.
44 'Stirring Period Recalled', *Clare Champion*, 14 November 1936, p. 1.
45 The American Commission on Conditions in Ireland, *Interim Report* (New York, Hardin and Moore, 1921), p. 52.
46 Teasie McCormack, 11 October 2011.
47 Michael Howard, 14 December 2010.
48 On the occasion when Ignatius O'Neill was preparing for a gunfight at the McCormacks' house, the British forces did not arrive. However, they came later and burned many of the houses in the townland, whose inhabitants they suspected of supporting republicans. Fortunately for the McCormacks, their home was spared.
49 Correspondence with P.J. Donnellan, Moy, Co. Clare, 4 July 2018. Ellie's younger brother, Tommy, although thirty-eight years of

age in 1921, older than the average Volunteer, was also an active republican and participated in a number of IRA actions during this period.
50 Micheál O'Connell, 12 October 2009.
51 Correspondence with P.J. Donnellan, Moy, Co. Clare, 4 July 2018.
52 Various, *With the IRA in the Fight for Freedom: The Red Path to Glory* (Tralee, The Kerryman Ltd, 1953), p. 36.
53 Teasie McCormack, 25 April 2012.
54 Tom McNamara, Crusheen, Co. Clare, 2 February 2012; Con Hogan, Tulla, Co. Clare, 14 March 2010.
55 Tommy Daly was a Tulla and Clare hurler who was killed in a car accident in Tuamgraney in 1936.
56 Tom McNamara, 2 February 2012.
57 Pat O'Halloran, 1 October 2010.
58 Con Hogan, 14 March 2010. Greaves offers a detailed treatment of Mellows' stay in Clare, see Greaves, C. Desmond, *Liam Mellows and the Irish Revolution* (London, An Ghlór Gafa, 1988), pp. 96–100.
59 Mae Crowe, Killimer, Co. Clare, 23 April 2013.
60 P.J. Clancy, 18 May 2010.
61 Mick Ryan, 10 December 2013.
62 Seán Kiely, 5 October 2009.
63 *Ibid.*, 22 March 2014.
64 *Ibid.*, 5 October 2009.
65 John Flanagan, BMH WS 1316, p. 15.
66 Michael Howard, 14 December 2011.
67 Jimmy Gleeson, 16 June 2011.
68 Patrick Kerin, BMH WS 977, pp. 4–5.
69 Jimmy Gleeson, 16 June 2011.
70 NFCS, Vol. 591: p. 363; contributor and collector unnamed, Bodyke National School, Co. Clare; teacher: Bean Uí Chadhla.

71 John Corry, Fermoy, Co. Cork, 26 May 2012.
72 Mick Ryan, 10 December 2013.
73 John O'Connell, 16 October 2012.
74 Pat O'Halloran, 1 October 2010; Bobby Hehir, Kildysart, Co. Clare, 11 October 2010.
75 Jimmy Gleeson, 16 June 2011.
76 Jerry Moriarty, Killaloe, Co. Clare, 3 August 2015.
77 John J. Walsh, BMH WS 1002, p. 6.
78 Gerome Griffin, 12 May 2005.
79 John Minogue, 6 May 2011.
80 The gravestone is visible in St Cronin's graveyard, Tuamgraney.
81 P.J. Magner, Ross, Co. Clare, 5 January 2012.
82 Pádraig Haugh, Doonbeg, Co. Clare, 16 April 2012.
83 Correspondence, Fr Martin Bugler, Auckland, New Zealand to me, 19 February 2014.
84 Johnny Doyle, 20 October 2011.
85 Jimmy Walsh, 5 May 2012.
86 *Ibid.*
87 Tommy Bolton, 11 June 1989 (copy in my possession).
88 Jimmy Walsh, 8 April 2018.
89 *Ibid.*
90 Correspondence with Joe Fitzgerald, Australia to me, 8 January 2018.
91 *Ibid.*
92 In 1938 William Jones recorded in the Schools' Folklore Scheme that Turkenna House 'was burned in 1921 by the Sinn Féin Volunteers who were "on the run" in the Black and Tan war', NFCS, Vol. 592: p. 322; Matt Moroney, Gortaderry, Co. Clare; collector: William Jones, Currakyle School; teacher: Bean Uí Innseadúin.
93 Joe Fitzgerald, Corragnoe, 6 July 2018.
94 'Stirring Period Recalled', *Clare Champion*, 14 November 1936, p. 1.

95 Tommy appears to be referring to P.J. Rutledge (1892–1952), a Sinn Féin and later Fianna Fáil TD, who was minister for justice under Éamon de Valera.
96 John S. Kelly, Private Collection, interview with Tommy Bolton, Tuamgraney, Co. Clare, 11 June 1989 (copy in my possession).

4 'Born wild'

1   Jimmy Gleeson, 16 June 2011.
2   CACA, interview with Ned Keane, Cahermurphy, Co. Clare, 2 April 2010 (also present was Pat Hayes).
3   Seán Moroney, BMH WS 1462, pp. 14–15.
4   Ned Keane, 2 April 2010. On 15 May 1921 Pat Houlihan was a key participant in the Ballyturin ambush near Gort in which the local district inspector, Captain Cecil Blake, his wife and two officers, Captain Cornwallis and Lieutenant McCreery, were shot dead as they drove away from Ballyturin House. Houlihan also fought in ambushes at Feakle, Kilrush and Dalystown (Galway). There are two songs composed in his honour by Pat O'Donnell.
5   Correspondence, Bernie Burchell, Cheshire, England, to me, 28 June 2013.
6   Tom Lynch, Kilkittane, Whitegate, Co. Clare, 11 May 2011.
7   Michael O'Gorman, 22 October 2012.
8   CACA, interview with John Queally, Roscrea, Co. Tipperary, 17 May 2011.
9   CACA, interview with Dympna Bonfield, Kilbaha, Co. Clare, 10 March 2011 (interviewed by Linda Quinn).
10 West Clare IRA Volunteer Michael Russell suggests that his body was bound and chained to the back of the lorry and dragged along the road: see BMH WS, 1226, p. 4. Martin Chambers held that McNamara was bayoneted by one of the escort: see BMH WS 1251, pp. 8–9. The military court of inquiry recorded

a ludicrous account, which claimed that after hitting a bumpy stretch of road one of the escort's rifles went off accidentally and hit McNamara in the back: see NAUK, CO 904/143, Summary of Police Reports December 1920, WO 35/154 Courts of Inquiry in lieu of Inquest, Individual Cases: MACA–MACV; WO 35/159A Courts of Inquiry in lieu of Inquest, Individual Cases: SAD–STO.

11 Willie Whelan, Killimer, Co. Clare, 16 April 2012.
12 Joe 'Jack' Sexton, 16 June 2009.
13 The ambush would seem to be an action undertaken at Decomade, Lissycasey in late June 1920; see Joseph Barrett, BMH WS 1324, pp. 20–1. 'Weanlings' is an agricultural term used to describe approximately eight-month-old calves that have been weaned from their mothers.
14 Gerome Griffin Collection, private diary of Seán Ó Griofa, Mid Clare IRA Volunteer.
15 Daniel Corkery, introduction to O'Súilleabháin (1965), pp. 8–9.
16 NFCS, Vol. 615, p. 201, Michael Jordan, Ballyvelaghan; collector: Brighíd Ní Shúrtáin, Ballyvelaghan National School, Co. Clare; teacher: Máire Ní Dheaghaigh.
17 'Strange Story from Clare', *Irish Independent*, 8 November 1928.
18 NFCS, 621: 306–7; Pat Garrahy, Dough, Lahinch, Co. Clare; collector unnamed, Lahinch National School, Co. Clare; teacher: Dónall Ó Ríordáin.
19 Dan McNamara, Ballymalone, Tuamgraney, Co. Clare, 3 January 2014.
20 Seán Crowe, Broadford, Co. Clare, 26 September 2011.
21 The story of Lendrum's death has been a controversial one, with multiple accounts emerging about how he was killed. The suggestion that Lendrum was buried alive facing the incoming tide has been rubbished by Eoin Shanahan, who indicates that an initial fictionalised account repeated by historians found its

way into the local historical consciousness of the area; see Eoin Shanahan, 'Telling tales: the story of the burial alive and drowning of a Clare RM in 1920', in *History Ireland*, issue 1, vol. 18 (January/February 2010).
22   Ó Ruairc (2009), p. 159.
23   CACA, interview with Senan Fitzmartin, Ennis, Co. Clare, 26 August 2011.
24   Kelly Cree, Co. Clare, 8 August 2012; Willie Whelan, Killimer, Co. Clare, 16 April 2012; Catherine Talty, Clounlaheen, Co. Clare, 13 November 2013.
25   Joe 'Jack' Sexton, Mullagh, Co. Clare, 16 June 2009.
26   Willie Whelan, 16 April 2012.
27   John and Phil Kelly, 8 August 2012.
28   Arensberg, Conrad M. and Kimball, Solon T., *Family and Community in Ireland* (Ennis, CLASP, 2001), p. xlvii.
29   See Browne, Kevin J., *Éamon de Valera and the Banner County* (Dublin, Glendale Press, 1982), p. 120.
30   Arensberg and Kimball (2001), p. xlvii.
31   NAUK, CO 904/145, Daily summary of police reports on outrages, April 1921; WO 35/89, Military operations and inquiries: Ambushes raids and casualties inflicted by rebels.
32   Terence MacSwiney, *Principles of Freedom* (Dublin, Talbot Press, 1921), p. 148.
33   Micheál Brennan, BMH WS 1068, p. 100.
34   'The Burning of Ennistymon', RTÉ Documentary on One, www.rte.ie/radio1/doconone/radio-documentary-ennistymon-burning-ira-war-independence.html (accessed 4 December 2013)
35   CACA, interview with Teresa Flynn, Mountshannon, Co. Clare, 21 July 2010 (interviewed by Frances Madigan).
36   Tommy Holland, 10 September 2010.
37   Peggy Hogan, 18 February 2013.

38   John O'Connell, 16 October 2012.
39   Five shillings equated to twenty-five pence.
40   Mellie Enright, Kilmihil, Co. Clare, 16 December 2008.
41   Palkie McNamara, Killaloe, Co. Clare, 22 November 2011.
42   Dan McNamara, 12 May 2015.
43   'Cattle Drives', *Clare Champion*, 9 February 1918, p. 3; for a detailed treatment of both the cattle drives and court case see, Tomás Mac Conmara, 'The Land for the People and the Road for the Bullock', *Clare Champion* (Living), 2 February 2018, p. 5; Mac Conmara, 'The Great Escape, *Clare Champion* (Living), 9 February, 2018, p. 3.
44   'Ennis Court', *Clare Champion*, 16 February 1918, p. 1.
45   Paddy Gleeson, 8 October 2008.
46   Seán Crowe, 26 September 2011. Michael Campbell was a shopkeeper and farmer from Cloncool in O'Callaghan's Mills.
47   Mike McNamara, Broadford, Co. Clare, 22 March 2005.
48   Dan McNamara, 12 May 2015.
49   Pat O'Halloran, 8 November 2008.
50   Arensberg and Kimball (2001), p. 153
51   Jimmy Gleeson, 16 June 2011.
52   'Fourth Battalion Mid Clare Brigade', *Clare Champion*, 31 December 1955, p. 3.
53   Nell Gleeson, *The Pub Down in Coore* (Clare, 2011).
54   Jimmy Gleeson, 16 June 2011.
55   Joe 'Jack' Sexton, 31 May 2010.

5 'A corner of the grave'

1   The Office of Public Works, Clare County Council, the British Commonwealth Graves Association and An Garda Síochána were the principal agencies involved in the exhumation.
2   Three British servicemen – Privates George Robertson, George

Duff Chalmers and Constable Daniel Anthony Murphy – were shot and buried by the IRA in Clare in three separate incidents: see Ó Ruairc, Pádraig Óg, 'Missing in Action: British Servicemen Secretly Buried in Clare during the War of Independence', *The Other Clare*, vol. 36 (2012), pp. 77–80.

3   The IRA had been waiting in ambush for the military convoy according to the then Mid Clare IRA's 4th Battalion O/C, Commandant Anthony Malone: see BMH WS 1076, pp. 14–15.
4   Correspondence with P.J. Donnellan, Moy, Co. Clare, 4 July 2018.
5   MAI, A/07304, Seamus Hennessy Military Service Pension application, 3 April 1935.
6   University College Dublin Archives, P7/A/20 Mulcahy Papers.
7   P.J. Clancy, 30 May 2012.
8   Dinny Costelloe, Knockneppy, Ennistymon, Co. Clare, 14 January 2011.
9   Micheál O'Connell, 12 October 2009.
10 *Ibid.* The interview was also attended by the historian Pádraig Óg Ó Ruairc, who subsequently examined the case and, after considerable research, established the name of Chalmers. Ó Ruairc also helped to mark the grave with a stone carving. This was not acknowledged as part of media coverage surrounding the exhumation.
11 Ballaun is the local name used to describe a hill area in the townland of Drumbaun and is the local description for the area in which Chalmers was buried.
12 Catherine Talty, 5 July 2013.
13 Ó Ruairc, Pádraig Óg (ed.), *The Men Will Talk to Me: Clare Interviews by Ernie O'Malley* (Cork, Mercier Press, 2016), Paddy 'Con' MacMahon interview, p. 99.
14 Ó Ruairc, 'Missing in Action: British Servicemen Secretly Buried in Clare during the War of Independence', pp. 77–80.
15 Francie Kenneally, 1 February 2012.

16 Ó Ruairc (2016), p. 99.

6 Carrying Wounds

1   The florin was an Irish coin, which preceded the 10p coin and was commonly known as the two-shilling coin.
2   Mary Dollard, 24 June 2013.
3   *Ibid.*
4   Matt Gleeson Papers, statement by Anthony McGuane (signed by Jeremiah Killeen, O/C 4th Battalion, West Clare Brigade).
5   Catherine Talty, 31 March 2011.
6   *Ibid.*, 31 October 2013.
7   *Ibid.*
8   Correspondence, Seán Cox, Michigan, USA, to me, 13 March 2016.
9   *Ibid.*
10 Dr Michael Hillery was the father of Patrick Hillery, president of Ireland from 1976 to 1990. In the War of Independence, he had cared for many wounded IRA Volunteers in north and west Clare.
11 Correspondence, Margaret McGuane Cox, America, to me, 9 April 2018.
12 Correspondence, Sr Catherine McGuane, West Leederville, Western Australia, to me, 6 January 2014.
13 *Ibid.*
14 In an illustration of how challenging it was for local IRA Volunteers to later receive recognition, two years before his death McGuane wrote to GHQ of the Irish Army complaining that his earlier claim for an IRA pension in November 1939 had not been acknowledged: Matt Gleeson Papers, copy of letter by Anthony McGuane (signed by Jeremiah Killeen, O/C 4th Battalion, West Clare Brigade).
15 Mick Killoury's mother, Mary, was still alive when her son was

buried in November 1945.
16   Liam Haugh, BMH WS 474, p. 37.
17   John and Phil Kelly, 8 August 2012.
18   'Fitting tribute to IRA Captain', *Clare Champion*, 29 December 1945, p. 3.
19   Joseph Clancy, BMH WS 1370, p. 5.
20   'Memorial Unveiled at Killaloe to Gallant Soldier', *Clare Champion*, 23 March 1963, p. 1.
21   Joseph Clancy, BMH WS 1370.
22   'Memorial Unveiled at Killaloe to Gallant Soldier', *Clare Champion*, 23 March 1963, p. 1.
23   J.P. Guinnane and Paddy Clancy, 3 November 2010.
24   Jack Quigley, Ballina, Co. Tipperary, 14 March 2012.
25   *Ibid.*

7 'Dormant sympathies'

1   Mellie Enright, 16 December 2008.
2   'Dear Susan' documentary surrounding the ambush in Kilmihil, Co. Clare, April 1920, first broadcast on Clare FM, 18 February 1997. There have been contrasting accounts about the composition of the group of attackers. In his BMH witness statement (1316, p. 11), John Flanagan named Melican, O'Dea, Breen and an unnamed fourth as being involved, while Ó Ruairc only named three (2009, p. 134). However, research undertaken recently by Eoin Shanahan supports the presence of McMahon and Killoury, including the identification of the latter by Constable Martyn in a subsequent statement: see Eoin Shanahan, 'Kilmihil's Bloody Sunday', *The Clare Association Yearbook* (2018), pp. 38–42. The latter account is reinforced by local tradition I have documented, both within Kilmihil and in the surrounding areas.
3   Ó Ruairc (2009), p. 134.

4   John Flanagan, BMH WS 1316, p. 11. NAUK CO 904/148, Weekly summary of outrages against the police to week ended 17 April 1920; HO 184/30, Irish Constabulary Records, Records and Services, General Register, Numbers 57001–59000.
5   'Dear Susan', Clare FM, 18 February 1997.
6   Michael 'Marshall' McMahon and John Cleary, 10 January 2011.
7   Eoin Shanahan, 'Kilmihil's Bloody Sunday', *The Clare Association Yearbook* (2018), pp. 38–42.
8   Michael 'Marshall' McMahon and John Cleary, 10 January 2011.
9   Patricia Sheehan Collection, interview with Morgie O'Connell, Cranny, Co. Clare, 18 July 2014.
10 Timmy Ryan, 21 December 2008.
11 *Ibid.*
12 *Ibid.*
13 Mellie Enright, 16 December 2008.
14 *Ibid.*
15 Williams and Breen (1989), p. 160.
16 Mellie Enright, 16 December 2008.
17 West Clare IRA Volunteer Martin Chambers suggested that 500 people attended the funeral, while John Flanagan put the figure at 800: see Martin Chambers, BMH WS 1251, p. 4; John Flanagan, BMH WS 1316, p. 11.
18 John Flanagan, BMH WS 1316, p. 12.
19 Mellie Enright, 16 December 2008.
20 Williams and Breen (1989), p. 160.
21 Catherine is referring to Archbishop Daniel Mannix, the Cork-born long-serving archbishop of Melbourne, who through his considerable influence behind Ireland's struggle for independence caused an international incident when he attempted to visit Ireland in the summer of 1920, only to be arrested at sea on Lloyd George's orders. Mannix had shared a platform with Éamon de Valera in

New York in July 1920, during which he strongly supported the republican position and called for Irish freedom.
22   Buffalo Private Collection (Kevin James O'Brien) Mrs Catherine Breen, Kiltumper, Kilmihil to Mrs O'Gorman, Buffalo, USA, 11 October 1923.
23   Flan Garvey, 24 October 2011 and 8 August 2015.
24   Ó Ruairc (2009), p. 101.
25   Flan Garvey, 24 October 2011.
26   *Clare Champion*, 23 August 1919.
27   Flan Garvey, 24 October 2011.
28   *Ibid.*
29   NAUK, CO 904/109, Inspector General's confidential report for the month of August 1919.
30   NAUK, WO 3/145/2, G.H.Q. Ireland, Disturbance, Death of F. Murphy, Ennistymon, 1919, Correspondence, W. E. Wylie to Commander-in-Chief (25920), 12 September 1919.
31   Michael Knightly, BMH WS 834, pp. 3–4.
32   *Clare Champion*, 30 August 1919.
33   Nora Canavan, 20 April 2010.
34   P.J. Clancy, 30 May 2012.
35   Flan Garvey, 24 October 2011.
36   Correspondence, Oliver McDonagh to me – handwritten responses to questionnaire of Clare MacDonagh, Australia.
37   Eilís Blake Collection, taped recording of Barney O'Higgins, 3 September 1978.
38   *Ibid.*
39   John Joe Neylon, BMH WS 1042, pp. 18–19.
40   Barney O'Higgins, 3 September 1978.
41   Ó Ruairc (2009), pp. 169–71; Hopkinson (2002), p. 130; O'Malley, Ernie, *On Another Man's Wound* (Colorado, Roberts Rinehart, 2001), pp. 64–90, O'Farrell, Padraic, *Who's Who in the War of Inde-*

pendence and Civil War (Dublin, Mercier Press, 1997), p. 83.
42 There is a slight confusion over Connole's age. In the court testimony of his wife in January 1921, Connole is listed as thirty-seven, while most accounts refer to him as thirty-one. According to the 1911 Census, Connole would have been twenty-eight. See 'Thos Connole's Death', *Clare Champion*, 5 February, 1921, p. 3; 'Fearful Occurrence in West Clare', *Saturday Record*, 25 September, 1920, p. 2.
43 'Fearful Occurrence in West Clare', *Saturday Record*, 25 September 1920, p. 2.
44 'The Burning of Ennistymon', RTÉ Documentary on One.
45 NFCS, Vol. 621: p. 359; James Queally, Cregg, Lahinch, Co. Clare; collector unnamed, Moy Lahinch National School; teacher: Dónall Ó Ríordáin.
46 'Ennistymon and Lahinch', *Clare Champion*, 2 October 1920, p. 3; interview with P.J. Clancy, Lahinch, Co. Clare, 28 November 2013.
47 Helena Connole was a native of Killaloe in east Clare. In 1926 she remarried in Kilkee, where she ran a guesthouse and had four more children, before eventually moving to Cork. Her first sons, Jack and Patrick, who were two years and four months respectively when their father was murdered, kept their father's surname: correspondence, Helena Marconetto to me, 1 February 2018.
48 'Where Terror Reigns', *The Freeman's Journal*, 11 October 1920.
49 'The Burning of Ennistymon', RTÉ Documentary on One.
50 Maureen Connole, 7 May 2008.
51 'Thos Connole's Death', *Clare Champion*, 5 February 1921, p. 3.
52 Maureen Connole, 7 May 2008.
53 Helena uses the common term 'Black and Tans' when instead it was the regular army that murdered Tom Connole. She also refers to a locally held belief that Tom had lent his coat to an IRA

Volunteer called Michael Nestor, who lost it during the Rineen ambush, implicating Connole in the action.

54 Correspondence, Helena Marconetto to me, 1 February 2018.
55 'The Burning of Ennistymon', RTÉ Documentary on One.
56 P.J. Clancy, 28 November 2013.
57 J.T. McMahon, BMH WS 362, p. 2.
58 'Ennistymon Memorial', *Clare Champion*, 1 November 1947; 'Sack of Ennistymon recalled', *Clare Champion*, 11 November 1947, p. 1.
59 Glynn, Enda, *Ennistymon Bridge Club and its Times* (Clare, 2007), pp. 85–90.
60 'Sack of Ennistymon recalled', *Clare Champion*, 11 November 1947, p. 1; 'Ennistymon and Lahinch', *Clare Champion*, 2 October 1920, p. 3.
61 'Sack of Ennistymon recalled', *Clare Champion*, 11 November 1947, p. 1.

Conclusion

1 Chang, Larry (ed.), *Wisdom for the Soul: Five Millennia of Prescriptions for Spiritual Healing* (Washington DC, Gnosophia Publishing, 2006), p. 509.
2 Paddy Gleeson, Clare FM, 12 May 2004.
3 Fitzpatrick, David, *Politics and Irish Life, 1913–21: Provincial Experiences of War and Revolution* (Dublin, Gill & Macmillan, 1977), p. 45.
4 Dáil Éireann, 3 June 1924, 'Ennistymon Bomb Explosion', www.oireachtas.ie/en/debates/debate/dail/1924-06-03/4/ (accessed 8 August 2018); 'The Burning of Ennistymon', RTÉ Documentary on One.
5 Nora Canavan, 25 April 2012.

Appendix: Exploring Memory

1 Neylon, Michael, and Kirby, Brid, *Our Elders: the Post-Independence Generation in Clare* (Clare, Clare County Council, 2010), p. 10; Beiner, Guy, *Remembering the Year of the French: Irish Folk History and Social Memory* (London, University of Wisconsin Press, 2007), p. 10.
2 Eamon Fennell, BMH WS 1252, pp. 7–8; Joseph Barrett, BMH WS 1324, pp. 11–13.
3 Neylon and Kirby (2010), p. 10.
4 Ritchie, Donald A. (ed.), *The Oxford Handbook of Oral History* (Oxford, Oxford University Press, 2011) pp. 287–8.
5 Perks, Robert and Thomson, Alistair (eds), *The Oral History Reader* (London and New York, Routledge, 1998), p. 1.
6 Abu Dheer, Ala, *Nakba Eyewitnesses: Narrations of the Palestinian 1948 Catastrophe*, edited by Liam Morgan and Alison Morris, Alison (Nablus, An-Najah National University, 2009), pp. 17–18; Kanaaneh, Rhoda Ann and Nusair, Isis (eds), *Displaced at Home: Ethnicity and Gender among Palestinians in Israel* (Albany, State of New York University Press, 2010).

BIBLIOGRAPHY

Primary Sources
Military Archives of Ireland
Brother Allen Collection
Bureau of Military History Witness Statements
Military Service Pensions Collection

National Folklore Collection, UCD
National Folklore Schools' Collection (Schools' Folklore Scheme)

National Archives of the United Kingdom (NAUK)
British House of Commons Parliamentary Papers
Colonial Office Papers
Home Office Papers
War Office Papers

Private oral history collections
Eilís Blake Collection, interview with Barney O'Higgins, Lahinch
John S. Kelly Collection, Tommy Bolton, Tuamgraney, Co. Clare
Shannon Social History Project, interviews by Olive Carey
Patricia Sheehan Collection, interviews with Morgan O'Connell

Newspapers

Clare Champion	*Limerick Leader*
Clare Journal, The	*New Ireland*
Cork Examiner, The	*Saturday Record*
Freeman's Journal, The	
Irish Press, The	

Irish Times, The

Correspondence

Martin Bugler (Fr), New Zealand, 26 December 2013, 19 February 2014
Bernie Burchell, Cheshire, England, 28 June 2013
John Corbett, Galway, 15 January 2018
Joe Fitzgerald, Australia, 8 January 2018
Helena Marconetto, England, 1 February 2018
Catherine McGuane (Sr), West Leederville, Western Australia, 6 January 2014
Margaret McGuane Cox, Michigan, USA, 8 April 2018
Oliver McDonagh, Australia, 12 May 2016
John Moroney, Bridgetown, Co. Clare, 13 March 2018
Michael O'Keefe (Fr), Florida, USA, 22 April 2013

Private collections in family ownership

P.J. Clancy Collection: Private papers of Maria Conneally and Micho Clancy, former members of Mid Clare Cumann na mBan and IRA, including pension applications, correspondence between former comrades, pictures, prison autograph book, handwritten song.
Billy Malone Collection: Photographs, family letters, correspondence between Anthony Malone and other former IRA Volunteers, newspapers cuttings.
Phil McGrath Collection: Handwritten account of family homes' burning during the War of Independence, private letters and correspondence between her father Tom McGrath and Shannon Development.
Mary Galvin Collection: Private papers of Kathleen Foley relating to the East Clare Cumann na mBan Brigade including correspondence between former Cumann na mBan members, membership lists, pension applications.
Gleeson Buffalo Collection: Correspondence between Buffalo, USA

and Coore in West Clare concerning republican fundraising and activities.

Seán Griffin Diary: Handwritten diary of Clare IRA Volunteer Seán Griffin from Ballyea detailing his experience in the 2nd Battalion, Mid Clare IRA Brigade.

Jack Hogan Collection: Family papers relating to Nan Hogan, Cumann na mBan.

Patrick McMahon Diary: Handwritten diary of West Clare IRA Volunteer Patrick McMahon, detailing IRA activity in Coolmeen.

Seán Murnane Collection: Collection of correspondence between Seán Murnane, East Clare IRA Brigade and both IRA and Free State forces during the War of Independence and Civil War.

Catherine Talty Collection: Correspondence between the US and Clounlaheen in west Clare from 1912 to 1924 including reference to the revolutionary period in both Ireland and America.

Secondary Sources

Abu Dheer, Ala, *Nakba Eyewitnesses: Narrations of the Palestinian 1948 Catastrophe*, edited by Liam Morgan and Alison Morris, Alison (Nablus, An-Najah National University, 2009)

Arensberg, Conrad M. and Kimball, Solon T., *Family and Community in Ireland* (Ennis, CLASP, 2001)

Beiner, Guy, *Remembering the Year of the French: Irish Folk History and Social Memory* (London, University of Wisconsin Press, 2007)

Breathneach, Seamus, *The Irish Police: From Earliest Times to the Present Day* (Dublin, Anvil Books, 1974)

Browne, Kevin J., *Éamon de Valera and the Banner County* (Dublin, Glendale Press, 1982)

Chang, Larry (ed.), *Wisdom for the Soul: Five Millennia of Prescriptions for Spiritual Healing* (Washington DC, Gnosophia Publishing, 2006)

Coleman, Marie, *The Irish Revolution, 1916–1923* (New York, Routledge, 2014)

Dwyer, T. Ryle, *Tans, Terror and Troubles: Kerry's Real Fighting Story 1913–1923* (Cork, Mercier Press, 2001)

Ferriter, Diarmuid, *The Transformation of Ireland, 1900–2000* (London, Profile Books, 2004)

Fitzpatrick, David, *Politics and Irish Life, 1913–21: Provincial Experiences of War and Revolution* (Dublin, Gill & Macmillan, 1977)

Gleeson, Nell, *The Pub Down in Coore* (Clare, privately published, 2011)

Glynn, Enda, *Ennistymon Bridge Club and its Times* (Clare, privately published, 2007)

Griffith, Kenneth and O'Grady, Timothy, *Curious Journey: An Oral History of Ireland's Unfinished Revolution* (Dublin, Mercier Press, 1998)

Greaves, C. Desmond, *Liam Mellows and the Irish Revolution* (London, An Ghlór Gafa, 1988)

Hopkinson, Michael, *The Irish War of Independence* (Dublin, McGill-Queen's University Press, 2002)

Kanaaneh, Rhoda Ann and Nusair, Isis (eds), *Displaced at Home: Ethnicity and Gender among Palestinians in Israel* (Albany, State of New York University Press, 2010)

Kautt, William, *The Anglo-Irish War, 1916–1921: A People's War* (America, Praeger, 1999)

Kearns, Kevin C., *Dublin Tenement Life: An Oral History* (Dublin, Gill & Macmillan, 2006)

Laffan, Michael, *The Resurrection of Ireland: The Sinn Féin Party, 1916–1921* (Cambridge, Cambridge University Press, 1999)

Leeson, David, *The Black and Tans: British Police and Auxiliaries in the Irish War of Independence, 1920–1921* (Oxford, Oxford University Press, 2011)

MacEoin, Uinseann, *The IRA in the Twilight Years, 1923–1948* (Dublin, Argenta Publications, 1997)

Mac Mathúna, Seosamh, *Kilfarboy: A History of a West Clare Parish* (Clare, privately published, 1978)

MacSwiney, Terence, *Principles of Freedom* (Dublin, Talbot Press, 1921)

Matthews, Ann, *Dissidents: Irish Republican Women 1923–1941* (Cork, Mercier Press, 2012)

McConville, Sean, *Irish Political Prisoners, 1848–1922: Theatres of War* (London, Routledge, 2003)

McKenna, Joseph, *Guerrilla Warfare in the Irish War of Independence, 1919–1921* (Carolina, McFarland & Co., 2011)

Murphy, William, *Political Imprisonment and the Irish, 1912–1921* (Oxford, Oxford University Press, 2014)

Narain, Savita, *The Jallianwala Bagh Massacre* (USA, Lancer Publishers, 2013)

Neylon, Michael and Kirby, Brid, *Our Elders: the Post-Independence Generation in Clare* (Clare, Clare County Council, 2010)

Ó Comhraí, Cormac and Ó Comhraí, Stiofán, *Peadar Clancy: Easter Rising Hero, Bloody Sunday Martyr* (Galway, Cranny Publications, 2016)

O'Farrell, Padraic, *Who's Who in the War of Independence and Civil War* (Dublin, Mercier Press, 1997)

O'Malley, Ernie, *Raids and Rallies* (Dublin, Anvil, 1982)

— *On Another Man's Wound* (Colorado, Roberts Rinehart, 2001)

Ó Ruairc, Pádraig Óg, *Blood on the Banner: The Republican Struggle in Clare* (Cork, Mercier Press, 2009)

— (ed.), *The Men Will Talk to Me: Clare Interviews by Ernie O'Malley* (Cork, Mercier Press, 2016)

Ó Súilleabháin, Micheál, *Where Mountainy Men Have Sown: War and Peace in Rebel Cork in the Turbulent Years 1916–21* (Kerry, Anvil Books, 1965)

Perks, Robert and Thomson, Alistair (eds), *The Oral History Reader* (London and New York, Routledge, 1998)

Ritchie, Donald A. (ed.), *The Oxford Handbook of Oral History* (Oxford, Oxford University Press, 2011)

Ryan, Meda, *Tom Barry: IRA Freedom Fighter* (Cork, Mercier Press, 2003)

Sheehan, William, *British Voices from the Irish War of Independence 1918–1921: The Words of British Servicemen Who Were There* (Cork, Collins Press, 2007)

The American Commission on Conditions in Ireland, *Interim Report* (New York, Hardin and Moore, 1921)

Various, *With the IRA in the Fight for Freedom: The Red Path to Glory* (Tralee, The Kerryman Ltd, 1953)

Walsh, J.J., *Recollections of a Rebel* (Tralee, The Kerryman Ltd, 1949)

Whelan, Bernadette, *United States Foreign Policy and Ireland: From Empire to Independence, 1913–29* (Dublin, Four Courts, 2006)

Williams, Niall and Breen, Christine, *O Come Ye Back to Ireland: Our First Year in County Clare* (USA, Soho Press, 1989)

Williams, W. J., *Report of the Irish White Cross to 31st August, 1922* (Dublin, Martin Lester Ltd, 1922)

Documentaries

'Dear Susan', documentary about the ambush in Kilmihil, Co. Clare, April 1920, first broadcast on Clare FM, 18 February 1997

'The Burning of Ennistymon', RTÉ Documentary on One, http://www.rte.ie/radio1/doconone/radio-documentary-ennistymon-burning-ira-war-independence.html (accessed 04 December 2013)

Journal Articles

Lowe, W. J., 'Who were the Black-and-Tans?', *History Ireland*, issue 3, vol. 12 (Autumn 2004), pp. 47–51

McGarry, Fearghal, 'Too many histories? The Bureau of Military History and Easter 1916', *History Ireland*, issue 6, vol. 19 (Nov/Dec 2011),

pp. 26–9
Ó Ruairc, Pádraig Óg, 'Missing in Action: British Servicemen Secretly Buried in Clare during the War of Independence', *The Other Clare*, vol. 36 (2012), pp. 77–80
Ryan, Louise, 'Furies and Die-hards: Women and Irish Republicanism in the Early Twentieth Century', *Gender and History*, vol. 11, No. 2 (July 1999), pp. 256–75
Shanahan, Eoin, 'Telling tales: the story of the burial alive and drowning of a Clare RM in 1920', *History Ireland*, Issue 1 (January/February 2010), pp. 36–7
— 'Kilmihil's Bloody Sunday', *The Clare Association Yearbook* (2018), pp. 38–42

Unpublished academic paper

Ainsworth, John, 'The Black & Tans and Auxiliaries in Ireland, 1920–1921: Their Origins, Roles and Legacy', paper presented to the Annual Conference of the Queensland History Teachers' Association in Brisbane, 12 May 2001

Websites

Dáil Éireann: www.oireachtas.ie
Hansard 1803–2005: http://hansard.millbanksystems.com
Irish Medals: www.irishmedals.ie
Kilkee History: http://kilkeehistory.com
Military Archives, Military Service Pensions Collection: http://mspcsearch.militaryarchives.ie
RTÉ Radio 1: www.rte.ie/radio1
The Cairo Gang: www.cairogang.com
The Victorian Web: www.victorianweb.org
Paul Markham, Michael Falahee Ballyguiry and late of New York: www.markhams-of-derryguiha.com/id6.html

INDEX

A

Anglo-Irish Treaty 25, 78
Arensberg, Conrad 198, 199, 210
Armagh 147, 237
Auxiliary Division 19, 29, 30, 81, 99, 114, 146, 183, 184, 185, 202, 203, 207, 208, 234

B

Baird, John 32
Ballaun 217
Ballyboucher 115
Ballydonaghane 61, 62, 184
Ballyea 155, 194
Ballygeary 153
Ballymacdonnell 152, 205
Ballynacally 177, 194
Ballyoughtra 168
Ballyturin 191
Ballyvaughan 176
Bell, Charlotte 147
Belvoir 103
Birmingham, Matthew 53, 54
Bleach, Bill 188
Bloody Sunday 19
Blythe, Ernest 116
Bodyke 40, 41, 61, 100, 156, 174, 182, 183, 203, 205
    Caherhurley 60, 182, 183, 184, 185
Bolton, Tommy 60, 61, 62, 184, 188
Bonfield, Dympna 192
Boyle, Peter 156

Breen, Catherine 162, 239, 248, 249, 250
Breen, Dinsey 240
Breen, Michael 238, 239, 243, 247, 250
Breen, Seán (John) 162, 230, 236, 237, 238, 239, 240, 243, 246, 247, 250
Brennan, Austin 112
Brennan, Elizabeth M. 113, 114
Brennan, John 157
Brennan, Mary 117, 118
Brennan, Micheál 101, 102, 112, 114, 117, 118, 187, 188, 200, 268
Brennan, Patrick 112
Brennan, Tom 31, 35, 112, 113, 114, 116, 118, 131
Bridgetown 83, 146
    Kilroughil 83, 84
Brien, Denis 79
Broadford 77, 102, 117, 152, 170, 181, 182, 197, 206, 208
Browne, Kevin J. 111
Browne, Thomas 90, 91, 92
Buchanan, Norman 68, 69
Bugler, Martin 180
Burchell, Bernie 191
Butler, Paddy 59
Byrnes, Ann 155

C

Caher 67, 190, 191
    Currakyle 67, 187, 190
    Doorus 191

INDEX 317

Caherfeenick 197, 198
Cairo Gang 19
Campbell, Michael 208
Canavan, Nora 38, 50, 52, 104, 145, 148, 149, 150, 254, 269
Cape, Thomas 31
Carey, John 241, 242
Carr, Michael 123
Carrigaholt 85, 86, 258
Carroll, Patrick 230, 237, 240
Chalmers, George Duff 212, 213, 214, 215, 216, 217, 218
Churchill, Winston 36, 56
Civil War 22, 26, 49, 86, 92, 106, 116, 119, 121, 124, 194, 223, 225, 227, 249
Clancy, Bridget 232
Clancy, Dossy 247
Clancy, Joe 75, 93, 94, 95, 102, 200, 232, 233, 234, 235
Clancy, John 232
Clancy, Michael 'Micho' 135, 170
Clancy, Paddy (brother of Joe) 93, 94
Clancy, Paddy (Coolmeen) 92, 93, 95
Clancy, Paddy (interviewee) 75, 76, 93
Clancy, Peadar 19, 83
Clancy, P.J. 33, 51, 132, 133, 134, 135, 170, 215, 254, 264
Clancy, Winnie 112
Claremount 25, 152, 170, 206, 208
Clarke, Tom 21
Cleary, Delia 125
Cleary, John 131
Clonderlaw 95
Clondrinagh 174, 175
Clonkerry East 55, 56, 64, 90, 203
Clonlara 47, 123, 174
Clonloum 106

Clonreddan 230
Clonusker 54
Cloonanaha 50
Clooney 176
Clooneyogan 216
Clouna 50, 52, 53
Clounlaheen 19, 22, 23, 88, 218, 225, 226
Clune, Matt 147, 148
Clune, Patrick 264
Clune, Tim 34
Clune, Tom 209
Collins, Daniel 237
Collins, Michael 70, 78, 223, 229
Conneally, Maria 132, 133, 134, 135
Conneally, Tom 134
Connole, Helena 258, 259, 260, 262, 263
Connole, Jack 262
Connole, Joseph 'Joe' 256, 259, 260, 261, 263, 264, 265
Connole, Maureen 34, 256, 257, 258, 261, 264
Connole, Nancy 257
Connole, Patrick 262
Connole, Pete 252
Connole, Tom 256, 257, 258, 259, 260, 261, 262, 263, 264, 265
Connolly 97, 215, 218, 219, 220, 221
Connors, Patsy 216
Considine, Brendan 151
Considine, Tull 151
Considine, William 'Dodger' 151
Conway, Michael 'Micho' 133, 134
Cooleen Bridge 48, 157
Coolmeen 90, 92, 93, 98, 151, 153, 239, 240
Cooraclare 161, 179, 192

Coore 25, 48, 49, 89, 128, 173, 189, 209, 210, 222, 223, 225, 227
Corbett, Jamie 55, 56, 204
Corbett, John 63, 64
Core 157
Corgrigg 58, 241
Cork 44, 60, 195, 196, 208
    Cork city 19, 20, 199
    Fermoy 174
    Kinsale 161
Cork No. 1 IRA Brigade 100
Corkery, Daniel 60, 195
Corragnoe 79, 185, 186, 187
Corry, John 174, 175
Corry, Martin 174, 175
Corry, Nora 218
Costelloe, Dinny 215
Cox, Seán 227
Craggaknock 158, 159, 160
    Cloonagarnane 159
Cranny 95, 174, 240
Cratloe 113, 115, 120, 201, 232
Crawford, Dan 48, 49
Cree 156, 198, 200, 229, 230
Cregg 259
Croom 81
Crotty, Elizabeth 160
Crotty, Michael 160
Crowe, Mae 170
Crowe, Seán 197, 207, 208
Crusheen 169
Cullaun 94
Culligan, Charlie 159
Cumann na mBan 26, 35, 47, 82, 109, 110, 111, 112, 114, 116, 117, 118, 119, 120, 121, 122, 124, 125, 128, 130, 132, 133, 144, 225
Cunneen, John 'Jack' 75

Curtin, Micklo 167
Curtin, Thomas 159, 160

D

Daly, John 200, 201
Daly, Tommy 169
de Montaigne, Michel 266
de Valera, Éamon 22, 111, 122, 227, 229
Delaney, Cornelius 19
Delaney, Jeremiah 20
Devitt, Martin 51, 52, 53
Devitt, Michael 84
Dillon, John 78, 79, 80
Dinan, Peter 209
Doherty, Francis 44
Dollard, Mary 222, 223, 224, 225, 226
Dollard, Pat 223
Donegal 185
Donnellan, Mary 167
Donnellan, Patricia 125, 126
Donnellan, P.J. 166, 167, 215, 217
Doonbeg 180, 193, 194, 198
Doyle, Bridgid 78, 181
Doyle, Edward 77, 78, 181
Doyle, Johnny 77, 78, 102, 181
Doyle, Katy 78, 181
Doyle, Maggie 181
Doyle, Paddy 78
Dromelihy 179
Drumbaun 212
Drumcharley 146, 147
Drumminnanav 34
Dublin 19, 32, 98, 101, 106, 135, 191, 223, 231, 268
    Grangegorman Military Cemetery 212

Kilmainham Gaol 21, 120
Mountjoy Prison 117, 122
Phoenix Park 29
Dublin IRA Brigade 253
Dublin Metropolitan Police 53
Dundalk jail 238, 249
Dundon, Michael 261
Dunleavy, Billy 98
Dunleavy, Jack 96, 160
Dunógan 19, 220, 225, 226
Durack, Bridget 'Baba' 81

E

Easter Rising 28, 120, 253
Effernan 90, 91
Ennis 22, 75, 85, 86, 91, 111, 114, 120, 122, 128, 149, 150, 153, 154, 155, 193, 194, 199, 204, 221, 240, 246, 268, 269
Ennistymon 34, 38, 51, 88, 100, 105, 116, 133, 148, 149, 196, 200, 216, 250, 251, 252, 253, 254, 255, 257, 258, 259, 260, 261, 263, 264, 265, 268, 269
Enright, Mellie 132, 204, 236, 243, 244, 245, 248
Eustace, Mick 218

F

Falsey, Micheál 156
Farrell, Jack 127
Farrell, Michael 'Hookey' 56, 57
Feakle 34, 43, 44, 45, 48, 66, 82, 83, 148, 190, 203
  Annagh 34, 203
Feeney, John 91
Feilding, Rudolph 38, 39

Fennessy, Joe 131
Fitzgerald, Joe 186
Fitzgerald, Martin 186, 187
Fitzgerald, Mary 31
Fitzgerald, Patrick 187
Fitzmartin, Senan 198
Flagmount 190
Flaherty, Joe 261
Flanagan, John 238
Flanagan, Susan 128, 129
Flynn, Teresa 201
Fogarty, Pattie 169
Foley (née McCormack), Kathleen 121, 122, 123, 124
Foley, Micho 122, 124

G

Gallagher, Steve 135, 214
Galvin, Mary 122, 123, 124
Galway 62, 112
Garrahy, Pat 195, 196
Garvey, Flan 250, 251, 252, 255
Garvey, Una 250, 251, 255, 256
Gaynor, Pat 35, 219, 294
Gifford, Grace 120
Ginnell, Laurence 206
Gleeson, Jimmy 25, 173, 174, 176, 189, 209, 210
Gleeson, Matt 173, 176, 177, 189, 209
Gleeson, Paddy 40, 99, 155, 206, 207, 267, 268
Glendine 210
Glendree 148
Glenwood 93, 94, 102, 103, 124, 146, 196, 197, 201, 232
Gortatreasa 170, 171
Grace, Ned 151

Greenwood, Hamar 69
Griffin, Ferrick 178
Griffin, Gerome 65, 155
Griffin, Michael 179
Griffin, Seán 65, 194, 195
Griffith, Arthur 253
Grogan, Gerry 97
Guinnane, J.P. 102, 103

H

Hanrahan, James 86, 87
Hanrahan, Jimmy 85, 86, 87
Hanrahan, Mary 87
Harte, Kate 89
Harte, Patrick 'Paddy' 66, 67, 89
Harvey, Paddy 52, 133
Haugh, Bill 95, 96, 97, 100, 230
Haugh, Pádraig 180
Haugh, Sini 95
Hayes, Maeve 84
Hehir, Hugh 219
Hennessy, Patrick 151
Hennessy, Seamus 214
Hill, Tom 80, 81, 82
Hillery, Michael 167, 228
Hillery, Patrick 167
Hoare, Bernard 237
Hoey, Margaret 39, 41, 42, 105
Hogan, Annie 'Nan' 110, 119, 120, 121, 122
Hogan, Con 169
Hogan, Jack 119, 121
Hogan, Jim 206
Hogan, Michael 78, 79, 80
Hogan, Peggy 34, 203
Hogan, Tom 238
Holland, Mary Joe 130, 131

Holland, Tommy 202, 203
Houlihan, Pat 190, 191
Howard, Michael 35, 45, 46, 165, 171, 172, 173
Howard, Patrick 46, 165
Howard, Susan 172
Hubbard, Elber 250
Hynes, Frank 169

I

Illaunbaun 166, 167
Inagh 105
    Kylea 50, 51
Irish Republican Brotherhood (IRB) 51, 70

J

Jones, Thomas 48, 157

K

Keane, James 191
Keane, Ned 190, 191
Kearney, Bill 196, 197
Keating, Patrick 86
Kelleher, Cornie 53
Kelly, John 158, 160, 198, 229, 230
Kelly, John S. 60
Kelly, Josie 160, 161
Kelly, Matt 58
Kelly, Patrick 'the soldier' 158
Kelly, Paul 57
Kelly, Phil 229, 230, 231, 232
Kelly, Teresa 31
Kenneally, Francie 163, 220, 221
Kennedy, Mick 95
Kerin, Patrick 'Pako' 174, 210, 211

Kerry 53, 88, 96, 177, 237
  Currow 177
  Kilsarcon 177
Kerry No. 2 Brigade 177
Kiely, Jack 170, 171
Kiely, Seán 25, 170, 171
Kilanena 62, 190
  Corbehagh 62
Kilbaha 179, 192
  Ross 179
Kilballyowen 85
  Cloghaunsavaun 85
Kilbane 109, 115, 183
  Clonconry 109
Kilbarron 43, 44
Kilcorney 176
Kildysart 86, 90, 91, 95, 96, 131, 153, 174
Kileen, Jack 111
Kileen, Madeline 111
Kilfenora 87, 116, 118, 130, 133, 164, 167, 168
Kilkee 197, 198
Kilkishen 74, 75, 93, 94, 95, 102, 110, 112, 146, 174, 232, 233, 234
  Teeronea 232
Killaloe 80, 81, 84, 150, 183, 192, 202, 233, 234
Killeen, Tomás 48, 49
Killernan 176, 177
Killimer 170, 172
  Burrane 172
Killoury, Mary 229
Killoury, Michael 229
Killoury, Michael 'Mick' 229, 230, 231, 232, 236, 237, 238, 239, 240, 243
Kilmaley 218

Furroor 218
Kilmihil 58, 59, 132, 162, 174, 204, 229, 230, 236, 237, 238, 239, 240, 241, 242, 243, 244, 245, 246, 247, 248, 250
Kilrush 45, 95, 96, 130, 155, 160, 161, 165, 192, 193, 199, 211, 227, 232
  Tarmon 45, 165, 171, 192
Kilseily 78
Kiltannon 147, 169, 176
  Cloondoorney More 147
Kiltumper 237, 239, 249
Kimball, Solon T. 199, 210
Knightly, Michael 253
Knockerra 46
Knockjames 147, 148, 168, 169
Knockroe 170, 254

L

Labasheeda 55, 63, 92, 95, 153, 174, 175, 203
Lacken 240
Laffan, Michael 145
Lahinch 100, 128, 132, 133, 196, 216, 259, 263
Larkin, Eddie 109
Larkin, Ned 115
Larkin, Paddy 109
Leitrim 44
Leitrim bog, Bridgetown 175
Lendrum, Alan 193, 197, 198, 225
Lenihan, Mollie 110
Lillis, Jim 191, 192
Lillis, Tom 'Brody' 191
Limerick 62, 81, 96, 100, 113, 114, 115, 117, 118, 120, 121, 122, 123, 124, 127, 171, 183, 222, 223, 232,

233, 270, 272
Lisdoonvarna 133, 253, 258
Lisheen 65
Lissane 77, 102
Lloyd George, David 264
Longford 209
Lynch, Charles 68, 69, 71, 72, 218
Lynch, Charlie 69, 70, 71, 72
Lynch, James 252
Lynch, John 70, 72, 73
Lynch, Katie 70, 71, 72, 73
Lynch, Ned 68, 70, 71, 72
Lynch, Pat 217
Lynch, Patrick 253
Lynch, Tom 192
Lynch, Wilson 103

M

Mac Clúin (Clune), Conor 19, 284
MacDonagh, Clare 256, 257
MacDonagh, Tomás 21
MacMahon, Tadgh 211
Mac Piarais, Pádraig 21
MacSwiney, Terence 199
Madigan, Frances 129
Magner, Patrick 179
Magner, P.J. 179
Maguire, Sam 70
Maherantaisce 222, 224, 225, 226
Malone, Anthony 37
Malone, Billy 37
Malone, Timmy 184, 185
Marconetto, Helena 262, 263
Markievicz, Countess 111
Marrinan, Nellie 132
Martyn, Patrick 237, 238
Mayo 209

McCormack, Jack 124
McCormack, Katie 87, 88, 116
McCormack, Mickey 116, 164, 165
McCormack, Norah 'Lala' 87, 88, 164, 165, 168
McCormack, Peter 164
McCormack, Teasie 87, 116, 118, 164, 168
McDonnell, Paddy 99, 100
McGough, Michael 51
McGough, Patrick 'Paddy' 50, 51, 105
McGrath, Dinny 179, 180
McGrath, Kit 107
McGrath, Kitty 106
McGrath, Mick 148
McGrath, Pat 'Thade' 106, 107, 181
McGrath, Phil 106, 107, 118
McGrath, Thomas 148
McGrath, Tom 106, 107, 118, 151, 181
McGuane, Anthony 'Murray' 222, 223, 224, 225, 226, 227, 228, 229
McGuane, Bridget 225, 227
McGuane, Catherine 'Kitty' 222, 228, 229
McGuane Cox, Margaret 227, 228
McGuane, Mary 225, 227, 228
McGuane, Tess 228
McInerney, Pa 'Fowler' 151
McKee, Dick 19, 284
McMahon, John 242
McMahon, Michael 231, 232
McMahon, Michael 'Marshall' 95, 239, 240, 241
McMahon, Molly 227
McMahon, Monsignor J.T. 264
McMahon, Murty 83
McMahon, Paddy 'Con' 221

INDEX   323

McMahon, Patrick 98
McMahon, Peter 236, 237, 238
McNamara, Bartholomew 'Batty' 206, 207, 208
McNamara, Jim 62, 63
McNamara, John 239
McNamara, Katy 125, 126, 127
McNamara, Martin 'Neighbour' 74, 75, 76, 93, 94, 200, 232, 233
McNamara, Michael 'Mac' 19, 180, 192, 193, 194
McNamara, Palkie 59, 205
McNamara, Sarah 62
McNamara, Thomas 125, 126
McNamara, Tom 169
McPherson, Alexander 68, 69, 72, 218, 219, 220, 221
Meaney, Jamsie 50, 51
Meelick 112, 113, 115, 117, 118, 201
Meere, Mick 218
Melican, Martin 236, 237
Mellows, Liam 87, 116, 168, 169
Melody, John 146, 147
Mescall, Paddy 46, 172, 179
Miltown Malbay 23, 31, 49, 51, 58, 68, 69, 98, 100, 105, 151, 157, 163, 210, 217, 220, 257, 258, 263
Minogue, Joe 201, 202
Minogue, John 47, 157, 178
Minogue, Mick 47
Molloy, Denis 261
Moloney, Dinny 188
Moloney, Ellen 83, 84
Moloney, Ellie 166, 167
Moloney, Jim 84
Moloney, Maggie 106
Moloney, Michael 169
Moloney, Sonny 152

Monaghan, Alfie 169
Moriarty, Jeremiah 177
Moriarty, Jerry 177
Moroney, Joseph 19
Moroney, Mary 19, 21
Moroney, Michael 'Casey' 97, 98
Moroney, Molly 19, 20, 21, 23
Moroney, Seán 190
Moughna 50, 213
Mountshannon 125, 201
Moy 135, 166, 196, 211, 212, 214, 216, 217
Moyasta 53, 54
Moynoe 181
Mullagh 35, 58, 194, 195, 198, 211, 225
  Creevagh 58
Mullins, Seán 161
Murnane, John 36, 76
Murnane, Seán 36, 76, 77
Murphy, Andrew 255
Murphy, Francis 'Francie' 250, 251, 252, 253, 254, 255, 256
Murphy, Humphrey 177
Murphy, John 252
Murphy, William 265
Murrihy, Mary 37, 49, 157

N

Nash, Kathleen 26, 35, 47, 48
Nestor, Micho 133
Nevins, Buddy 59
Newmarket-on-Fergus 36, 76, 119, 152
Neylon, John Joe 'Tosser' 51
Neylon, Sino 95
Ní Bhrian, Máire 31

Noonan, Joe 80, 81, 82, 120, 184, 185
Noonan, John 185
Nugent, Joe 55
Nugent, Kevin 54, 55, 56
Nugent, Tom 55

O

O'Brien, Catherine 130
O'Brien, Flan 32, 78, 79, 80, 81
O'Brien, James 150
O'Brien, Jimmy 150
O'Brien, Johanna 78
O'Brien, John 78, 79, 80
O'Brien, Paddy 60
O'Brien's Bridge 110, 187
O'Brien, Willie 197
O'Callaghan, George 100
O'Callaghan's Mills 40, 106, 152, 206, 207
O'Connell (née Corbett), Bridget 56
O'Connell, Daniel 22
O'Connell, John 55, 56, 64, 90, 92, 175
O'Connell, Micheál 18, 37, 145, 166, 216, 217
O'Connell, Morgie 83, 96, 240, 241
O'Connor, William 153
O'Dea, Jimmy 83, 96
O'Dea, John 236, 237
O'Donnell (née Howard), Mary 130
O'Donnell, Seamus 67
O'Donoghue, Jimmy 130
O'Dwyer, Máire 100, 132, 133
O'Dwyer, Nora 101
O'Dwyer, Paddy 200, 260, 263
O'Gorman, Michael 65, 66, 127, 192
O'Grady, Francis 203

O'Grady, Margaret 203
O'Grady, Rodger 203
O'Halloran, Pat 115, 146, 147, 148, 169
O'Halloran, Seán (nephew) 36
O'Halloran, Seán (uncle) 120, 121
O'Hanlon, John 96
O'Higgins, Barney 257, 258
O'Kerin, Gerry 153
O'Malley, Ernie 87, 100, 165, 166
O'Neill, Ignatius 166, 167
O'Neill, Sonny 151
Ó Súilleabháin, Micheál 60
O'Sullivan, Seán 128, 129
O'Sullivan, Tomsie 129

P

Percival, A.E. 161, 162
Plunkett, Joseph Mary 120
Powell, John 43, 44

Q

Queally, James 259
Queally, John 192
Quigley, Jack 234, 235
Quilty 71, 156
    Seafield 156
Quin 176

R

Raheen Hospital 40, 61
Redmond, Willie 111
Reidy, Patrick 152
Reidy, P.J. 152
Rineen 35, 37, 50, 51, 69, 128, 166, 167, 210, 211, 225, 257, 259, 260,

INDEX   325

264, 265, 268
Robertson, George   215, 218, 219, 220, 221
Robins, Maurice   120
Ross Rose, Major   196
Royal Irish Constabulary (RIC)   20, 21, 28, 29, 30, 33, 37, 44, 51, 53, 54, 65, 70, 71, 88, 91, 95, 96, 102, 115, 126, 128, 132, 134, 145, 154, 159, 162, 183, 197, 204, 225, 230, 234, 236, 237, 238, 240, 242, 245, 246, 248, 253, 258, 267
Ruan   154
Rutledge, P.J.   188
Ryan, Dan   47, 115
Ryan, Jackie 'Bishop'   46, 108, 175
Ryan, John   241
Ryan, Johnny   185, 186
Ryan, Mary   108
Ryan, Michael   47
Ryan, Michael 'Mike'   186
Ryan, Mick   46, 47, 108, 109, 115, 170, 175
Ryan, Nora   47, 170
Ryan, Noreen   47, 130
Ryan, Patsy   185
Ryan, Timmy   58, 59, 241, 242, 243

S

Scanlon, John 'Shang'   85, 86
Scanlon, Tom   188
Scariff   26, 39, 47, 48, 54, 57, 59, 65, 66, 89, 127, 150, 151, 157, 178, 179, 180, 183, 192, 205, 234, 267
Scariff Martyrs   47, 48, 131, 192, 202
Second World War   22, 197
Sexton, Joe 'Jack'   35, 36, 194, 198, 211

Shanahan, Marty   173
Shanahan, William 'Willie'   19, 159, 173, 180, 192, 193, 194
Shannon, Dinny   95
Shaughnessy, Kate   199
Sixmilebridge   102, 103, 112, 113, 114, 117, 131, 196
Skeehan, Batt   145
Skeehan, Patrick 'Brud'   145
Spackman, Alfred   120
Spellissy, James 'Sham'   151
St Flannan's College   75
Stanley, William   44

T

Talty (née Moroney), Catherine   21, 22, 23, 24, 36, 37, 88, 97, 218, 221, 225, 226
Tipperary   28, 145, 202
   Ballina   202
   Roscrea   47
   Templemore   100
   Thurles   100
   Upperchurch   100
Tobin, John Michael   82
Tottenham, Frederick St Leger   173, 174, 219
Tromra   156
Tuamgraney   32, 40, 60, 78, 80, 81, 99, 110, 120, 155, 156, 179, 183, 184, 186
   Ballymalone   32, 62, 78, 82, 186, 270
   Kielta   99
Tulla   43, 115, 146, 148, 168, 169, 176
Tullaha   87, 116, 118, 164, 165, 166, 167, 168

Tullycrine 130, 157
Tuohy, John 83
Tuohy (née Powell), Mae 43, 44, 45
Turner, Charlie 202
Tuttle, Tom 213, 216
Tyrone 197

W

Waldron, Eamon 116
Walsh, Jimmy 182, 183, 184, 185
Walsh, Margaret 185
Walsh, Martin 36, 57, 153, 156
Walsh, Michael 'Sonny' 182, 183, 184
Ward, Bridget 118
Ward, Paddy 118
Whelan, Willie 194, 198
Whitegate 56, 79, 80, 125, 130, 202
    Tintrim 56, 57
White's Bridge 167
Wilson, Henry 32
Wimberley, Douglas 32
Woulfe, Joe 31
Wylie, William Evelyn 253

Y

Young, Micho 66, 67

ABOUT THE AUTHOR

Tomás Mac Conmara is an oral historian born in Tuamgraney, Co. Clare in 1980. He completed a PhD at the University of Limerick in 2015 which explored the social memory of the Irish War of Independence. He began recording memory and folklore as a teenager in his townland of Ballymalone and is now recognised as one of the leading oral historians in the country. In 2016 he was commended by President Michael D. Higgins with a Comhaltas Forógra na Cásca Centenary Award for his contribution to Irish culture. In 2008 he founded Cuimhneamh an Chláir, the Clare Oral History and Folklore Group, to record the memories of Clare's oldest citizens. He was appointed by UCC as Manager of the Cork Folklore Project in January 2016 and also runs a heritage consultancy with clients including Waterways Ireland, the Defence Forces and Dublin Port. Mac Conmara is the author of several publications, including *High Prestige: The Story of Clare's All Ireland Hurling Champions of 1914*; *Paddy Brennan's Book: An Irish Rebel Autograph Book from Frongoch Internment Camp*; *The Ministry of Healing: St. Mary's Orthopaedic Hospital, Cork*; *An Oral and Historical Record*; and *Days of Hunger: The Clare Volunteers and the Mountjoy Hunger Strike of 1917*.

www.ingramcontent.com/pod-product-compliance
Lightning Source LLC
Chambersburg PA
CBHW052052230426
43671CB00011B/1875